Lynn H. Saint

Mists from the Waterfall

Guarding the Wellsprings of Life through Sorrow and Joy

Published by
At the Waterfall
Gresham, Oregon 97080-9395

For privacy reasons, some names, locations, and dates may have been changed.

Scripture translations are referenced, starting on Page 251.

Book cover photograph by Leon Burkholder
Page and cover design by Ariel Jiménez Saint
Proof editor and consultant: Janet Albers
First edition, August 2023

Print ISBN: 979-8-218-00385-2
Ebook ISBN: 979-8-218-00386-9

Printed in the USA

Table of Contents

Endorsements

It was my privilege to function as Jim and Lynn's attorney for the adoptions of two of their children. Their experiences are genuine as well as the faith exhibited in their lives. You will encounter a Savior who makes a difference, not only in times of joy but in seasons of heartache.

Duane Olson, attorney at law, Phoenix Arizona

I feel as though I spent the weekend with her! Her manuscript kept me ravished with the details of her life and with deep relationships, mainly with our Lord. Her spiritual gifts are evident: hospitality, teaching, caring and understanding. Furthermore, her love for our Lord and His children and those incubated to become His own is such an evident characteristic. She has been anointed to walk in the good works that God has prepared.

Nancy Advocaat, former missionary in Germany, Siberia and Uzbekistan, counselor with Navigators, Bible study teacher

The courage, endurance and grace reflected in Mists from the Waterfall challenge me to walk in more courage and faith in my life as well.

Lynn has taught her own children, coordinated lessons and taught other children/young people, spoken at Women's Retreats and Bible Studies, led prayer groups/ministry, worked with and tutored international students.

Through the life experiences reflected in her book Mists from the Waterfall, you will know God is alive and cares for every detail in our lives!

Sharon Hazlett, friend, prayer partner, Bible study hospitality coordinator

I deeply appreciated the author's honesty in the emotional experience of the ups and downs of her life story. I wish Lynn lived close enough for tea! Our family has been through what seems like a lot in the last 5 years, but especially the last year and a half. Her wisdom and transparency were a balm.

Heather Frazier, wife and a mother of four children, one of whom is medically fragile.

When hard times come and life seems terribly unfair, we choose whether to get bitter or better.

During her pain, my dear friend Lynn has found God's recipe for faith, hope and peace.

Her testimony of God's faithfulness is authentic, raw and pure, overflowing with God's grace. May you be encouraged as you read!

Pastor Candy Brandstetter (Four Square International), wife, mother, grandmother, pastor, mentor, teacher

Introduction

Swimming Upstream

My dear reader, this has been a labor of love for you. Each word has been prayed over, while entrusting God's plan for you as you read through this story. I don't know the parts that will move you, but there are portions waiting to leap into your heart to help clarify your journey. I've worked on this for years. Some words are recent additions. Others have been resting in the unfinished manuscript, within the pages of my journals and in my mind for decades, waiting. They are also waiting to encourage you, to weep with you, to smile with you, to identify with you.

Fifty years ago, after a biology lab, our instructor chatted with three or four of us coeds about our lives and what was happening in them. He mentioned something that impressed me, but I didn't catch the meaning behind his observation for a long time.

"Lynn, whenever I see you, a butterfly comes to mind. Just as I get ready to reach out and touch you, you flutter away."

When he expressed it, I said nothing, but inside the words echoed, *What a beautiful sentiment. I'm like a butterfly. Wow!* I loved being a butterfly—fluttering here and there, not staying long enough to be touched and especially not wounded. What a delightful life! I failed to see my need to rest as a caterpillar—a creature meant to crawl on the ground. Staying down to earth and learning to be real. That was going to take time. More than time, it required life experiences. The experiences were coming.

With time's passing, I am thankful for his observations, but not because I flutter by. Physical action is not what causes me to fly; it is my emotional interaction. How do I engage with others? Am I more relatable than I was decades ago? Hopefully. I pray you will also understand my heart and will grasp the meanings within the pages. I do not intend to take flight. I have had a reverse transformation. Instead of flapping my wings, I've reverted to caterpillar life, awaiting my graduation day when He allows me to take flight in heavenly realms.

Years ago, I presented a Bible study on humility and shared a few points that resonated within me. An essential ingredient for the growth of plants is humus. It holds water and nutrients. Humus was once earth, but through amendments of decaying matter, microbes have transformed this less than fertile soil into a nurturing medium for seeds as they sink into its dark embrace. What is my job now? I need to dig into the soil, helping to prepare it for new plantings and fresh growth.

Section 1. Taking the Plunge: *New Plans, People and Places*

"The land is... Mine, and you are only foreigners and temporary residents on My land"
(Leviticus 25:23 HCSB).

Turning the Stream

The king's heart is a stream of water in the hand of the LORD; he turns it wherever he will
(Proverbs 21:1 ESV).

On a morning hike, I encountered a young couple pushing baby carriages down Lovhar, a road with a steep incline situated close to our neighborhood. As I climbed the hill, vainly attempting to look buff and fit, I greeted the young woman who was wearing a cross-country ski shirt (that should have been a red flag if I were expecting sympathy). She extolled, "It's a wonderful walk!" As my heart pounded from exertion while gasping for breath, I thought she was referring to the warm breezes, the radiant sunshine and the azure skies. I responded, "It's a gorgeous walk, isn't it?" Her husband, who knew what she was saying (*God bless him*), moaned, "It's painful, dreadfully painful."

That man had the walk figured out. The more I walk, the more painful the walks become when I enter newer and more difficult areas. No longer content with the house and the yard, I need the uphill climb to test and rebuild my strength. The easy course doesn't encourage my legs and body to stretch and improve. When my strength increases, I can do the inclined path, but more often it is dreadfully painful.

Life is the same way. When we try to stay within our cushioned comfort rooms, we don't experience the challenge of the higher life, the firmer faith, the greater fortitude. When we venture out and prepare our emotional and spiritual muscles, those challenges hurt, but they often show increased strength, not weakness. Allowing the Lord to change the direction permits new experiences one might avoid to escape the pain. Sometimes, there's no choice. The comfort zones cease to exist, and a new hill obstructs our path. We must move forward, painful or not.

Learning to listen to His voice

In July 1973, I faced a predicament. My position as youth leader and secretary at my home church was ending. A default to higher education appealed to me as a practical option, so I applied to Arizona State University for a place in their master's degree program. They sent me a letter of acceptance, which cleared my future course. As the days passed, peace dissipated. I sought God for clear direction. A voice, not audible but discernible, breathed into my heart. *"Trust Me, I have something better for you."* With no alternatives open and no clear path for my future, I wrote a letter of rejection for my acceptance letter, explaining that I needed to wait for another time. They acknowledged my refusal with a response, explaining they would keep the position open in the program for a later date. Although they never heard from me again, the open invitation was a gracious and encouraging gesture.

Several days later, while visiting a Christian bookstore, I spied a book entitled *Amazing Saints*, by Phil Saint. I didn't know him but had heard of Nate Saint, martyred in Ecuador while serving as a missionary and jungle pilot. Flipping through the pages, I realized Phil Saint was one of Nate's older brothers. I bought the book and immediately read it. The family adventures intrigued me and piqued my curiosity. The author, a captivating storyteller, engaged my interest with his descriptions of their daily life as missionaries in Argentina. I sensed a nudge upon finishing the book and wrote a letter to the headquarters of Saint Evangelistic Crusades in North Carolina. Besides explaining my appreciation for the book, I also asked if there were a possibility of serving as a short-term missionary in Argentina. Then I mailed the envelope with my letter tucked inside.

This account records events from the last century. The postal system moved sluggishly with international transmissions. Letters still travel slowly between the hemispheres, but now communication relies on texts and emails via tablets, cell phone apps and the computer. At the least, a two-week delay for letters going one direction, from the States to Argentina or vice versa, presented a threat and a promise. Additionally, my letter was on its way to the mission office address here in the States, not to Argentina. There was no telling how long mail would park in the post office box before the mission secretary retrieved it and then forwarded it south. I wrote in mid-July. Because I didn't understand the unseen mountains, the possibility of mission work nestled firmly in the back of my mind. I penned the letter, believing God wanted me to. After that, He would handle the details. He did.

Invitation to join in the work

On my birthday, four weeks later, I received a letter from Phil Saint inviting me to travel to Argentina to work and stay with the family for a short term. Although I read the letter with excitement, the subsequent stages seemed planned and designed, keeping me calm. I didn't have nagging questions or curious thoughts. The door opened and beckoned me to enter.

In my second letter heading directly to Argentina, I explained my willingness and excitement to fly down and live for a season, I asked if there were any supplies the family might need or use. My future boss's only response was that he wanted a moose head someone was keeping for him back East. Traveling with a moose head didn't rank high on my priority list. Without further direction, I pondered which household items and practical tools might prove useful. In reexamining his reply, a second check with his wife might have given clearer guidance. Not discerning the subtleties of the family dynamics, I missed the opportunity to bring specific goods. Fortunately, trusted missionary friends furnished me with solid suggestions, which proved useful for practical gift giving.

Shortly, a rush of activity replaced the calmness as I prepared for this new adventure. My home church encouraged me; several helped through generous financial support over the months of my stay. The youth group held a newspaper drive, earning funds by turning in collected papers for payment by the pound. I still owe a debt of gratitude to those who sacrificed and offered such unconditional love for my benefit, ultimately reflecting His glory and His plans.

Flying South

Within two months of opening the initial letter from Phil Saint, I boarded my first flight to South America. My expected arrival in Córdoba met with a snag, as I missed the Buenos Aires to Córdoba flight the previous day through misinformation. Buenos Aires hosted (still does) two major airports, one for international flights, Ezeiza, and the other, Aeroparque, for domestic transportation. Neither the travel agent nor I knew of that airport quirk. Thanks to the good graces of a missionary family, I spent the night at their home and took a flight to Córdoba the next morning.

From the airport in Córdoba, a taxi took me to the Saints' home address, written on a piece of paper, which I had shown to the chauffeur. Ruth Saint greeted me outside and paid the driver with her pesos (maybe they were mine). In looking at the pesos in my hand, I realized my concept of the monetary value was nil.

When I tumbled through the door, I had little idea of the plans God had in store for me in the coming years. After a couple hours of rest, the family at home—Doña Ruth, David (25) and Evelyn (14)—introduced me to their lives. I expected to meet Phil Saint, who had invited me to try my wings as a short-term missionary. However, he was at the Christian family camp in the mountains, supervising builders, bricklayers, painters and gardeners. As its founder, he took much pride in this retreat center, sometimes to the dismay of his family, as he devoted every extra ounce of energy to maintaining the area and by engaging innovative ideas for changes and improvements.

Evelyn, the youngest member of the household, assisted me countless times with her excellent grasp of English, which she had learned from her parents and through her voracious appetite for books. With Eve's limited exposure to North Americans and her only visit to the States as a toddler, she often pummeled me with questions about life in the USA. It was odd for me to realize I represented the States. I expected to be absorbed into the activities without being noticed, at least not as much as I was. Had I known, I would have studied a lot more about American idiosyncrasies before leaving the homeland.

Since their arrival in South America, the Saints had insisted on speaking English at home as they worked to ensure their children would communicate in their parents' language as well as that of the Argentines. Thanks to parental diligence, their offspring speak both English and Spanish without an accent in either tongue. Even though their American English pronunciation was precise, it soon became obvious that some common terms were from a book or from idioms which had fallen into disuse. The entire family had only visited the States one time in 1960 since their move to Argentina in 1957, thus preventing much interaction with Yankees other than a few North American missionaries and even fewer businesspeople who remained in the vicinity.

Once I settled in, Evelyn supplied me with a grand tour of all the rooms. The living room, a sitting and visiting place of respite, held a piano, several older couches, a few pieces of odds-and-ends furniture and throw rugs. She pointed out a *Waodani* spear gracing one wall along with her dad's paintings on others. Red earthen Italian tiles, *mosaicos*, covered all the floors throughout the house. Months later, I discovered those tiles were the only layer above the dirt foundation. While meandering into the bedrooms and through the hallway, I noticed the floor rugs scattered in the hallways and a few rooms. Those small rugs provided a distant semblance to carpeting; the family was pleased with the ambience.

Bedrooms had no built-in closets. My room had an old, decommissioned water closet for extra storage, later revealed by the toilet seat's black image emblazoned on my yellow suitcase. Reminiscent of *The Lion, the Witch and the Wardrobe*, larger bedrooms were afforded a wardrobe for collecting clothes and other treasures. In fact, the wardrobe in Eve's room accumulated dozens of eggs on the top until the cook, Mom Saint, needed them.

The kitchen and dining rooms displayed well-aged and well-used furniture and kitchen supplies. School-green Melmac dinnerware graced the table at every meal unless there was a special occasion or a Sunday dinner. On those days, Ruth served family and guests with her mother's Noritake dinnerware. She reserved goblets for iced tea and lemonade, demitasse cups for Turkish coffee and a teapot for English tea. Silverware and special plates remained in the credenza until Sundays or celebrations.

Covering most of one wall in the dining area, the resident artist (Phil Saint) had painted an enormous mural of snow-capped mountains. The dining room table attracted many visitors who came for counseling and/or a home-cooked meal. Often, college students dropped by to bask in the home atmosphere and to consume the home-cooked food which Ruth prepared for invited and unexpected guests a minimum of three times a week for years. Organized and efficient, she counted kitchen duties among her many skills.

In my North American eyes, nothing looked luxurious. Material things didn't push the family to accumulate objects of monetary value. The possessions they had were often worn, albeit well-cared for. In part, their disregard for luxury moved my heart. To me, their life was far richer and more complex than one with stateside creature comforts. They lived at a level commensurate with their neighbors, not flaunting what they owned.

A few days after my arrival, Phil Saint returned from *Valle del Lago* (Lake Valley) with glorious stories about the environment in the sierras of Córdoba. Days earlier, during my unexpected night at the Swindoll home, that family asked what responsibilities I would have at camp. I wasn't aware of any camp commitment, but they assured me I would spend a good amount of my summer there. And they were right. Their talk introduced me to the months ahead, as *Don Felipe's* focus on the camp had captured the interest of many Argentines.

Before departing for summer camp two months after my arrival, I faced more supplemental education. The family discussed my future at length. Finally, they agreed on my next assignment.

Glimmers of sunshine and rainbows through the mist

When I realize how brave my parents were to let me travel such a far distance, my heart swells in gratitude for their encouragement and confidence. Argentina's volatile political climate created an unsafe environment for Americans.

American-owned companies had left the country, along with the American executives in their employ. North Americans needed to stay under the radar to avoid identification. A few Argentines showed considerable animosity toward Yankees.

Gathering grace gems from the bubbling waters

- Have you encountered dead-end times when you were unsure of your future?
- How did God speak to you? How did you find a way out?
- Have you had to keep climbing even though the efforts were taxing, mentally and spiritually, and possibly physically? Where did you end up?
- What events or circumstances showed you there was divine intervention, not human machinations?

Hilltop Springs

For the Lord your God is bringing you into a good land, a land of brooks of water, of fountains and springs, flowing forth in valleys and hills; a land of wheat and barley, of vines and fig trees and pomegranates, a land of olive oil and honey; a land where you will eat food without scarcity, in which you will not lack anything; a land whose stones are iron, and out of whose hills you can dig copper

(Deuteronomy 8:7-9 NASB).

One of our agreed-upon first-agenda items was for me to secure more Spanish instruction. Even though a tutor had worked with me for months while in the States, I had absorbed little of the spoken language. When taking a taxicab from the airport after landing in Buenos Aires, the only phrase I could speak to the driver was, "*Buenos Aires es una linda ciudad.*" (Buenos Aires is a lovely city.) Beyond that, words failed me, and I am sure the driver was less than impressed with my bilingual attempt.

The family suggested hiring a professional translator to provide Spanish tutoring. To arrive at his family's apartment, I took a bus to downtown Córdoba from *Cerro de las Rosas*, a barrio, or suburb, where the family lived.

Some who wander are lost

One day after class, I waited for the bus for more than twice the expected time. Many light blue buses that barreled past us could have let the passengers board. One bus after another pressed on, ignoring eager and weary commuters. To no avail, I searched for the "G" and finally spotted one that had a "G" along with an inconsequential, smaller number attached to it. To my way of thinking, close was as good as spot on. Besides, it was the right color. So, I boarded that bus. After half an hour, I realized the bus was not traversing the familiar avenues of the Cerro, neighborhood. Not only did I possess few Spanish skills, but I was ill equipped with a poor sense of direction.

Dear Lord, please help me find my way. I don't know when I should get off and which way I should walk once I'm back on the ground. As my heart settled, I finally took the plunge and stepped from the conveyance. Although I recognized no familiar landmarks, after a short time, I identified the home where we had Bible study and prayer gatherings on Wednesday nights. Continuing, I spotted the street where the Saints lived. Home at last! God had prodded this gringa, foreigner, to the right spot without assurance she was anywhere close to the goal. Despite my disorientation, He knew my destination. I just needed to move and keep listening.

A few weeks later, after arriving downtown for my tutoring session, I realized the street I walked on was clear of pedestrians. This meant I could reach my destination faster and easier. Thankful for the clear path, I rushed down the street, quickly passing a hospital as I continued unimpeded by oncoming pedestrian traffic. Armed militia with automatic machine guns guarded the medical facility. Not knowing the usual procedures, I figured they were commonly present to protect the hospital. Later, I learned they were defending the area as a guerrilla fighter had been admitted to the medical center for wounds received in a gunfight with government soldiers. The guards were positioned in vigilance to make sure no counter groups would attack the facility or the environs. God purposed to protect me from harm, despite my ignorance.

Camping out

Classes with my tutor ended in December before the family made its annual trek through the hills of Córdoba to Valle del Lago, where Argentine believers and non-believers, alike, arrived from around the country for church, family and individual retreats. The route through *Pampa de Achala* held more excitement and danger than any carnival ride. Pampa de Achala, filled with over 1000 hairpin curves on a single-lane width of gravel road, provided access to the main shortcut through mountain passes. The rules of the road dictated that a vehicle climbing possessed the right of way when encountering one descending. With no guard rails, sheer drop-offs and little wiggle room, motorists responded with astuteness and agility in handling the low-traction and rutted route with buses, cars, trucks and motorcycles. Occasionally, a brave and adventurous bicyclist would hazard the route, but not very often.[1]

After I had settled into my camp apartment, Don Felipe returned to Córdoba, leaving me with the cook and other workers who were preparing for the coming summer season of guests. With a month and a half of rudimentary *castellano* (the dialect of Spanish spoken in Argentina), panic set in with the realization that I didn't understand what my new acquaintances were saying. Even when they repeatedly spoke the same phrases to help me, I didn't always "get it." They exhibited great patience as I bumbled my way into and out of conversations.

Many people from around the world are accustomed to eating animals and animal parts. As someone who had not ventured to try tongue or heart, I was not ready to eat more adventuresome foods. My boss had warned me not to offend anyone by refusing to eat what they offered. My marching orders spelled out my responsibilities. I was determined to drink mate (the traditional Argentine herbal tea consumed with a metal straw out of a special mug or gourd) and eat all foods. One night, while still on my own with camp workers, the group announced they were making an *asado* (barbecue). In preparation, they would roast the meat over an open wood fire for many hours, cooking it to perfection. The meat on the barbecue that night was goat, baby goat. Having never eaten goat meat before, I was both curious and apprehensive. My resolve to eat anything had to hold firm. After hours of waiting for the delicacy to reach its tenderest state, the chefs served an entire baby goat on a platter with its head listing to one side and its eyes looking at me. As they cut meat from the little goat, I took what they gave me, cut it into tiny pieces and then carefully chewed and swallowed each morsel while staring into the kid's eyes. That was the only time anyone presented me kid meat to eat, thankfully.

Campers and workers at Valle del Lago extended their love and friendliness. The warm and open Argentine culture drew me in closer and tighter. I enjoyed spending time with them, learning how their minds worked, watching them interact, listening to them speak and working alongside them.

After settling at the retreat center for the first month with only a few campers, I met a lady from the main province of Argentina, Buenos Aires, who longed to hike the hill beyond the cabins and the camp itself. Someone had told me she was lonely, so I figured this hike would provide me a chance to become better acquainted with her and to take advantage of fresh air and excellent exercise. The trail opened to an easy climb toward the top and gave us the opportunity to explore the hilltop ambience, which included a gaucho on horseback and a half dozen stray cattle. For the first time in my life, I watched a spring bubbling from the ground. Water oozing from the earth's pores intrigued me as I gazed at the wet meadow. The gurgling waters filled a small field, gathering into rivulets and descending toward a stream.

Once we had taken in the highland scenes, and after checking our watches, the time arrived to wend our way back down. As the light faded, the return trek became complicated when I couldn't figure out where the path up was, which should have returned us to the camp below. Unfortunately, I chose a more direct path, straight down, not the best option. Once committed, we had to proceed with our descent. After an hour of cautiously sliding on the downgrade (had the actual trail been located, this should have taken 15 minutes), we reached the campgrounds where worried staff and campers had started looking at their watches every few minutes. What a relief for them and for us when we dragged into camp at last!

I suspected I had ruined the day for this lady. To my surprise, she confided to others that our adventure was the best one she'd had in years. Although relieved, I didn't recommit my services as a tour guide. I enjoyed talking to her and spending time with her, but opted to leave hiking in parts unknown to others who showed greater aptitude in understanding the terrain, along with possessing an inner compass to provide fine-tuned positioning and orientation.

New roommate

A young woman, in her early 20s, arrived from the States at the start of the camp season. She became my roommate at camp and at the house when we returned. Having worked with Youth with a Mission, Cheryl evidenced a deep understanding, trust and love for God and His word. During the months we lived together, she taught me ways to refine my relationship with the Lord. We challenged ourselves to a three-day fast as we sought God's direction for our next move. Her spirituality was stronger than mine as we denied ourselves food. I counted the days, hours and minutes before eating again. Diplomatically, Cheryl observed that perhaps my heart was not committed to the discipline. She was right. I have since become more adept at fasting, but the exercise was not my forte then.

Cheryl and I intended to leave from Córdoba in May, assuming we would both attend language school together in Mexico. However, God had other plans. She moved to Mexico while I stayed behind. I still needed to exit Argentina to renew my tourist visa, which, by law, demanded that I leave the country after a half year of residence. Paraguay offered a solution as my next stop for visa renewal, so I made plans to travel there.

Glimmers of sunshine and rainbows through the mist

Getting on the "*G*" with the extra number required a lapse in judgment. I realized, too late, that my bus's destination was a mystery. Thankfully, God is not harsh with us and often provides a way out. He could shout, "I told you so." Rather, He may permit us to make ill-advised decisions because we don't know any better, but He doesn't *rejoice in the wrong*[2] which reveals our Father's commitments to His promises in the written word.

Walking down the street with soldiers guarding the hospital exposed another incident of divine protection. It was not until hours later, after I had returned home, that members of the family commented about the situation downtown. Then I recognized the danger. I doubt if I shared about my encounter with the police and the hospital.

I have become lost on more than a few occasions. Somewhat perplexed and hoping for more knowledge and wisdom the next time around, I have found my way back. God has also guided me when I have lacked direction in my life decisions

Gathering grace gems from the bubbling waters

- Have you ever felt lost or disoriented? Sometimes this is not a physical lostness, but an emotional or spiritual one.
- How did you find your way back?
- Are there any promises you depend on when lost?

Paraguay, Paraná, Paraclete

And now why do you wait? Rise and be baptized
(Acts 22:16 ESV).

I had renewed my visa in an ersatz queue in downtown Córdoba months earlier, but a stay beyond six months required that I leave the country. Although I could have traveled to any international border, had my visa stamped and then returned to Argentina, this regulation presented an opportunity to visit Paraguay. After planning and connecting with others, I made my way north towards the Paraguayan border on a passenger bus. The trip lasted a day and a night with a few stops at bus stations along the way. I had made friends with Anglican schoolteachers at Valle del Lago months before and looked forward to learning about them while in Asunción, especially because they had invited me to their mission station.

Not there yet

Although the 20-plus-hour bus trip was uneventful, a surprise awaited me upon arrival in the capital city. Unbeknownst to me, there was a city-wide *paro*, a general workers' strike. Because of the strike, the expected city buses and taxicabs were not available to transport me to the mission compound. I wasn't expecting anyone to meet me, so I tried to think and pray my way out of this new dilemma. A gentleman at the bus station treated me courteously and engaged in a conversation upon realizing I was in a quandary. Although I tried to take precautions with strangers, I was clearly in a predicament beyond my own maneuverings. He presented me with his business card in the event I might need extra help in the future. Before giving me his information, he lectured me on how to protect myself and warned me to watch out for Americans. Then he opened his satchel and handed me his card. I glanced at the open briefcase. On top of an assortment of papers, I spied a large revolver. He had told me he was close to the country's president.

Regardless of whether he was, that gun must have worked as an enforcer for more people than I realized.

Somehow I contacted the ladies at the mission compound. Upon receiving the address and directions on how to get there, one of the few available cabs drove me to the large home where the teachers lived. After an inauspicious arrival, I enjoyed several beautiful and meaningful days at the mission station.

Local buses push for new encounters

Two days following my arrival, Niki, my Anglican[3] friend, decided we should contact a lady with whom she was ministering. The woman lived on the outskirts of Asunción, so we had to travel for close to an hour. This was my first bus ride while hanging from the outside of a bus. The other passengers had crammed themselves into every likely and unlikely space, so Niki and I dangled out the side door. It was a prayer adventure, as I called on the Lord for His help while we clung for dear life. We finally arrived at the lady's home, where she served us tea and biscuits with a visit and prayer time.

Following the adventurous bus ride, someone told me that in Asunción, and more than likely the entire country, it is not illegal to hit and kill a pedestrian. Their laws stipulate a vehicle can kill a pedestrian and not risk any jail time if the driver pays to bury the victim. I speculate that falling off a bus and getting run over would have caused me to meet with the same fate as any other unsuspecting pedestrian who impeded a moving vehicle.

Immersed in a new culture

The first days of my stay, the Anglican teachers discussed the fisherfolk and their pending baptism that coming Sunday. One pastor from their mission was preparing for the service, as he frequently ministered to these people. My ears perked up. *Maybe I can be baptized and take care of business.* The Saints had teased me back home in Argentina because my pastor had sprinkled me as a teen and had not immersed me. They spent the conversation at many meals informing me how important immersion was. In jest, I was told that the river in heaven was there for all those who had only been sprinkled. The idea of being baptized in Paraguay created a welcome opportunity to avoid further discussion.

My thinking was that I could quickly get this "out of the way" and go on with whatever else was ahead. However, the teachers were more conscientious.

They didn't want me escaping Argentina to emerge in Paraguay for a "quickie" baptism. This required a phone call to Córdoba to seek permission for the next action in my life. After talking with family members in Argentina, I received the go ahead. Then the teachers prayed with me for at least an hour as we petitioned God for His blessing on my baptism. Their submission to God stands as a reminder to walk slower and think more carefully in matters of eternal significance.

When Sunday morning arrived, we loaded ourselves into an open, doorless Land Rover, which resembled an African safari vehicle. Our trip to the river village did not traverse a distinguishable (to me) road or path, as we bounced through miles of grasslands. To my knowledge, there weren't any wild animals ready to attack us, but my imagination worked overtime contemplating what might lurk in the brush and trees. Snakes and a few big cats must have been watching us.

After almost an hour, a half dozen of us exited our conveyance and headed toward the river. We walked along the river's edge to a small village with huts made of grass roofs and mud walls. Shortly, a group of people gathered for a church service of preaching and singing. The pastor had scheduled three of us for baptism that day. A husband and wife had elected to experience the waters of baptism together. Previously, her parents had not allowed her to marry so young, even though they already had two children and were expecting a third baby. The church had granted them permission to be baptized once they married.

Before the baptism, the husband shared (in *Guaraní*, the national language of Paraguay) his encounters with Jesus and how God's protection influenced his decision to become a Christ follower. Because he fished for a living, he frequently encountered dangerous conditions while on the Paraná River. One time a squall caught him, causing his boat to capsize, tossing him into the swirling waters. While he struggled in the river, a school of piranhas surrounded him. Many have heard that a large school can consume a cow[4] in seconds. As a fisherman, he knew the dangers of the toothed fish in the turbulent waters and realized he could not save himself. He cried out to Jesus to rescue and save him. Within minutes, the storm subsided, and the fish disappeared. He climbed back into his boat and returned to shore, unscathed and grateful.

We changed our clothes after the baptismal service. I put on my dry clothes in the home of the newly baptized couple. Their abode consisted of one room, furnished with a bed and a chest. A thatch roof covered the mud-walled home. Once we were in fresh clothes, the pastors conducted another prayer time. Rodney, the English-speaking, baptizing minister, offered me a new promise verse which has reminded me of God's providence several times in my life. *"Your ears shall hear a word behind you, saying, 'This is the way, walk in it,' whenever you turn to the right hand or whenever you turn to the left."*[5]

An indigenous pastor from the local congregation also prayed for the three newly baptized individuals as he received a vision for each person. He first prayed for the couple, assuring them of God's pleasure and love, as he watched clouds of protection hovering over them. Then he prayed over me, and in Guaraní, he described a scene the Lord gave him of a waterfall, a man dressed in a white robe and a green tree. Rodney interpreted the pastor's vision into English. He explained the waterfall revealed the desire of the Holy Spirit to fill me with His presence; the man in white was the Lord overseeing my life; the tree symbolized spiritual growth.

Glimmers of sunshine and rainbows through the mist

Several years after my baptism, while browsing in a bookstore, I opened a book on name meanings. Until then, I didn't realize what my name meant. In this book, the explanation for the name *"Lynn"* was *"pool at the base of a waterfall."* I thought, *This sounds like the vision the man had for me in Paraguay.* He didn't speak English. I didn't speak Guaraní. The Holy Spirit communicates in all languages and perceives how to touch each heart. God cared about my name, and He cared about me.

Gathering grace gems from the bubbling waters

- What encounters have you experienced that evidence God's care for you?
- Do you know the meaning of your name and what it implies?
- Have you heard God call you by name? Have you experienced the meaning of your name? How has your name influenced your life?

Engaging Encounters

Behold, I am standing by the spring of water, and the daughters of the men of the city are coming out to draw water. Let the young woman to whom I shall say,

"Please let down your jar that I may drink," and who shall say, "Drink, and I will water your camels"—let her be the one whom you have appointed for your servant Isaac. By this I shall know that you have shown steadfast love to my master (Genesis 24:13-14 ESV).

More discussion, more comprehension

Enrique *"Chilo"* Gaggiotti and I devoted three hours to talking together several days a week. Instead of my returning to the downtown tutor, the Saints suggested I learn Spanish from their neighbor and former employee. I could pay him, and he would benefit from the funds and the companionship.

He loved to sing and share the songs learned while growing up. He recognized and sang Argentine tangos and Carlos Gardel (an Argentine singer and songwriter) songs. Although I didn't learn any of the lyrics, I found Chilo endearing as he waxed poetic and expressive in conveying their beauty to me. He also rehearsed the Argentine national anthem, much slower and heavier than the *"Star-Spangled Banner."* We practiced choruses from church, which helped me memorize more words in Spanish and in the songs. Hymnals and songbooks rarely appeared at gatherings, forcing me to fine tune my ear for the lyrics. Well-known hymns from English supplied me with cues about what the worshipers were singing.

This gentleman taught me to respond with greater grace. Chilo had many reasons to shake his fist at life and perhaps question God because of his current condition. He had experienced more of the "good life" in his younger years. With time, the progression of multiple sclerosis robbed Chilo of the ability to move about freely, to leave his home and to go out with old or new friends. He depended on his sister to prepare his meals, clean his home and shop at the market. He didn't complain but maintained a kind and caring heart despite his physical afflictions.

Fritz Halbers lived across the street from the Saint home. A Jewish man, he had escaped from Germany but had lost most of his family during the Holocaust. Having lived in the United States at one time, Fritz liked to practice English, so prevailed upon me to hold conversations with him.

As kindly as Fritz behaved towards me, he held an enormous amount of anger and bitterness. I do not understand what he endured when escaping from Germany and losing so many loved ones. His grief was more than I could grasp.

However, he handled his anguish by turning against God. He spent hours during the day working on a book to exonerate Judas Iscariot and to vilify Jesus. When we talked, I shared what I knew and prayed his heart would change. He never attacked my personal beliefs, but made certain I knew where he stood.

It's cold outside

During winter, we wore layers of sweaters, woolen pants and warm socks to keep out the chill inside the house. With central heating in my American home, I had never experienced space heaters other than a radiator in an old apartment while living in Chicago one summer. Many Argentine homes had either oil heaters, like our old radiators, or *pantallas*, small wall panels which radiated heat into the room. In the past, the family must have used the oil from an oil drum outside my room to heat the house, or at least several rooms in the home. The gas cook stove in the kitchen warmed that room and the dining area. Family members carted small box-shaped space heaters from room to room to keep their feet warm while working at their desks.

A new door of opportunity opened when my typing assignments slowed. Students who wished to improve their English came to interact. One young woman, a university undergraduate, visited to engage in conversations. To show her appreciation, she explained she enjoyed me because I was so simple. In Spanish, "*simple*" refers to someone who is fresh and transparent. She spoke to me in carefully crafted English and didn't understand why I grinned at her compliment. We straightened out the misunderstanding, but it serves to remember that cognates are not always intuitive.

Related to word confusion is a memory of a brief conversation during winter. It didn't seem unbearably cold to me, so I hadn't bundled up with more than a light sweater. While standing at a bus stop, a lady asked if I were cold. I responded, "*No, me siento bien.*" ("No, I'm fine.") Her response shocked me. "*Dichosa.*" At the dinner table, Doña Ruth often used the word "*dichosos*" when she prayed about how we stand before God's presence. I mistakenly translated it as meaning that we are unworthy before our almighty Father. Later, I learned the word connotes "favored, fortunate, privileged." Before discovering the meaning, I was hurt by the bus stop lady and thought, *Why is this stranger calling me a liar?* Most uncomfortable, I weakly smiled. Communicating in one's birth language creates enough barriers; adding a foreign tongue to the mix complicates matters even more.

Lost, found, lost

"My husband's boss is leaving the country and has paid Alberto in dollars. We need pesos. Do you know how I can get pesos?" the maid asked Ruth.

Overhearing her request, I jumped in and offered, "I can help with that. I've visited Exprinter to do an exchange several times."

After work a few days later, Emilia and I took the *"G"* to downtown Córdoba to retrieve her pesos. After kissing her goodbye when we left the exchange office, waves of thankfulness washed over me in realizing how I could reach out in kindness. My euphoric feelings were short-lived. Several days later, while going through my clothes on the shelves in the nightstand, I noticed my stationery supplies were in disarray. After checking in the box which held my cards and secreted cash, I realized that most of my concealed funds were missing.

"Missionary friends had told me to have extra dollars in case I couldn't always get my checks cashed," I informed Mom and Dad Saint. "Now that money is missing. What's happened to it?"

Both quickly concluded, "The only person who has entered your room is the maid. We will contact her husband to verify what she has told us."

Thus, the family began careful sleuthing. They contacted her husband and requested he come with Emilia on her next workday.

In an adjoining room, I listened to the Saints' conversation with Alberto and Emilia.

"Alberto, did you receive dollars from your employer?"

"No."

"Did Emilia tell you about the dollars she had in her possession?"

"No."

After a bit more discussion, one of them asked, "Emilia, where did you get those dollars?"

Finally she confessed, "I took them from the bedroom."

Sadly, they explained to her, "We cannot continue to hire you as our maid. You have been dishonest in our home, and we cannot trust you anymore."

In taking my money, and although she had a temporary gain, Emilia lost her job and the chance to use the family as a solid reference for other positions. My heart broke for her as I felt responsible for not taking more precautions with my cash. My naivete might have tempted her and caused her to fall. It's one of those imponderables. How responsible am I for the actions of others? In the historical novel *Les Miserables*, Victor Hugo explains the importance of not owning something which might cause another to covet or to sin. The story about the thief who took the bishop's silver revealed God's mercy to Jean Valjean through the bishop's pardon.[6] *What could I have done to change the outcome with the maid?*

Train ride to B. A.

Haydée, the camp cook at Valle del Lago in the summer, stayed with us from August to October in 1974. Along with Haydée, David, Evelyn and I kept the home fires burning while Dad Phil traveled to the States for evangelistic and fund-raising events. Mom Ruth left in late winter (in Argentina, but late summer in the States) to retrieve her twin sons, Jim and Joe, who had been serving in the U.S. Army in Germany since 1972.

In October Eve and I took a train to Buenos Aires to meet the plane with her mom and her brothers on board. We rode to the airport with another missionary family to receive the three travelers. Once in the parking lot after disembarking from the plane, Jim remarked to his mom, "*Está linda, mami, ¿no?*" I looked at him and smiled, knowing he did not realize the *norteamericana* had absorbed enough Spanish to understand a compliment about looking pretty.

Camp beckons: we follow

Within a week, the brothers engaged me in conversation and outings. Jim showed an interest in me, but he sat on the fence in his relationship with Christ. Months later, at Valle del Lago, he took a stand to follow Jesus during a camp meeting led by the father of Joe's future *novia* (bride). On that warm February night, Jim's determined frame headed towards the fireplace in the *comedor* (dining room). Before hundreds of campers and worshipers, he made his choice. Within days, his twin brother Joe also made the same decision, awakening his parents in their room in the middle of the night at their bedside as his father had dreamed, months beforehand. Two weeks after Jim's eternal decision, we announced our engagement at the camp before the entire mealtime crew of 300 people applauding in anticipation of a Saint family wedding.

On a warm and sunny day during camp that summer, Jim and Joe drove to a cliff for diving and swimming. A new Stateside friend (another recent roommate) and I stayed at camp and climbed the infamous hill (the one I had hiked with the lady from Buenos Aires) with a handful of teens from a church youth group. On our return from the hike, we learned that, as Joe was diving from *Nido de Aguila* (Eagle's Nest), he had misjudged his head position during his last dive and had broken his eardrum on impact with the water. In the coming days, putting drops into Joe's ear as he muffled his moans from the pain, became my nursing duty. Thankfully, except for the agony of those few weeks following the mishap, his hearing and eardrum were restored.

Although Jim and I socialized at camp, working in the kitchen occupied hours of time. The head cook and we assistants prepared most of the foods from fresh ingredients except for enormous cans of tomatoes used for creating Italian sauces for *fideos* (noodles), *ñoquis* (little potato dumplings made from scratch) and *polenta* (thickened cornmeal mush). Enormous quantities of food and many hours of preparation were required when 200-300 campers devoured hefty portions at each meal. Cleaning dinner plates, glasses and flatware also consumed hours with hand washing and drying. Willing and able campers also assisted, which shaved off a few minutes of work for those of us laboring in the kitchen.

Simple morning breakfasts offered French bread slathered with either *dulce de leche* (a caramel as thick as peanut butter but much smoother, better tasting and more highly caloric) or peach marmalade. Besides *café con leche*, guests sometimes enjoyed *mate cocido*. *Mate* (MAH-tay), a traditional tea from Argentina and a few other South American countries, is composed of healthful herbs; the liquid is usually sipped through a filtered metal straw inserted into a special container, such as a gourd, holding the herbal mixture mixed with water. The prepared mate cocido, with milk as a base instead of water, resembles a mate latte. To prepare for the breakfast gathering, the cook poured gallons of milk into enormous cauldrons to heat on open gas flames, adding scoops of either the coffee or the mate, plus many cups of sugar. We ladled out thousands of cups each summer season. Before many campers came, in December we welcomed the countryside children who arrived on a buckboard hauled by a tractor. They also inhaled the traditional breakfast, followed by Bible stories, games and activities on the campgrounds.

The Saints made *Valle del Lago* their main headquarters over many summers, from most of December to the first week of March. Camp positions beckoned volunteers and workers to fill the void of required labor. During my first summer, *Doña Ruth* sometimes asked me to accompany her to the warehouse in *Villa Dolores*, a small town about half an hour's distance from the retreat center. While we shopped and took in the sights of the town, workers loaded the truck with supplies for both the kitchen and the snack stand. Besides kitchen orders from the cook and workers, campers also requested special purchases from the town. After Jim and Joe's arrival, their mother willingly released herself from that assignment.

Not only did Ruth often conduct a shopping expedition when she didn't have extra drivers, she also engineered the room placement of all campers. Accommodating hundreds of guests kept her constantly counting and figuring who was coming and who was going. People traveled by bus or car from hours away. In those days there was no telephone at the camp, so someone needed to drive to or connect with the small-scale telegraph and telephone office in *Los Pozos*, several miles away, to receive dispatches advising of guest arrivals. Many accepted the job of retrieving messages—workers, casual visitors, campers, camp caretakers. There was no way of guessing when messages would reach the phone station or when said messages would arrive at their intended destination, i.e., Ruth Saint, room coordinator. Getting notices required divine intervention. Sometimes campers appeared at the same time as their messages. Rarely did guests turn up before their estimated arrival.

Goodbye, for now

After camp season, we returned to Córdoba two months before my visa expired. I continued to work on typing projects for Phil Saint. In off hours, Jim and I got to know each other better, along with relating to his friends. In one of their unguarded, spontaneous moments, Jim and Joe discovered an exotic animal farm where they bought a young puma. The pet lasted about 20 hours in its cage at their home as it exhibited aggression and discipline problems. Shocks, surprises and spontaneity presented my future.

In the middle of May, Jim and I took the train to *Buenos Aires* where he said "Goodbye" until our August wedding. Upon reaching home in the States, I listened to a song repeatedly, *"Te quiero como nadie te quiso"* ("I love you as no one has loved you"), a romantic ballad which made my heart flutter. Jim's go-to song, which did not carry the same romantic message, was from Glenn Campbell's rendition of "By the Time I Get to Phoenix." At least it had my hometown in the lyrics. Repeatedly listening to the record put him into a melancholy state of mind. As he listened to the "Phoenix" song on the only record player in the house, the family endured patiently, perhaps through gritted teeth.

Glimmers of sunshine and rainbows through the mist

Working at camp granted me the opportunity to know my future husband in ways many don't have. Our interactions took place over hours every day. I recognized his natural skills and ideas. He had honed his practical aptitude for home repairs and automobile maintenance over years of living with items that broke down. Agility was and is one of his strong points as he can easily maneuver his body or a vehicle on narrow pathways or high cliffs.

More than his outward abilities, Jim lives with a heart of passion. He exhibits a transparency and vulnerability observable in few others. Often, people who meet him have intense feelings about him. Some are negative; others are positive. He doesn't apologize for his stance. His personality moves him to go where the action is. Their dad, referring to James and John in Scripture, often called Jim and Joe the *"Sons of Thunder."* [7]

Living with the family before meeting Jim allowed me to observe interactions, which gave me an understanding of the family psychology, especially after we were married. Insight is not always an instant revelation. It can be hard won and time delayed.

Missionary kids, as a missionary once shared with me, are tricultural. They belong to the culture their parents were raised in. They belong to the culture they were raised in. And they end up blending the two into a unique culture.[8] It helps to know these propensities when living with someone who is tricultural. It doesn't always fix things, but it helps to understand... sometimes.

Gathering grace gems from the bubbling waters

- Have you ever learned a new language? How did you attempt it?
- Languages comprise words, but of additional importance are the values and ideas nuanced into conversations. What kind of body language or innuendoes do you identify in others?
- When we walk with the Lord, we learn a new way of thinking. In what ways are your thoughts different in these days than they were before?
- How do you communicate to show you care about someone else?
- When there are cultural issues, how can you work at developing stronger ties?

Desert Vows

Water will gush forth in the wilderness and streams in the desert
(Isaiah 35:6 NIV).

My return flight first landed in Miami, Florida, where I opened my luggage for the customs agent and then checked my bags for connections to Phoenix. Miami resembled Buenos Aires, as there were enough Spanish-speaking people to remind me of Argentina. Landing in Dallas, Texas, my next stop, brought unexpected experiences with newer technology. Dallas possessed a modern system of airport trams with a disembodied voice advising of the next terminal stop. No humans overseeing the rail cars left me uneasy. The sterile atmosphere in Dallas introduced my first taste of reverse culture shock. This was not Latin America.

The old familiar–brand new

The concept of culture shock had prepared me for living in Argentina. I had steeled myself for a different locale in adapting to the expected challenge of landing and living in the Latin country. Like a sponge, I soaked in the Hispanic ambience. The physical surroundings and the people drew me in. Admittedly, living with the Saints provided a buffer as they spoke English and explained many subtleties I might not have recognized on my own had I stayed with others solely from that Latin culture.

Because the Phil Saint family had moved from the States almost two decades before my arrival, they used unfamiliar American terms. Jim's mom frequently peppered her conversations with idioms from the 40s and 50s. Many of her phrases mystified me, which led to absorbing a different facet of American culture.

Certainly, many details in communication have escaped my notice. In fact, I am now grasping what was unperceived then. After years of adapting and changing, I now comprehend eccentricities and mannerisms of people with whom I grew up, attended school and worked. Relating to one another encompasses a peculiar mystery that keeps us constantly questioning, growing and learning.

Upon returning home, reverse culture shock stunned me. Within a week of my arrival, Mom took me to Metro Center, a large mall in North Phoenix. Oddly, this felt foreign, and I wasn't prepared. Within minutes of entering the extensive structure boasting a myriad of stores, dizziness and nausea enveloped me. Too much stimulation. Too much wealth. Too slick. The electricity and air conditioning kept the environment controlled and inviting, at least for the customers frequenting the shopping center. It took me weeks to adapt to shopping and making purchases from a cashier at a cash register. In Argentina, I had to stop and think about how I was going to request something in Spanish. Back in the States, I still hesitated and formed my thoughts; then I remembered to ask in English as I suffered from a nano paralysis in communication.

Not only did shopping centers throw me into conniptions, but homes did, too. In Argentina, most homes and businesses had tile floors. In the Saint home, throw rugs decorated and improved the environment. Doña Ruth rolled up the rugs, carried them outside and shook them out on cleaning days as she swept and mopped the floors. I had forgotten about vacuum cleaners. In the States, it was rare to encounter a home that didn't have wall-to-wall carpeting. Down there, carpeting represented wealth. Here, even economy apartments provided carpeting. Our Stateside church also had carpeting, along with central air conditioning and heating.

After adapting to the initial surprises, I enjoyed spending time with friends from church who had been strong encouragers while I was away. Many had helped support my stay, financially and spiritually. Sharing on the phone or in small groups allowed me to nurture our relationships.

A moment of chagrin involved a duet that Mom insisted Doug and I sing for the church congregation. My brother has a superb voice and a fine ear for music. I like to sing but cannot attempt creative vocal arrangements, thus limiting my musical abilities. On that fateful Sunday, we sang a song in English and Spanish. I didn't hit the right notes with an "Alleluia" descant but fumbled on through. Thankfully, no one asked for a reprise. Doug never said another word about the performance, feigning no memory of the debacle.

Wedding plans

From May until August, I spent days in wedding preparations. One chore was to compose invitations in English and Spanish. Without seeking advice, I had corrected something in Spanish before printing off the letters and sending the copies to Argentina. Once they arrived in Argentina, a family member detected my grammatical error. Too late. Mail took weeks; phone calls took hours for connection. I never learned if the family shared the imperfect invitations with friends. Printing costs were exorbitant, so my guess is that they gave out the flawed cards just the same—only a guess.

To purchase wedding attire, Mom and I shopped for days, looking for the right prices, colors and styles for ladies' dresses and men's suits. Leisure suits made a fashion statement for men in the 1970s. Most gentlemen would hesitate to don the clothes now, but my husband has kept his suit, either in case the style returns or because of sentiment. To avoid a wedding dress storage quandary, my wedding gown accompanied Eve to Argentina within two years of our marriage in anticipation of her future wedding in 1982 (she didn't know it then but planned ahead).

The nuptials took place in August, one of Phoenix's hottest months. Jim, coming from winter in Argentina, arrived at the airport in a fashionable woolen suit with a high turtleneck sweater. Thankfully, he reached Phoenix two weeks beforehand to acclimate himself and his wardrobe.

Within a day or two of Jim's arrival, my brother took him outside to play tennis in the unrelenting Arizona sun. Morning temperatures often hit the high 90s before climbing to the afternoon 100s. By the time they returned, Jim was suffering from heat stroke. His face had turned beet red as he perspired profusely and complained of nausea. As a nurse who had lived for years in the desert climate, Mom knew how to provide him with the best first aid. She made sure he drank copious amounts of water and waited until his symptoms resolved before pulling back on the liquids. Undeterred, he played tennis again… in the winter.

To continue with home settling, we purchased our first vehicle, a manual transmission, mustard yellow Vega. Once the contract was signed and approved, the salesman, running and shouting congratulations at us with the contract flapping from his fist, left me mortified. The dealership must have gleefully rubbed its corporate hands to find someone willing to buy the car, which had a few lemon flaws we failed to recognize. Fortunately, at the time of purchase we also signed an extended warranty which eventually served us well, as we needed to replace the entire engine when the aluminum block melted in the heat the year following.

Off and on again

A week after Jim arrived, I started taking birth control pills to help with family planning. On a Monday night, we visited new Argentine friends. I returned home in a foul mood, not realizing the pill's hormonal changes would take a toll and shatter my plans. After downing one or two pills, I did not want to get married and wanted nothing to do with my fiancé. This ushered in a dark two days for me and for Jim. The entire household remained in dire straits. I purchased Jim's ticket to fly back to Argentina and could not bear to talk to him. It was the strangest experience. From loving him deeply and then suddenly entering a state of complete apathy and rejection towards him confused Jim, my family and me.

My mother brought in friends to talk with me, to dissuade me from a rash decision. It became almost impossible to articulate my feelings. The presence of people assigned to reason with me did not improve my attitude, but seemed to cause the clouds to darken. The sense of sadness and emptiness left me drained. Lying on my bed for hours, I remained depressed. My mother came in and tried to brighten my outlook, insisting I change from my dark blue clothes into brighter, happier ones. Inexplicably, Mom seemed to believe she could order me to exhibit a sunnier attitude. The lecture didn't faze me; I remained in a maelstrom of emotions.

Two days after the dark, disturbing clouds had descended and enveloped me and a few hours before Jim's scheduled return plane trip to Argentina, a palpable lifting came over me. I sensed the clouds drift away. Suddenly, the heaviness dissipated. The darkness vanished before the light. Upon leaving my bedroom dungeon, I entered the den to talk to my mom and simply said, "I love Jim. I want to marry him."

She responded, "Well, you had better get in there and tell him."

I did. He stopped packing. We all stopped crying. The airlines refunded the canceled plane tickets. We proceeded with plans for the next week and a half before our wedding. During that time, we found an apartment. We arranged for hotels and cabin stays for our honeymoon.

Throughout the pre-wedding week, we welcomed family members and guests, including Jim's sister, Martha, and her husband, Sam, and their children, Steve and Elizabeth. They were the only ones representing Jim's family and friends, as most lived in Argentina. The Berberiáns, by divine arrangement, spent several years in the States before relocating as missionaries and professors to Guatemala; those years overlapped our first years of marriage.

Upon entering the family, I became the only North American in-law. Sam was born in Greece during World War II and moved with his family after the war to live in Argentina. Two of the other future Saint daughters-in-law were Argentines. Eve later married Humberto, originally from Peru.

One more setback occurred on Friday, two days before our wedding. Before obtaining our marriage license in the morning, the officials informed us that Jim needed to have a physical exam before they could approve the marriage. At that point, I was envisioning a sham wedding, one that would not be honored until we could follow the rules. However, my mom called St. Joseph's Hospital where she worked and found a nun who approved the physical Jim needed, along with the blood test. The result: we had a valid marriage license when needed.

The wedding ceremony held so much meaning for me… the music, the Scriptures, the people. For the reception, I baked many quick breads and prepared special mint candies. We had ordered a small, tiered cake with candied daisies and forget-me-nots for us (I put the rest of it into the freezer for a year to be savored on our anniversary… freezer burn rendered it a sad celebratory remembrance). The sheet cake for our guests displayed one minor flaw. A four-year-old, lacking parental supervision, took his finger and ran it down the middle of the cake for a finger-sized taste of frosting. His action left an odd and unforgettable divot in the dessert.

Life as a pair

After our honeymoon on the White Mountain Apache Indian Reservation in eastern Arizona, we settled into a little furnished apartment in a complex that housed retirees. While Jim attended school under the G. I. Bill, homemaking skills became my focus—cooking full meals, decorating the apartment and sewing clothes.

Most of the time, our dinners were tasty and made from scratch, although my husband only recalls the homemade chili I served five days in a row, starting with crunchy beans and ending with soft ones by the end of the week. My time in Argentina had gifted me with a greater appreciation for preparing food, cleaning the kitchen and organizing the house. Jim's mom had tackled household tasks with energy and delight. She danced and sang as she did her chores. An instant menu could be called up every day, no matter when unexpected guests showed up. I needed that training and her attitude.

Because we both loved spending time with children, church families and their friends offered us babysitting jobs. We also house sat every few months. Leaving the apartment meant we would have food to eat and could take advantage of someone else's water and electricity. Our budget squeezed us tightly, but God's provision kept our bills paid and food in our mouths with small childcare responsibilities or house-sitting jobs.

Glimmers of sunshine and rainbows through the mist

The two days of battling hormonal changes showed me it was possible to enter a depression and feel powerless to combat it. I prayed hard during that time and still endured such a vacuum in my soul. From that experience, I can more easily identify with those who live with this on either a daily basis or as a periodic event.

Because my situation was abnormal, identifying the root cause initially eluded all of us. *Intervention* did not improve the situation. It is hard to face others who make assumptions about us, especially when the *obvious* is not the truth. *Nobody understands me.* My situation was not the presumed bridal jitters; it was a chemical change in my body. Others' stories only left me more estranged and alienated during the dilemma.

Once we were married, wedded bliss didn't overwhelm either of us. Adapting to one another is work, a dreadfully painful amount of work. Besides gender differences, adjusting to someone from a different culture adds an extra dimension to marital harmony and/or disharmony.

Before we took our vows, a book extolling the virtues and ease of "*two becoming one*" gave me hope for the glorious blending of two diverse individuals. Imposing the book application created a chasm of unreality when looking at real life. We had craters in places intended to reveal jagged edges. The author of the book used an illustration of puzzle pieces, each one filling the space the other lacked. We were full of jagged, three-dimensional pieces that couldn't find a suitable space within the other one, outside of major revision. That revision warranted painful cutting, sanding and refitting. Later, much later, we melded together.

While in 8th grade home economics class, I had cut out two left pieces for the back of a dress. No one has two left sides. A new right side was required to complete the outfit, costing extra time and extra expense, adding frustrated tears to the entire project. With relationships, people do not blend perfectly. Fitting and adjusting requires incredible refining, removing and readjusting. It helps to recall that God is the ultimate "Re"—He will do it again. We rejoice in His skill as He redeems, renews, revives, reclaims and restores. We remain a dynamic rework in progress.

Gathering grace gems from the bubbling waters

- Have you ever faced a situation in which you knew you were powerless? How did you come to a resolution?
- If others were involved, how could they have encouraged you to change or at least have eased your discomfort?
- Was there a specific turning around that you can pinpoint as an "*Aha*" moment? How would you describe it? How do you remember it?

Footnotes

1 Phil and Ruth's twin sons, Jim and Joe, and their friend challenged the Pampa de Achala road on bicycle for a three-day trek from Córdoba to Valle del Lago, transporting tents and camping supplies in their backpacks and inside a makeshift box on the frame of each bike. After the grueling days and nights, they opted to hitch a ride when they finally returned home.

2 1 Corinthians 13:6 (paraphrase)

3 The Anglican Church originated as the Church of England, also known as the Episcopal Church here in the United States.

4 Piranha Guide

5 Isaiah 30:21 (NKJV)

6 Layton.

7 James the *son* of Zebedee and John the brother of James, to whom He gave the name Boanerges, that is, 'Sons of Thunder' (Mark 3:17 NKJV).

8 Hopkins. The author offers a thorough explanation of the challenges and complexities faced by missionary kids who have been largely ignored by supporting churches and sometimes, their own parents, regarding their unusual circumstances in their host country and in their homeland. Even defining "homeland" can create an ambiguous perception of where home resides in the hearts of those living in a foreign land.

As an example of the confusion, both my husband's parents are buried in Argentina. Although this was not the land of their birth, this became the land of their heart. My father-in-law had strong feelings about too much intermingling with Americans. He wanted his family to identify with Argentina.

Section 2. Troubling the Dark Waters:

The Lord Gives, and the Lord Takes Away

The LORD gives, and the LORD takes away. Blessed be the name of the LORD
(Job 1:21 CSB).

Gift from God

He will swallow up death [and abolish it] for all time. And the Lord GOD will wipe away tears from all faces, And He will take away the disgrace of His people from all the earth; For the LORD has spoken
(Isaiah 25:8 AMP).

Excitement and anticipation filled the days of waiting for our firstborn's arrival. Before conception, I had fasted and prayed for a child. I sensed the Lord directed me to read the account of Hannah and of her begging God for a son. Also, while reading in Isaiah, a verse impressed me, *Make a large signboard and write on it the birth announcement of the son I am going to give you.*[1]

Unexpected gift

A month before our baby was born, we agreed on the name *Nathaniel* if we had a boy, in memory of Jim's uncle, Nate Saint. Two weeks late, Nathaniel finally showed up on September 10th. Eight hours after his birth, as I was recovering from an emergency C-section, a pediatrician came in to advise me there was something wrong with our baby. In a clinical fashion, he reported, "You may not nurse or hold the baby. We don't know why he has so little movement." And then he promptly left. Alone with the pain of surgery, I now faced the pain of an ailing child.

Three days later, after performing a battery of tests, a pediatric neurologist informed us Nathaniel had Werdnig-Hoffman's[2] syndrome, or muscular atrophy. This is a rare genetic disease which recent medical findings relate to the adult onset of ALS (amyotrophic lateral sclerosis), Lou Gehrig's disease. There is little to no muscle tone as the nerves and muscles fail to transmit messages over the synapses (like open bridge crossings), thus preventing the muscles from reacting to stimuli or improving in strength. One pediatrician explained, "His muscle tone is like that of a rag doll."

The neurologist gave us a negative prognosis and counseled that Nathaniel would live only six months at the most. He also, and I believe to protect us, insisted we should not love him too much because he would soon die. In the consultation room, the doctor introduced us to a medical student, furiously taking notes about our reactions to the news of our baby. From my perspective, the information, which carried such a dire outcome, invites medical voyeurism. The shock is so heavy and intense. It is too private and sacred to expose as a medical study. And I understand scientists appreciate data and studies. However, to value the individual, it would be my preference not to exploit the reactions of the sufferers. It reminds me of news reporters shoving microphones and cameras into the faces of disaster victims. In the confusion and turmoil, raw pain needs time to process. Then again, that doesn't make the sensational news.

After our consultation with the neurologist and his assistant, the hospital discharged Nathaniel into our care. We had received permission to hold him within the first day of his birth as other staff determined his condition did not warrant isolation from us. Whenever we wanted to visit him during his stay in NICU, the newborn intensive care unit, we washed our hands, arms, faces and necks with Betadine solution and then covered our clothes with a sterile hospital gown before entering the unit. We didn't have to bathe in yellow fluid or don a sterile gown after taking him home.

Caring for him in our own apartment gave us a sense of relief. As the days passed, Nathaniel's personality developed. He thrilled us with his sweet disposition. Within two weeks, he first smiled at Jim. Because of Nathaniel's weakness, we determined to focus on Jesus. Emphasizing the baby's illness would have kept us perpetually depressed. Instead, we immersed ourselves with Bible verses and prayer, clinging to the Healer of our bodies and our hearts.

Nathaniel developed pneumonia at six weeks of age. We continued to care for him at home and learned to replicate PT maneuvers on his lung quadrants. The technique required cupping our hands and tapping his chest and his back. Although it made more noise than we thought he could endure, the activity must have helped to loosen the infection in his lungs as he cooperated with the treatments and didn't grimace during the sessions.

Put him back. He runs so fast.

On Sunday, November 13th, he gave us his last two smiles at our church. The next two days entailed a life and death battle. We took him to his pediatrician who soberly told us, "Apart from divine intervention, his course is fatal." By Tuesday afternoon, after many sleepless hours, we drove him to Phoenix Crippled Children's Hospital where we left him in the hands of the medical staff and God's intervention. We expected to return the next morning.

Late that evening, after we had gone to bed, I couldn't sleep. Although I closed my eyelids, my eyes stayed wide open on the inside. As I prayed for Nathaniel, I visualized Jesus walking down the corridor of the hospital. At first I thought the picture was in my mind, but the scene changed to what I was not imagining. My first thoughts echoed hope for his recovery. *Good, now Jesus is going to heal Nathaniel.*

While watching, I asked Jesus to first bless the other babies, which He did by placing His hands on these little ones. He stood at the side of their beds as he touched them. Then Jesus walked over to the foot of Nathaniel's bed, leaned over, picked him up and embraced him. Brilliant light bathed the entire setting. I examined the picture carefully and realized that Nathaniel's body was still on the bed while he was also being held in Jesus' arms. This was not my plan. I cried out, silently, "Put him back!" With that, the scene vanished. I opened my eyes and looked at the alarm clock—11:35. I lay in the silence and cried.

Close to midnight, the phone rang. I hurried from the bedroom to answer the call.

"Mrs. Saint, this is Dr. Jones. The hospital called me to report that Nathaniel has expired."

"I already know. I just saw Jesus take him."

We called my mom and dad, who drove over to get us. Together we left for the hospital to see his little body. When we entered the room, Jim asked the nurse, "Would it be all right for me to hold the baby?"

She reacted. "I don't think that would be advisable."

My emboldened mother, seasoned by years of hospital work, refuted her, "He will be fine; he needs to hold him."

Mom had ways of interfering at the right time. Her interventions were not always welcome, but sometimes they were necessary. This was one of those times. Jim held and embraced Nathaniel's earthly body, his temporary tent, as we cried together.

We held a funeral/memorial service within a day and a half of Nathaniel's passing. Jim wanted to dress the baby one last time. We selected clothes to put on our little boy. My mom had given us knitted duckie slippers earlier, along with a light blue, velour onesie. She knew what we would choose for his going-away outfit.

After Nathaniel slipped from earth, we remembered that a few people, including Jim, had dreams of his running fast through vibrant green grass. Several weeks after he died, friends welcomed us to their home for dinner. After we related several dream stories, they confided they had cautioned their two-year-old not to ask us about little Nate.

She questioned, "Why?"

"Because he's gone."

She brightly answered, "I know why he's gone. It's because he runs so fast." She knew he was a baby. Did God give her a dream, too?

Expiration date

One other area I was laboring over related to the word the doctor had used to let me know Nathaniel had died. He had said, "Expired." The word was one I couldn't speak or repeat. Two weeks after the baby's death, my obstetrician's wife came to interview me to record the details of our experiences with Nathaniel to close her book, *Talk with us, Lord.*

Jayne asked, "What did the doctor say to let you know about Nathaniel's death?"

I answered, "He simply said he had died."

"Were those his exact words?"

I could not bring myself to even say the word "expired" out loud and insisted, "He just said, 'He died.'"

Thinking of my child as having expired left me with a cold and sterile sensation. I grappled with the word for a month. In mid-December, I recognized God directing me to write a thank-you letter to the neurologist. I carefully worded my correspondence, expressing our gratitude as we were indebted to him for intervening on our behalf and for allowing us to have the baby cared for, albeit for only a few hours, at a special, critical needs children's hospital. We could not afford the expense of the facility, so we recognized his word helped us receive better medical help to provide more comfort and less pain for Nathaniel during his last hours.

After I mailed the letter, my thoughts returned to "expired." In mulling over the word, I grasped the deeper meaning. In Latin, *ex* means *out of.* The *spired* syllable relates to *breath* or *spirit.* God showed me Nathaniel's "expiration" as Jesus gently took his spirit out of him. No longer does the word hold any pain. In God's tender mercy, He took the sting away as He reminded me of the word meaning and the vision He had given me.

My mother composed a poem dedicated to Nathaniel weeks before he died. Presenting us with soft leather, baby moccasins, she included her poetry to us to give us hope for the future.

Rolling beat of tom-toms
Indian feet are shod

In softest deerskin leather
Dancing on the sod.

Papoose, your feet are tender
As you dream in cradled care.
You walk on forest pathways
In footsteps of the bear.

You're tracking all the creatures
Down piney woods, you've trod.
And sun—in blue-skied heaven—
Is shining down from God.

Blow softly, wind, on little boy.
And sun—beam, oh so tender.
He'll soon grow up and watch with you
These things in all their splendor.

Joyce Hulstedt
October 16, 1977

Glimmers of sunshine and rainbows through the mist

Jim faced the loss of our son with incredible strength. Perhaps because his sister had died of cystic fibrosis when he was nine years old, he showed more fiber in confronting the death of our firstborn. He addressed certain emotional aspects which were uncomfortable for me. He wept freely and suffered openly.

Losing Nathaniel was the first time I had seriously looked death in the face. Although I had lost a few people I cared about when I was younger, my ability to reconcile death did not resonate from within. Emotionally I ran from death and from addressing the issues surrounding it. In facing Nathaniel's death, I entered a time of grief, much of it experienced while he was still alive. God granted me a deeper understanding of His kindness and grace through the sadness. He had given us visions and dreams, ones we could not have invented. God's reassurances helped me understand the course we are all on, as some finish sooner than later. We don't number our days.[3] He holds a divine calendar for each one.

God's Word amazes me at its appropriateness for any season. Psalm 84:6 (TPT) brings renewed comfort: *Even when their paths wind through the dark valley of tears, they dig deep to find a pleasant pool where others find only pain. He gives to them a brook of blessing filled from the rain of an outpouring.*

Almost ten years after Nathaniel's death, we placed a headstone on his formerly unmarked grave. The Scripture we chose comes from Psalm 116:15 (KJV) *Blessed in the sight of the LORD is the death of His saints.*

Gathering grace gems from the bubbling waters

- Was there an incident that confronted you, personally, about God's ways in this narrative?
- Are there places in which you detected God was speaking and addressing the family and others?
- Have you lost someone close? How have you received comfort and consolation?
- What helped you deal with this person's passing? Is there something you can share with someone else that helped you?

Our Valentine

For the Lamb in the center of the throne will be their shepherd and will guide them to springs of the water of life; and God will wipe every tear from their eyes (Revelation 7:17 NASB).

Joe, Susy, and their one-year-old son, Martin, arrived from Argentina two months after Nathaniel's death. Martin moved like a spinning firecracker. He gave us delightful days; he helped fill in the open wounds we endured after losing our little boy. We still wanted another child and welcoming Martin into our lives increased our desire to parent so that we, too, could participate in the joy of child-rearing.

Having a second child seemed a matter of course. We welcomed Jeremy into our family on Valentine's Day in 1979, 15 months after losing Nathaniel. At his dedication, our pastor cryptically commented, "He will always be a heartthrob in your lives."

Jeremy, at birth, appeared healthy. However, by March we realized his muscle tone did not seem as tight as it should be. During those doubtful days, I learned to listen more directly to the voice of God. I filled a journal with notes from times of meditation, spending an hour a day, praying and listening.

And He talks with me

My little babe is but a caterpillar. How I want him to stretch his wings and soar. But he does not have his wings yet. He still must learn to crawl. I am so impatient and don't want to plod through transitions. Yet, how many times in my own life have I been a lowly caterpillar, not even crawling? Teach me and instruct me in Your ways, O my God.

One thought invaded my thoughts as I looked at our little boy, not seeing any advancements in his physical development. There were mothers all over the world who had children whom they truly could not help. They might not have enough food to feed them. Or perhaps their children were ill with a disease that could have been curable in a Western culture, but they had no access to medication for their little ones. There were millions of mothers experiencing helplessness.

God had given His only Son, who was sent to earth to die. In a small way, God's heart for Jesus and for the entire world gave me a glimpse of His love. There is a world of individuals that He longs for, who will not open their arms to receive Him. I could only focus on my baby but realized God had sadness, too.

How great must Jesus' heart and love be? I can care about a precious few people and truly care for my family. As a mother once again, I love Jeremy deeply. How immense is God's love, as He loves ALL so very much! As I sit meditating, the song is playing on the radio, "God, How It Must Have Broken Your Heart to Send Your Son Away." Lord, fill me with Your love that I may reach out and touch the hurting and the sorrowing. Let me reflect Jesus' love to all... there's so much of me.

As the days and weeks wore on, there was more apprehension than confirmation. I recall taking Jeremy to a meeting at a church on the westside of Phoenix for a healing prayer. Perhaps God would choose to heal him through this avenue. A few family members encouraged us to declare healing and wholeness for Jeremy. I prayed as earnestly and as filled with faith as I knew. I tried to speak declarations of God's healing. Not that God does not honor such prayers but for us, we didn't see what we were so desperately seeking.

Same diagnosis, same prognosis

In June, we took Jeremy to the baby's pediatrician.

"Jeremy is on the same trajectory as his older brother."

"Is there anything we can do?"

Repeating the words he had given us with Nathaniel, the doctor stressed, *"Outside of divine intervention, there is nothing else that can be done."* There was nothing else we could do but wait for him to get sicker. Or wait for God to heal him.

Traveling in the States with Dad Saint, Jim's mom stayed with us close to the time our doctor gave Jeremy's diagnosis. One day I was spent and exhausted from caring for our little boy, not just caring for him but caring about him. I broke into sobs while talking to Mom Ruth. Only four months old, Jeremy absorbed my emotions as he also burst into tears. My reaction confused him, and he responded to my cries with his own. Through this experience, I resolved to minister to his tender heart and to shield him from my pain. He was too young to carry my burdens.

How could I change my ways? My answer came in pursuing thankfulness. Purposing to look at what Jeremy could do, not at where he was losing ground, allowed me to repent and turn around. This exercise changed my focus from despair to anticipation. Every movement, every breath, every smile and every cry gave me reason to respond to the light.

Light chases the darkness

In one of his last weeks, Jeremy had an episode in which he evidenced convulsions. We thought we were going to lose him, but he rallied. Our pastor and his wife drove to our home to pray for him the following day. My mind raced. I could hardly form two thoughts in a row without questioning where we were or why we were not getting better answers. As they were preparing to leave, our pastor's wife mentioned, "I see Jim is at peace." That is all she said, but it made me think—hard.

If he is at peace, why am I struggling? That night I had another serious talk with God. A Scripture verse illustrates what He and I worked on. *"Search me, O God, and know my heart; Try me and know my anxious thoughts."*[4] I sensed a searchlight. I had not faced God's displeasure so acutely in the past. It was not His intention to leave me in this place, but He also wanted me to see that my own judgments against others, especially my husband, were a grief to Him.

Because of His light beams, I recognized two areas in which I held judgments against Jim. Whether God was judging or correcting him was truly not my business. The Holy Spirit does His work. He never assigned that task to me. I am a human with my own flaws and disconnects. I prayed, *Dear God, You are in control of our defects. I am not here to restore and reconcile areas that are lacking in others, especially in my husband. You do the work, and I will trust You. My hands are off.*

On Sunday morning, I asked our minister and his wife if I could share what God had shown me about judgment. They gave me permission to open my heart and speak. During prayer time for healing, a woman named Grace stood and gave us the exact words given after my baptism in Paraguay. *"And your ears shall hear a word behind you, saying, 'This is the way, walk in it,' when you turn to the right or when you turn to the left."*[5]

Once the prayers and Scripture exhortation ended, I took Jeremy to the nursery to change his diapers and to feed him. A woman followed me with an urgency in her manner. I didn't know how to respond to her after she spoke to me. I have no memory of either her name or her face, but her words stayed and penetrated.

"Why would such a nice young couple go for prayer again? I knew you had lost your first little boy and was concerned for you. But deep inside, I knew what it was. It was sin." She seemed delighted with her revelation. I thanked her but wasn't sure what I was thanking her for. That she had determined I was a sinner? That I needed to repent? That she had such insight into my heart? To this day, I don't harbor any feelings against her; she revealed some of what had been in my heart. The remarks have, hopefully, kept me tenderer and less judgmental toward others and toward those close to me. Nonetheless, this is not a recommendation for glibly sharing words of reprimand with the mother of a very ill child.

Because of the experience, I recorded areas of more learning in my journal:

- *Never accuse or assume the spiritual problem of another. I open myself for deceiving pride and self-righteousness.*
- *I am not the Holy Spirit. Lord, help me see what You would have me understand.*
- *Saying something is so doesn't make it so until God reveals it.*

- *There is no "magic formula" to healing.*
- *God has promised to write (engrave and carve) His words on our hearts.*
- *God says, "What I want is obedience, not sacrifice."*
- *I, once again, comprehend in a small way, Abraham's experience when placing Isaac on the altar... the wrenching in my heart of leaving my baby on the altar.*
- *I somewhat understand why Moses could not enter the promised land. God will accept a multitude of sins in those who haven't been with Him as intimately, but those who experience close communion with Him will be held more accountable for their actions and reactions. As we mature, we are to act more mature.*
- *I must not blame my husband for my critical attitudes.*
- *My rights are not my own. I need to be emptied of myself so that God can fill me, not rest on my own supplies to keep me full.*
- *I can praise God for His work, not because praising is a way to get God to do something, but because God is at work, and I choose to trust Him.*[6]

Clinging to Him in praise

Within weeks, Jeremy became so ill he stopped breathing in my arms. We resuscitated him, but his condition remained tenuous. That week, we had visits and calls from our immediate family members and from those who knew him. However, a day came when he became sick once again. He could not swallow and had trouble breathing. The ambulance arrived to transport him to Phoenix Baptist Hospital, the nearest medical center on our side of town. My mother came to take me to the hospital. Because he was so ill, the staff at PBH decided to Life Flight him to a larger, better equipped facility, St. Joseph's Hospital, where Mom worked as an ICU nurse. As Mom and I were traveling to the designated hospital, we saw his helicopter flying overhead. I thought, *That's his flight to heaven.*

Little Jeremy lay in a hospital bassinet with his eyes wide open as staff hovered over him. He'd never spent time away from family; this was an intense place. I ached to see needles with IV lines in each of his temples, presumably for nourishment. It bothered me that Jeremy experienced more pain as he labored to breathe. Soon after our arrival, someone asked if I would like to hold him. *This makes no sense. My hands haven't even been washed.* Still, I longed to hold him, to reassure him.

The staff offered me a rocking chair, and then gently placed Jeremy into my waiting arms. He nestled close. As we sat and rocked together, he relaxed. Instead of crying, I determined to look to Jesus. A song filled my mouth and my heart, *"Praise the Name of Jesus."* The words assured me that Jesus is my Rock, Fortress, Deliverer and the One Whom I can trust. I sang it through several times. A dozen people gathered around, watching. Then Jeremy's body remained in my arms as his soul left for heaven. Just minutes later, Jim arrived from work and joined Mom and me in the infant ICU. Our pastors came soon afterward, along with Joe and Susy. We comforted each other and prepared for another memorial service.

At the funeral home, Jim, as he had with Nathaniel, dressed our little boy. Although he asked me to join him in this last act of honor, it was more than I could handle. He and Joe prepared Jeremy's earthly body for burial. The twin brothers experienced another bond in their lives as they wept over our little one, so soon departed.

We held a service in the scorching July sun, next to the gravesite. People from our church, from our circle of friends and from our family supported us as we said goodbye to another one of our precious children. In talking to a group of friends afterwards, I told them of my grief in observing the medical staff had put needles into his head, but then I recalled the thorns thrust into Jesus' head as He suffered for us. It became a more intimate understanding of something God had shown me months before as I journaled about God's love for His own Son.

On Jeremy's headstone, the words from Isaiah 40:11 read, *He shall carry the lambs in His arms.* While he was alive, our church fellowship often sang those words. It made me think of Jeremy, but I told no one. Confirmation came after he died when a friend from church confided that the song always made her think of Jeremy. For financial reasons, we did not place a grave marker for several years, but the verse from Isaiah still fit for our little lamb when we finally put a headstone at his body's resting place.

Through Jeremy's brief life, God taught me to listen more attentively to Him. I devoted time to writing out the words He was giving to me. The words continued to give me solace and comfort years following. I recognized God's yearning to communicate with me. The book of Jeremiah highlights words Jeremy might have left with me as a charge to share messages from his brief stay. *"Before I formed you in the womb, I knew you. Before you were born, I set you apart; I appointed you as a prophet to the nations." "Alas, Sovereign LORD," I said, "I do not know how to speak; I am too young."*[7]

God's creation

And yet it was never whole—not complete nor wholly functional. It came with a defect—made that way, I guess—and yet in Your mind it was perfect, Lord, and beautiful and just right. And since it was prayed into Your care long before You allowed it life, how can we think of it as other than your perfect creation, made in Your image, brought for a purpose—the fruition of a plan?

And so, we are broken, too, Lord—broken to serve You and glorify You through the imperfections that we are, for we know that despite the pain of brokenness, there is joy in knowing that this is not all there is. There is more—a higher joy You've planned for us. A triumph of the spirit, for this life house is only a shell to be shed by us all, sooner or later.

So thank You, Lord, for even the short visit of a little boy we love.

Joyce Hulstedt, 1979

Glimmers of sunshine and rainbows through the mist

In my own life, God has not spoken to me in the same way in each season. During Jeremy's days here, I collected a journal full of notes which were God's directives for me. He taught me to heed His voice, to listen to His whispers, to quiet my thoughts.

At the time Nathaniel died, I believed I could never love another baby as much as I had loved him. He was the culmination of all my dreams since I was a little girl. All I ever wanted, from my earliest memories, was to have a baby and be a mom. Extremely ill from birth, Nathaniel showed little to no muscle tone and cried weakly, like a small kitten. Nathaniel was my firstborn, my dream, my son, my joy and my delight. However, in two months he was gone—never held in my arms again on this earth. I even worried months later when I was expecting Jeremy that I wouldn't be able to love this new baby with the depth and intensity that I had for Nathaniel. But I did. Not in the same way, of course. No one is ever loved in the same way. Each one is special, and each one is different. It's a new and distinct relationship every single time. Recently I read speaker and author Lisa Bevere's statement, "God does not love us equally; He loves us uniquely." [8]

Gathering grace gems from the bubbling waters

- Has God's light shone intensely into your heart as you have sought to point out another's flaws? How did it feel? What did you do to come into a gentler light?
- How does God communicate with you?
- How does God talk to you? In His word? In your dreams? Through worship? With His still, small voice? Through circumstances?

Comforter or Confronter

O God, you are my God; I earnestly search for you. My soul thirsts for you; my whole body longs for you in this parched and weary land where there is no water (Psalm 63:1 NLT).

When I shared about Jeremy's illness with Amy, a former and older neighbor, her response left me numb. "Well, that shouldn't come as a surprise. You knew the probability of having another sick baby, like your first one." "Yes," I replied, not knowing what else to say. This lady did not know Jesus, so I am unsure what I thought she would say when I told her. My sadness remained hard for her to handle. She answered in a way that allowed her to avoid further communication. Perhaps her response kept her own heart from hurting.

A meeting with a mixed message occurred one Sunday after church, within a month of Jeremy's death. As the congregants gathered to talk following the church service, Lois came over to ask, "How are you doing, after losing your baby?" I was living both on earth and in heaven and paused before responding. I gave a candid reply, "For now, reality is based in heaven. This life looks like a shadow. The real world is still waiting for me." She quickly answered, "Oh, you're in a state of shock." I sensed my feelings were dismissed. Admittedly, God was covering me and keeping pain from overwhelming me. I sensed a deeper intimacy with Him in those days. Perhaps she hadn't had that experience. A reaction came quickly to satisfy her own question. Sometimes answers arrive too easily for others. Maybe the words fill in the awkward, empty pause.

Pastor and writer Randy Alcorn penned a blog lesson entitled, "Heaven as Substance, Earth as Shadow." In the article he explained the support of Scripture to view the greater reality of heaven to the lesser reality of earth. He quoted John Milton using the angel's question to Adam from Paradise Lost,

What if Earth
Be but the shadow of Heav'n, and things therein
Each to other like, more than on Earth is thought?[9]

Rev. Alcorn referenced the book of Hebrews in which the author explains how earth results from the pattern set by heaven. In some ways, heaven and earth mirror the essence of each other, with heaven holding the master design.[10] Perhaps God allows the one grieving a glimpse into what is real and genuine for a brief time to encourage and console the broken heart.

Days after reflecting on my confusion about reality, my mother's friend contacted me and asked if she could bring a young woman over who wished to encourage me. Mom's friend assured me I would be as excited about this young woman as she was. Not wanting to miss an opportunity for blessing, I invited them over.

Unwanted gifts of insight

Within two hours, the ladies arrived and walked in. We exchanged introductions. Then I took them to the back bedroom and showed the cradle Jim had fashioned in woodshop class. I related some incidents that had occurred in both Nathaniel's and Jeremy's lives. The recollections were facts, not a ploy for sympathy. God had worked remarkable miracles during their short earth stays, and I longed to share. My heart, still raw from the recent loss, acknowledged His special encounters; and I longed to let others know of the hope He had given me.

When I paused, this new acquaintance turned to face me and stated, "At least you can be thankful your children are in heaven." It seemed like a reprimand. A hailstorm pelted me. Neither refreshment nor comfort washed over me. As the desert sun dried my skin, so the comment dried my soul. Instead of water, I received ice rocks, dry ice. Over the years, I have pondered what the truthful, but perhaps insincere, comment showed me.

This young woman didn't know me personally; she had never heard most of my story. To my knowledge, she had not experienced the loss of any children. Perhaps she had lost family members who were close. Sometimes when we have experienced loss, it doesn't seem necessary to explain to others. From the phone discussion with Mom's friend, I knew she was married and had three children. Beyond that, her life and her past remained a mystery. She accepted her mission, which I suspect centered on eliciting a response from me. I thank God for each of my children, and I have never doubted they entered heaven. Evidently her heart didn't yearn to bring life to my parched heart. She wanted to perform her duty. She wanted to evangelize me. She wanted to make sure I was on the right path. At least that is what I perceived.

Platitudes and clichés offered no refreshment. I yearned for a person to mourn with me and to identify with me. Although I rarely cried openly, I gained solace when someone wept over me. Those tears offered life and sustenance. When my pain touches another's heart, and I see the results in eyes brimming with tears, I heal from my own wounds.

Nurturing my heart

Walking in communion with the Holy Spirit does not mean we don't have problems. Carefully listening to the Lord changes what a person believes is true. Truth, blended with His compassion and love, nurtures and restores the soul and the spirit. Not only is the person benefitted, but those around can thrive, too. Intellectual understanding, which puffs up, does not nurture. Knowledge provides insight, but not comfort. Jeremiah 8:11 (KJV) warns of empty consolation, *For they have healed the hurt of the daughter of my people slightly.*

This leads me to think of psychological experiments performed on baby monkeys years ago. Scientists used surrogate mothers—one, a metal contraption with milk bottles and the other, a soft comfortable stuffed pillow—to gauge emotional development and to assess psychotic behavior. Although each baby monkey nursed from milk bottles which fed its body, it received comfort and nurturing from the stuffed pillow. It didn't go for protection from the one with the milk when distressed or afraid. Instead, it ran to the soft pillow. Those baby monkeys, with no soft pillow, demonstrated extreme emotional damage. The ones, who at least had a soft pillow mother, adjusted far better than the ones who drank milk from the sturdy metal milk providers but had no other comfort except to cling to the cold wire frame.[11]

The milk is like knowledge. Even though it will help us grow intellectually, we will not mature in other ways without the nurturing. The Holy Spirit is the Nurturer and Comforter. He isn't a pillow, an artificial provision. God's Spirit lives and provides us with nourishment and insights, making us whole, which is something surrogates, even the soft ones, can never give.

Some empathize without hurting

The interaction with my new acquaintance serves to caution me. When I minister to others, am I acting as a surrogate without life-giving comfort? I can perform by mechanically handing out platitudes which outwardly appear to fit the situation and might bring me encouragement. However, they lead to superficial spiritual understanding without offering life. How can I provide…? How can I provide life-giving balm and food to a wounded and hungry soul? To someone who is longing for a rope of hope?[12] It requires and demands a tenderized heart.

A stirring card came from a young mother of two small children at about this same time. She wrote. "I have tried to put myself in your place. I cannot imagine what you have been through." Her words showed me she identified with my pain, if only for a few moments. They touched my heart. She didn't provide any answers, but simply exhibited a willingness to suffer with me.

Glimmers of sunshine and rainbows through the mist

It is difficult to respond to people who have answers, answers that satisfy them when looking at another's circumstances, at the expense of the person walking through a hard season. For me, I have needed to handle the hows of these encounters. I want the grace to respond without insulting the other individual, without diminishing that person's value, without ignoring that person's pain.

Keeping my heart genuinely guarded will prevent unheeded and unneeded advice from muddying the waters in my life or in the lives of others. My prayer becomes, *Lord, You are the guardian of my heart. Help me release any offense I might take. Let me show Your love to those who don't understand my journey. Let me be wise with my time, my energy and my words. Thank You for Your help, Lord. I need it today.*

Gathering grace gems from the bubbling waters

- What is the good news I must share? Am I sensitive to the heart of the other person? Is his or her heart prepared to receive my good news?
- Am I in a place that simply wants someone else to hear from me and learn about my ideas? Is my heart tender to the heart of the other person? Have I listened for His voice to motion me in either direction?
- Our former pastor often cautioned us with the question, "Is the bridge of relationship you have with that other person strong enough to bear the weight of truth you have to share?"

Helper or Helped

So, he arose and went to Zarephath, and when he came to the gate of the city, behold, a widow was there gathering sticks; and he called to her and said, "Please get me a little water in a jar, that I may drink"

(1 Kings 17:10 NASB).

God poured fresh water into my outstretched cup as I tried to fill the empty hours after Jeremy died. Occasionally, greater holes of aloneness bore into my soul. My need to the hollowness arrived in several unexpected ways and left me more fulfilled, encouraged and comforted.

New job

Jenny Elven taught me many lessons in the days I spent with her. More than a contemporary of my mom's, at least 10 years her senior, Jenny exuded compassion and understanding. A former redhead (stunning in her wedding photo), she presently possessed a soft, round figure, twinkling eyes, a cocked head and a ready smile. She never showed anger in her actions or her words. Her character qualities have given me cause to reflect and ponder. Thankfully, years after working at Jenny's, my mother once mentioned that Jenny wanted to help me through my season of grief after we lost Jeremy. If Mom had said nothing, I might have believed I was helping Jenny, not the other way around.

On a hot, quiet day in August, Jenny called me and asked if I could assist her a couple of days a week. Jenny and her husband, Stan, lived in their home, next to the apartment complex they owned and managed. Her sister, Doris, afflicted with cerebral palsy from birth, also lived with them. Doris evidenced multiple issues, which included brain damage and physical weakness, as she lived her days in a wheelchair. In assessing her intellectual skills, Doris probably understood little beyond a second-grade level, if that. She did, however, have an incredible ability to recall dates and times, always informing me of the precise details. Whenever I visited, she reported the day, the date and the time I had arrived previously, even if months had passed.

Because we owned one car and Jim used it to drive to work or to school, I rode my bike over to their place, a few miles away. What did I do to assist her? I helped with washing clothes, dusting furniture, cleaning the floors and preparing meals. One dilemma I was unaware of until we talked about it was her husband's pants. I chose the quickest way and folded them as they came out of the dryer without a knee seam. His pants splayed out. After weeks of lackluster folding, Jenny cautiously revealed that Stan wondered how Jim wore his pants. After that, they received a proper fold.

Shopping for sewing material together allowed us to choose something suitable for her patio furniture. Thus, she prevailed upon me to recover her patio chair cushions. After measuring and calculating dimensions, I spent hours piecing fabric into expandable slip covers on my home sewing machine. Unfortunately, those beauties fit cock-eyed and misaligned because of my inability to understand how to make slipcovers out of stretch fabric. Jenny gushed, "They'll work perfectly on the patio." I know better. I don't recall they ever used those misshapen stretch tubes. She could have employed someone far more capable than I. However, she accepted her mission. For those days, I became her mission. She gave me her attention and her wisdom.

Sharing hearts

We talked and shared for hours during those months. Jenny had lost a little girl before the baby's first birthday because of an illness. I remember seeing a photograph of her beautiful child. One day we talked about a television teaching I had heard about people losing their babies. The pastor, Jack Hayford, quoted a verse expressing why Job wasn't ... *taken directly from my mother's womb into the Lord's presence?* (Job 3:11 WEB). In discussing the reference with her and what this would mean to parents who had lost children, she took a breath and then quietly remarked, "Why, that means I would have at least eight children waiting for me." She must have miscarried at least seven babies. Jenny didn't look for sympathy. In her matter-of-fact way, she shared how she expected to meet her little ones again.

After Jenny and Stan lost their little girl, they chose adoption. They made it clear to the agency they were not looking for a healthy child. They specifically asked for a baby showing "failure to thrive" syndrome. They adopted a little girl who must have had what is now known as a reactive attachment disorder.[13] I remember seeing their grown daughter with her children at church. Elena overcame her earlier challenges as she grew into adulthood. To me, her health showed how much Jenny and Stan had cared for her and had made sure she received nourishment—physical, emotional and spiritual. Eventually, Jenny and Stan had two healthy birth children, a son and a daughter.

Exhibiting inordinate kindness, Jenny rarely, if ever, said anything negative about anyone. She held a deep faith in a loving God which propelled her forward in life, even when times and events made her heart sad. When others presented problematic personalities, she chose a gentle, forgiving response.

Jenny's mother had died when she was a young girl, leaving Jenny's dad with a son and a daughter to raise. He married a second wife, whom Jenny portrayed as *"sensitive."* However, after hearing stories about how she treated Jenny and her brother, I think the word *harsh* offers a more apt description. If it were available, that woman could have applied for the ugly stepmother position and gained good standing against the competition.

This lady's only birth child was Doris. With Doris's severe physical and mental challenges, Jenny's stepmom must have suffered incredible personal pain.

After recounting memories about her and how she had treated Jenny and her brother, Jenny didn't malign her. She understood the woman lived out her grief and often unleashed her misery onto Jenny and Alfred. Doris's presence may have complicated the picture. Her stepmother probably compared her own compromised birth child with her two healthy stepchildren.

Hearing loss, via an illness or an inherited disorder, plagued Jenny. As a young woman, she attended Moody Bible Institute in Chicago for her training and education in Bible studies. Jenny became proficient in reading lips and appreciated her professors. In retrospect, she explained her challenges during a lecture when an instructor would turn his head away. Missing the culmination of the speech, tears would stream down her face when she lost the crucial details.

A new lesson

One morning Jenny and I discussed some money the church of my youth (the one Jenny, Stan and my parents attended) had given us after Nathaniel died. Because we were attending another fellowship, I couldn't accept such a large sum of money. As soon as we could, we reimbursed the deacon fund, asking the church to use it for someone who truly needed the money. To be honest, I didn't see us as being *"needy."*

Uncharacteristically, Jenny pointedly asked, "Don't you realize you are a daughter of the church? You grew up here. We care about what happens to you." Over 40 years later, I now realize she spoke about their sacrifice and their love for me. I assumed the church deacon funds were from the general fund and failed to associate the money with individuals who wanted to help us. However, it has finally sunk in. Jenny and Stan put that money into the benevolence fund, and I am too late to offer my words of gratitude for their thoughtfulness and loving kindness. Heaven awaits.

Jenny claimed favored status at our church. She taught preschoolers for years in Sunday school. Her reasoning about teaching them was that little ones believed in fairies so they should have no problem understanding God. I could never quite understand her explanation, but I loved her heart and her faith. Her walk was no accident and came at a price. She emanated a deep trust in the One who loved her most. When she talked about Jesus, her face shone. Even if little ones didn't believe in fairies, they could believe Jenny because she knew Jesus intimately.

Kindness from a new friend

Sheryl, another friend whom I knew briefly for a year, worked as a resident advisor at a women's home near where we lived. New Life for Girls was founded by Cookie Rodriguez as a response to other organizations which lumped males and females into the same group. Cookie intended to address women's unique needs. Several homes were distributed in various locations in the country. The place close to us housed about seven residents who needed to recover from substance abuse and/or life abuse.

Scars covering Sheryl's arms and face betrayed undisclosed injury, pain and hardship. After we became friends, she divulged more of her story. She had been raised in foster care homes. I don't recall if she ever had much relationship with her birth family. The homes where she had lived offered little spiritual or emotional support. When in her early 20s, the car in which she was a passenger crashed. That accident left lasting scars on her body. With the automobile broken and in pieces, her boyfriend forced her to crawl out of the wreckage and made her walk to the nearest place for help. Sheryl recounted, "I had to lift and support my head in my hands while we trudged those miles. I was afraid I had a broken neck." She was right. She did.

This young woman exuded great kindness as she reached out and showed me His heart. Sheryl lived with others who had endured similar life stories. However, her experiences did not define her behavior. She loved the Lord and constantly gave Him credit for all the benefits she had gained in life. One of her responsibilities at the home was to prepare meals. In fact, I believe that is how I got to know her, as she had called one time to see if I could bring over some basic provisions, such as eggs, milk and flour. In a conspiratorial manner, one day, she divulged the secret to her cooking success. Often, she wasn't sure if all the ingredients would suffice for the meal, meaning there might not be enough, or the blend might not be tasty. Every time she prepared food, she prayed, "God, this is Your food for us. I ask You to make it tasty and filling. Thank You for Your help. Amen." And, according to her report, He always answered with better than she could have expected.

Sheryl developed severe stomach pains and started visiting doctors. The medical community subjected her to many tests. Finally, the ministry staff decided Sheryl should return to Pennsylvania to live out her last days as physicians had determined she was dying of liver cancer. For a brief time, we exchanged letters. Through contacts at the home where she had lived and worked, I received word that God had healed her and that some fortunate man asked to marry her.

The following year, after Sheryl returned to Pennsylvania, Jim and I experienced a season of financial difficulty. Inexplicably, I received my last letter from her during those lean days. In it, she included a $10.00 bill. That money contributed to our grocery budget when we needed it. Why did she send me the money? It was surely an act of faith for her, who had so little surplus, to slip that bill into the envelope.

Glimmers of sunshine and rainbows through the mist

Mr. Rogers, the popular children's television show host, advised people to look for the helpers. In each of our lives, there are those who have encouraged us on our journeys. They aren't thinking of themselves as helpers. They are simply people who work out their love by serving others in the middle of their own journeys. Perhaps you have had some hidden helpers who have lightened your load. Ask the Lord to show you who they are. They may be gone, but their memories may still live in the recesses of your heart.

Gathering grace gems from the bubbling waters

- Are there people who have impacted you? What are your memories of them? How might you be able to honor them?
- Have you ever received a meaningful blessing from someone? From someone whom you expected to bless, but who blessed you instead?
- How is God using you to speak words of grace to others in situations that are challenging? What can you say to help lift the burden?
- Do you need others to speak into your life? What do you need to hear?

Bitter Waters to Healing Streams

Then Moses led Israel from the Red Sea, and they went out into the Desert of Shur. For three days they walked in the desert without finding water. And when they came to Marah, they could not drink the water there because it was bitter. (That is why it was named Marah.) So the people grumbled against Moses, saying, "What are we to drink?"

(Exodus 15:22-25 BSB)

On the last day, that great day of the feast, Jesus stood and cried out, saying, "If anyone thirsts, let him come to Me and drink"

(John 7:37 NKJV).

Bitterness in my heart created an unwholesome rift in the family. When Joe and Susy learned they were expecting a second baby about the time of Jeremy's passing, my bruised heart reminded me of my failure to bear a healthy child. Handling my vulnerable emotions proved difficult. The pain of our recent loss drew away my ability to look up to God. The verse in Romans 12:15, referring to "weeping with those who weep and rejoicing with those who rejoice," is far easier to implement during a time of weeping with someone else. It is hard for me to rejoice while I am weeping, and someone else is rejoicing. Why can't I rejoice as easily? How can I rejoice?

Susy was experiencing difficulties of her own, as she didn't want to shame us by having another baby. Her sadness was her own, and this was a time in which we could not take part as intimately and joyfully as we had previously. Joe and Susy had shown remarkable support for us in prayer and petition during Jeremy's life. Jeremy's death cut their souls, too.

We still spent meals and family times together, as well as attending the same home church. Our pastor's wife wisely counseled Susy to understand the baby she was carrying was God's gift to their family. There was nothing they could do to change the course of their family, and God would give evidence of His love to them with this new life in their home. Marge further explained that God had a particular plan for our lives. In His providence, God opened a different pathway for Joe and Susy that was not the same one He had selected for us. The danger existed in making comparisons and contrasting the differences.

Jim's mom and dad visited us in August, within a month of Jeremy's death. Because she was experiencing ambivalence with her pregnancy, Susy talked to Mom Ruth about her feelings and apprehensions. "I don't want Lynn to resent my pregnancy. I'm not comfortable, myself. This is hard for me, too."

Mom Saint told me what Susy had shared. Then she reassured me with the words, "You wouldn't have jealous or resentful feelings. That is not who you are." Did she believe that, or did she wonder where I was and expect her words would change my path?

When I heard the reaffirming words, my heart recoiled. I wanted to cry out, "But I am bitter. Why did God take a baby from me again?" Resentments had taken root in my heart, and I truly could not uproot them on my own. It is curious I had dealt with those feelings two months previously regarding my attitude toward my husband, and now I was facing them again. My learning curve wasn't on an upward course. What was God teaching me?

Caring for others

Michael Jr., a Christian black comedian, shared about an experience he had at his apartment complex when he was only 19 years of age. When he arrived late from work one night, police officers surrounded him, accusing him of involvement with a drug ring across the hall. This wasn't the case, and they finally left his apartment, which they had entered illegally, but only after threatening his life. Who could he call to help him? He was tired, sad and angry as he mentally reviewed the incident. Soon his thoughts were interrupted by the lady from across the hall who came knocking at his door, distraught that the police had arrested her boyfriend and taken him into custody. In broken English, she tried to explain her plight. Caring for two small children, she had no visible means of support. Perplexed by how to help her, Michael Jr. emptied his wallet of all the funds he had. Grabbing his money, the young woman quickly left. In the silence he realized his attitude had changed. She had given him a gift. By helping her, his own hurts began to heal. His compassion replaced the bitter feelings he had justifiably entertained.[14]

In the ensuing months after Jeremy's passing, I found others for whom I could care and minister. Perhaps they found me. They were God's gift to me. They helped me look beyond myself and my pain so that I could recognize their griefs and difficulties. Their human condition broke my heart and helped me heal. They gave me spiritual and emotional gifts by showing me a well from which to draw. My own well had not run dry; the Giver of life was replenishing it with living water.

Baby girl with a health dilemma

In February of the next year, Susy started labor, right on time. We watched three-year-old Martin as they raced to the hospital. Although we lived in Phoenix, the Valley of the Sun, Mikaela arrived during a thunderstorm. Jim adeptly maneuvered the car through flooded streets to Good Samaritan Hospital to get a glimpse of our new niece and Martin's baby sister.

My damaging heart attitudes had melted away. A month earlier, I had listened to a riveting sermon which addressed my broken heart and helped me heal. Reaching out to others and not focusing on my hurt feelings helped me overcome what threatened to affect me and our family relationship. Sometimes we must move in response, not working on our heart issues, but doing what needs to be done.

Mika, at 6 pounds, 4 ounces, was a small baby. At first she didn't nurse enthusiastically, which proved a trial for her mom. The baby often gave up suckling after a few minutes and then returned to sleep. Eating made her tired. When Joe and Susy took Mika for her first medical visit at a week old, they learned she had a fever. The pediatrician prescribed antibiotics for her. He determined she had a bladder infection and needed medicine to eliminate it.

For many days, Mika continued to run a fever throughout her tiny body. Even though the antibiotics were continued and were reinforced with a stronger prescription, her fever did not cease. Her parents took her to the doctor every few days. The initial prognosis had been positive; the doctor predicted it would quickly clear up. However, the infection remained.

In due course, her pediatrician recommended that Joe and Susy take her to a specialist for further interventions. Medical experts determined that Mika's bladder infection was not limited to her bladder. It had either traveled to or originated in her kidneys. Because the physicians considered her condition so serious, the doctors reviewing her case warned Joe and Susy that Mika would probably have to deal with renal struggle and intervention her entire life. Prognoses of multiple surgeries and a life of medical and drug dependence for their baby daughter loomed over these young parents.

Our church committed to prayer. Our family committed to prayer. Loved ones in the States and in Argentina committed to prayer. Declarations of God's Word covered Mika and her parents. As we prayed, we searched every avenue possible to present her to the Throne Room.

Several weeks after detecting her infection, Joe and Susy took Mika to yet another specialist for further testing and diagnosis. Even though various doctors had seen her, this visit would lend more definition to her prognosis and the protocol the medical community would adopt for her treatment.

This time the emotional and spiritual pain wasn't about me with concerns for my immediate family. Through their pain and anguish, God opened a window for me to witness what it was like for them to walk in similar pain, with a potentially life-threatening and life-altering illness. I anguished over my helplessness to alleviate their wounds.

God speaks, and He intervenes

Before that significant appointment, I devoted myself to fasting and prayer for Joe, Susy and little Mika. Sleep was hard won as I agonized over the situation and the dire possibilities. Early on the morning of the medical visit, I awakened from a dream, unsure of its significance. Mika sat in the middle of a circle of flames ready to consume her. Susy rushed past the outer ring of fire to her daughter. She leaned over and plucked Mika out of the blaze, whole and complete.

A few hours later, Mom called me to read a portion of a Bible verse that had impacted her while praying for them. She read, "*save others, snatching them out of the fire*" (Jude 1:23 AMP). Incredulous, I told Mom about my dream from three hours earlier. God was speaking to us about Mika; He was liberating her from the flames of this illness.

That afternoon, we learned what happened when Joe and Susy took Mika to the medical appointment. At one point, a technician tried to catheterize the baby. Joe put a stop to the procedure as Mika screamed in pain from a tube that was too large for her. Finally, a nurse took her temperature to verify the fever and the infection. The fever was gone. After weeks of unsatisfactory results, the fever had left. To this day, decades later, Mika has not experienced a recurrence of the ailment. God saved her and snatched her from the fire.

Glimmers of sunshine and rainbows through the mist

A deep lesson God taught me from this time is that someone else's blessings are not my curse. In 1 Corinthians 13:4, a portion of the verse states, *[Love] refuses to be jealous when blessing comes to someone else.* It is not always easy to embrace, but I now recognize a hidden agenda when I endure twinges of jealousy. In some ways, it reminds me of forgiveness. With repeated opportunities to forgive an offense, the weaker the hold of the grievance. Jealousy, left to grow, becomes covetousness. To refuse to covet, I choose godliness with contentment. Great gain![15]

Gathering grace gems from the bubbling waters

- Have you ever felt resentful of someone else's blessings when you aren't on the receiving end of something similar?
- How have you reconciled your own emotions? What has God shown you that has helped you realize He has a unique plan to prosper you?
- Is there a new perspective you have gained in this story? How is it helping you face those empty cracks in your own life? Have you tried to find ways, on your own, to stuff the cracks? Perhaps God has a better way. What is God using to fill the cracks?

Footnotes

1. Isaiah 8:1 (LB)
2. Goldberg

Werdnig-Hoffmann disease is the most severe type of spinal muscular atrophy (SMA). Known as "infantile SMA," Werdnig-Hoffmann is a rare, inherited, autosomal recessive neuromuscular disease. Both parents unknowingly carry the gene for the disorder, and when the child inherits the defective gene from both parents, the disease develops. Approximately 1 in 50 people or 1 in 2,500 couples in the United States are carriers. When both parents carry the gene, the likelihood of the child inheriting the disease is one in four or a 25% chance with each pregnancy. Since the 1990s, prenatal and carrier testing have been made available to families.

SMA type 1, also called Werdnig-Hoffmann disease, is evident before birth or within the first 6 months of life. There may be reduced fetal movement in the final months of pregnancy. Symptoms include floppiness of the limbs and trunk, feeble movements of the arms and legs, swallowing and feeding difficulties, and impaired breathing. Infants with the gravest prognosis have problems sucking or swallowing. A twitching of the tongue often is seen. This is the most common and severe type of SMA. Affected children never sit or stand and usually die before the age of 2 years.

3. Referenced in Psalm 90:12 (KJV)
4. Psalm 139:23 (NASB)
5. Isaiah 30:21 (ESV)
6. In Psalm 84:11, the Passion Translation interprets the verse as, "O LORD, how blessed are the people who know the triumphant shout." The term, "triumphant shout," uses a homonym for "brokenness." In our brokenness, we can also lift up a voice of praise.
7. Jeremiah 1:5-6 (NIV)
8. Bevere period
9. Alcorn.
10.Alcorn.
11. Talmon.
12. Gallagher, K. Because Hebrew does not use abstract words and chooses concrete ones, the word for "hope" represents a woven cord or rope. Also implied in the word is "expectation."
13. Mayo Clinic.
Reactive attachment disorder can start in infancy. There's little research on signs and symptoms of reactive attachment disorder beyond early childhood, and it remains uncertain whether it occurs in children older than 5 years.
Signs and symptoms may include:

- Unexplained withdrawal, fear, sadness or irritability
- Sad and listless appearance
- Not seeking comfort or showing no response when comfort is given
- Failure to smile
- Watching others closely but not engaging in social interaction
- Failing to ask for support or assistance
- Failure to reach out when picked up
- No interest in playing peekaboo or other interactive games

14. Michael Jr. pp.45-53
15. 1 Timothy 6:6

Section 3. Surfing the Waves:

Adopting a New Way of Life

Then you will say,
"The branches were broken off so that I can be grafted in"
(Romans 11:19 ESV).

Son of My Right Hand

At least there is hope for a tree: If it is cut down, it will sprout again, and its new shoots will not fail. Its roots may grow old in the ground and its stump die in the soil, yet at the scent of water it will bud and put forth shoots like a plant
(Job 14:7-9 NIV).

A*doption* soon became a new and familiar word in our home as Jim and I began talking about that possibility in the fall of 1979. How does one go about finding a baby? For some, it involves going through an agency and filling out endless forms. The answer for us came quickly and simply. We were and are blessed to have a fine, godly friend, Duane Olson, an attorney. In December, Duane informed us that a doctor whom he represented was looking for couples who could adopt an infant. From time to time, this obstetrician had patients who would ask him to find homes for their unborn babies. We gladly added our names to the list of prospective adoptive parents.

Healing and waiting

In March, close to the time Mika was healed, a young woman entered Dr. K's office and asked him if he knew of a couple who could adopt her soon-to-be-born child. She already had a little boy, about one or two years of age, and was experiencing a difficult time raising him. She felt it was important to carry this second baby, even if she couldn't keep him. She enumerated several specifications for the doctor before he proceeded with his search.

1. They could not come from her town in Northern Arizona.
2. The couple needed to share a similar ethnic background.
3. They must be Christian.

We met all three criteria. After her office visit, Duane called to inform us about this birth mother and what she wished for her unborn child. Her baby was due at the beginning of June. Our time of confinement began.

Relinquishment and reality

During those months, my heart yearned for peace and reconciliation. Relinquishing self-interest and passing the predicament into God's hands became a silent crusade between God and me. Three specific areas lacked God's full say and sway in my life.

The first challenge was to acknowledge this child was not mine but the Lord's. Because he or she belonged to God, He needed to decide who would raise this baby. Haltingly I prayed, *Lord, You know how desperately I want to have a baby. If this little one is not destined for our home, then place this child into the best home You select.*

A second obstacle was my desire to be a birth mother. This wish had to be "placed on the altar."[1] Bearing and having a child had been my desire for as long as I could remember. To adopt meant that I would not ask God any longer for the privilege of having a birth child. Grafting a child into our family tree would be His answer for parenthood. *Lord, I accept adoption as Your perfect plan for us. You may take away my desire to bear any more children.*

As a small child, one of my first uttered words was *baby.* At least that was Mom's memory. As far back as I recall, I loved little babies. I wanted to have babies most of my conscious life. Hence, my last declaration, during this waiting time, was to affirm, *Lord, You may take away my motherhood if that brings You honor and glory.* This pronouncement broke my heart. Feelings wavered, but there also remained a firm conviction that I must trust God "even if." Even if that child didn't come to our home. Even if I stayed barren. Even if we never had another child.

Despite dealing with inner struggles, we prepared our home. I made and hung new curtains in the nursery. Jim's hand-crafted baby cradle stood ready in our bedroom. We bought bottles and diapers. A new dresser held T-shirts, blankets, burp pads and sundry items.

It's a boy!

Duane called us on a Sunday evening, June 1st, Ruth Saint's birthday. Early the day before, a little boy had entered this world. Duane told us to meet him on Tuesday. In the state of Arizona, a birth mother has three days in which to reconsider her decision regarding the release of her infant. Feelings of nervousness, ecstasy, apprehension and incredulity filled the next day and a half.

Monday evening, we readied a homecoming outfit—hat, booties, dress shirt, short pants and diapers. We awakened at 4:00 a.m. to drive north. Three and a half hours later, our car rolled into Kingman. Duane met us in the hospital parking lot and directed us to a nearby restaurant to have a bite to eat. He told us to meet him again in an hour at the hospital. Glitches in releasing the baby had occurred. Evidently the hospital had allowed the birth mother to return home without giving her the required forms to sign. With extra information swirling in our heads and excessive emotions coursing through our bodies, the buffet breakfast table held as many foods as our thoughts. None of those foods looked appetizing. They were probably tasty, but cardboard would have held as much flavor for us at that point.

As we finished our meal, Duane and a nurse walked in with a tiny bundle—our son! The nurse kept telling us what a beautiful baby he was. We had a few doubts initially. Our first two babies had bald heads, but this one came with a load of soft, brown hair sticking up and out in all directions, making his head look more like a baby hedgehog.

Immediately, we left the restaurant with our newest addition and headed back to the hospital, as we also needed to sign authorization papers. Upon arriving at the medical center, Jim reached into the glove compartment to grab his IDs and discovered they were gone. After a thoughtful search, we recalled the last place we remembered seeing his billfold was at the restaurant. We made a mad dash back to the buffet. It appears several people, noticing the commotion we were making, saw his wallet and left it in the care of the restaurant manager. One inconvenience and calamity—averted.

The trip back to Phoenix seemed much shorter, perhaps because of our preoccupation with another passenger. Our newest addition soiled his fancy outfit within the first ten minutes of wearing it. His cap wouldn't rest stylishly on his head, caused by his constant wiggling. This newcomer didn't enter arrayed in the finest apparel. Instead, he came into our home with no fancy attire, clothed in a lackluster T-shirt and diapers.

We named him Benjamin,[2] after Jim's youngest and tallest uncle. Knowing he was a godly man, we figured Uncle Ben represented a perfect role model for our little Ben to emulate. Jim and Ben shared the same middle name, Vreeland, of Dutch origin, a nationality which they also shared. Middle names for our first two held a different ethnicity than Benjy's. A small difference, but one in which our Creator and divine Orchestrator must have gently guided.

The first few days after his arrival in our home, with a newborn's sleeping and eating schedule, were tiring. As new parents can attest, adopting can wear out and wear down the parental caregivers faster than actual bearing. Although one doesn't have to endure all the physical trauma of carrying a child for nine months followed by the ordeal of labor, there are some natural consequences which assist the birth mother in her task of caring for a new infant. The insistent cries of a new baby are foreign to adoptive parents, who, only days before, had enjoyed eight hours of uninterrupted sleep. Birth parents have this ordeal as well, but at least the mother has probably been getting up throughout the night for months prior to her infant's arrival. Having nursed our first two, I discovered that fixing bottles in the early morning hours and trying to calm the baby while waiting for the bottle to heat took more time and effort. Ignoring the adage, I cried over spilled milk, frequently.

Unexpected responses

Of more import were the emotional issues. Love didn't well up from within me like a spring of effervescent water. This condition disturbed me immensely. Five years earlier, when first married, Jim and I discussed the subject of adoption. I had rashly avowed, "I will love any baby God gives me." Now I faced the stark reality that I did not produce love. The Scripture, "God is love," [3] became real when I saw love was not in vast supply, overflowing from my innermost being. What happened?

I tried to process my lack of love through much prayer and submission to God. One main issue was that in accepting this baby, I was telling God that I would not ask for any more birth children. From what I could determine, that door was shut. For the first three days, I took care of him as a caregiver, but not as a mom. My heart felt empty, but I continued to trust that God was doing a work. The feelings were not there. They couldn't be worked up or invented. I could not give birth to love.

When Ben turned one-week old, I took him to the doctor for his first well-baby check-up and a circumcision. That evening, following this "minor" surgery, the poor baby cried copious tears in his pain and distress. Something in me broke, and love took root. Suddenly, care and concern replaced duty. His hurt became my own. His pain seared my soul, and I became his mom. I never wanted to see him hurt or in pain again.

During the week of Benjy's arrival, I helped supervise the apartments Joe and Susy were managing. They, along with 3 ½-year-old Martín and 3 ½-month-old Mikaela, had journeyed to California with Susy's parents who were visiting from Argentina. Jim stayed home with Benjy while I made several trips across town to attend to the needs of the complex for three days. On their return from Los Angeles, we had the most delightful surprise for Joe and Susy. We told them to check in our bedroom. Upon seeing a baby in the cradle, they responded with puzzlement. At first, they questioned who we were babysitting. It took some time before the truth dawned. Then we all laughed and cried with delight over our newest family member.

After we welcomed Benjy into our family and our home, we forwarded the following letter to his birth mother.

My Dear,

How can one express gratitude for the opportunity of being a family once again? Even though it does not nearly say what lies in the depths of our hearts, "Thank you."

Thank you, not only for allowing us to have this precious child, but thank you for respecting the life of this little one many months before his birth time. God bless you for bearing him and for not casting him aside before he, too, could experience the wonder of life, first as a babe and then as he grows to maturity.

We make a promise to you, as the special young woman who gave him birth, that we shall love him and care for him with our best capabilities. He shall know from an early age that we have him because of an unselfish act and because God chose each one of us for each other.

Do you know that we have been praying, not only for our future child but also for his mother? We started praying months before we knew about the possibility of this baby. When we learned a baby might come into our home, we started praying even more earnestly... for you and for your welfare in each area of need. Please be assured, you shall continue to be brought before our loving Father as we ask Him to cover you with an anointing of His love and comfort.

We both love children. The Lord blessed our home with two dear little lambs for a short time. Each baby was called to heaven after a handful of weeks here on earth. They were both afflicted with a rare genetic illness. During their lifetimes, we believed God would heal them. He healed them by giving them brand new bodies in heaven.

Although healing did not come in the physical realm as we'd expected, it came to our spirits. Where our hearts were broken, God came, in loving kindness, gently pouring His balm of comfort.

Dear, dear one, we pray that you, too, may know the "healing in His wings" as the Lord wraps you in His everlasting arms. May you sense His comfort and peace for the ache in your heart.

Once again, please know that we pray for you, in love, thanking God for your life and for how you have helped to bless our lives.

We love you,
A "grafted tree"

God's Word had encouraged and ministered to me while we were waiting for Benjy's birth. We shared the following Bible verses in our baby announcement:

"God decided in advance to adopt us into his own family by bringing us to himself through Jesus Christ. This is what he wanted to do, and it gave him great pleasure. So, we praise God for the glorious grace he has poured out on us who belong to his dear Son" (Ephesians 1:5, 6 NLT).

The children you lost will yet say in your ears,
"The place is too cramped for me;
Make room for me that I may live here."
Then you will say in your heart,
"Who has fathered these for me?
Since I have been bereaved of my children
And cannot conceive, and I am an exile, and a wanderer?
And who has raised these?
Behold, I was left alone; Where are these from?"
This is what the Lord GOD says:
"Behold, I will lift up My hand to the nations
And set up My flag to the peoples;
And they will bring your sons in their arms,
And your daughters will be carried on their shoulders.
Kings will be your guardians,
And their princesses your nurses.
And you will know that I am the LORD;
Those who hopefully wait for Me will not be put to shame"
(Isaiah 49:20-22, 23a, c NASB).

Additional concern

In November 1980, when Benjy was six months old, Jim started to lose his eyesight. He noticed, while driving his truck, that he wasn't seeing stop signs. To help correct the situation, he first made an ophthalmological appointment for prescription glasses. When his vision continued to deteriorate, Jim's ophthalmologist referred him to a neurologist. The doctor ordered a CAT scan to determine the potential causes of this disorder. We feared a brain tumor, partly because a close friend of the family had died four months earlier of brain cancer. We sought God desperately for direction and healing. Several days later, the neurologist again examined Jim's eyes, noting optic neuritis, an inflammation of the optic nerve. Jim took medication for several months and never experienced a recurrence of those symptoms. Little did we suspect that years later we would again face grave fears for another member of the family—the next time with far more complicated interventions.

Glimmers of sunshine and rainbows through the mist

Adopting Benjy was one of the best and hardest experiences. I dealt with relinquishment and acceptance at the same time. Surrendering my will into God's hands kept me humble and out of the picture, mostly. It all depended on Him. I found out when I finally held Benjy with my feelings of ambivalence, there was nothing I could do without God's direct involvement. I couldn't even love! On the other hand, when the love started to flow, there was nothing that could hold it back… springs of water from the rock. And the rock became flesh.

Gathering grace gems from the bubbling waters

- Have you found yourself in a place of surrender? Of acknowledging there was little or nothing you could do to change or help a situation?
- In what areas have you learned to surrender? What does it look like?
- Is God showing you any areas of hurt so that He can bring healing?
- Where has God brought blessing after surrender?

We'll Fly to You, Argentina

Behold, how good and pleasant it is when brothers live together in harmony! It is like fine oil on the head, running down on the beard, running down 'Aaron's beard over the collar of his robes. It is like the dew of Hermon falling on the mountains of Zion. For there the LORD has bestowed the blessing of life forevermore

(Psalm 133:1-3 BSB).

"Jaime! Jaime!" the voice called out while we stood in line, waiting to board our first flight on the way to Argentina. We turned to search for the person shouting in the distance. At last we spotted who was yelling Jim's name in Spanish. Joe came running toward us with Martin and Mika in tow. Minutes before, Susy had delivered a baby girl at the hospital on our departure day, and coincidentally, on my dad's birthday. Joe had raced to the airport and made it in time to see us. Within a short time, we boarded the plane, clutching a fresh Polaroid photo of minutes-old Becky.

Once we landed at the Los Angeles airport, we disembarked our state-side flight, searched for our bags, retrieved them and dragged them outside the domestic airport to the intercontinental one. As Jim and I lugged a few hundred pounds of crammed suitcases, our 2 ½-year-old traipsed behind, holding onto his stuffed dog, Whitey. I looked back, in our hot pursuit of the next departure gate, to see that Benjy had tripped and fallen. I stopped and begged him to get up. Neither Jim nor I had any hands or arms left to help him. He had to keep on walking/running to match our mad pace.

We checked our bags for the destination of Asunción, Paraguay, not Buenos Aires, Argentina. Our travel agent had told us the least expensive flight down to South America would be one that landed in Paraguay. So, to save hundreds of carefully guarded dollars, we opted for Asunción. A few years later, to our chagrin, we learned there actually were flights to Buenos Aires for the same price. In those days, the yellow pages and travel agents supplied our only travel options. No one else had known of any easier way of getting to Córdoba. Besides, our next adventures would never have made it in print. Win. Win. Kind of.

Jim's youngest sibling, Evelyn, planned to marry Humberto Jiménez on December 25, 1982. Mom and Dad Saint sent us funds to purchase needed supplies and gifts. We had shopped for many weeks in anticipation of our travels and had packed our suitcases to the utmost limit of weight, size and quantity. I had shopped retail, thrift store and yard sale, making more use of the latter than the former.

Landing in unfamiliar territory

Our plane finally arrived in the capital city of Paraguay, after 20 hours of travel time. Once we disembarked, we waited anxiously for our baggage to emerge from the plane. Craning our necks, we spied all six suitcases slowly moving down the conveyer belt. We watched, aghast, as the bulkiest and largest piece burst open at the seams. Thankfully, oh yes, thankfully, this accident had not happened inside the plane's cargo compartment. After retrieving the sorry bag, we secured the contents with all Jim's belts. The other suitcases held their own, which was a perfect solution as we had exhausted our supply of straps.

We heaved sighs of relief as we glimpsed Jim's dad waving at us beyond the customs counter. Emerging from the terminal with our bulging and battered suitcases, we hauled ourselves and our luggage to the parking lot just outside the building. Tired but excited, we boarded the familiar Ford station wagon and rode to the border crossing about half an hour away.

Ready to enter Argentina—not so fast

Alas, Argentines at the outpost did not pander to the U. S. tourist trade. The Falkland Islands war with Britain had ended bitterly months before, giving Argentina a jaundiced opinion of Britons and Yankees. The customs official took one look at our passports.

"Where is your visa to enter the country?" the agent sternly demanded.

"We don't have one. It's not required."

"Yes, it is. You must have one to enter Argentina."

"We were told it wasn't necessary."

"You must have visas, or else I cannot allow you to come into the country."

"How do we get a visa now?"

"There is an Argentine embassy in Asunción. You will need to speak to the ambassador there."

Although not a legitimate decision, according to international travel guidelines, in that outpost the agent could make his own rules. What to do? Dad Saint knew a pastor in the next town who would put him up for the night. Our option was limited to returning to the Paraguayan capital for a required stamp of approval from the Argentine embassy. Jim's dad instructed us to find him in the designated town the following day if everything proceeded according to plan.

We bid all our luggage and Dad goodbye before trudging back down the dirt road to hail a taxi to take us into town. Beside the clothes on our backs, our main possessions comprised American dollars and a guaraní bill Jim's dad handed us, the value of which we were clueless. It could have been one, ten or a hundred dollars.

That night we stayed at a Mennonite mission. A fresh bed in a sparsely decorated, clean room welcomed our weary bodies. We washed the outer clothes we wore for the trip and slept in underwear. A tropical rainstorm, battering down with steady rata tat tats on the tin roof, gave us music to sleep by, accompanied by thunderclaps and lightning flashes. Mosquitoes found Benjy's skin and drilled in during the night. By morning, bites peppered his whole body, causing incessant itching. (Later in the week, with Benjy accompanying us, we found a drugstore. The pharmacist insisted Benj had chicken pox and wanted to treat him for the illness. The man was tough to convince, but we prevailed with our mosquito story.) After we crawled out of bed in the morning, we put on our damp, but clean, clothes, and prepared for a new day.

Following breakfast, we walked to the embassy. Someone in charge gave us a number for our place in the queue to request our visas. Within two hours, the representative stamped official Argentine visas onto the pages of our passports. We thanked God that the official came to work that Friday. Government employees often took three-day weekends, and we had no assurance the ambassador would make it in that day. I am positive he showed up for us.

Our hopes soaring, we reached the border only to meet another setback. As we prepared to walk out of Paraguay, the Paraguayan official stopped us and asked another unexpected question.

"Where is your exit visa?"

"We don't have one. We never heard of it."

"I cannot allow you to leave without an exit visa."

"How do we get that visa?"

"Any police officer in Asunción can grant you the visa. You just have to ask."

The previous day, no one had requested this. New day. New rules. Seeing we had no options, we turned and headed back towards the Capital. Just outside the Paraguayan exit center, a gentleman sauntered over to us.

"Do you need an exit visa?" he asked.

"Yes, we do."

"I have one you can have."

"How much does it cost?"

"How much do you have?"

"We only have this guaraní bill."

"Good, I'll take it. Here's your permit to leave the country."

The Paraguayan officials may have been privy to the transaction; we certainly returned quickly. Without questioning how we secured the visa, they simply accepted it and waved us on to the next encounter.

After walking a few more yards, we arrived, once again, at the Argentine outpost. We met the same representative who had performed his duties the previous day. He looked at our passports and approved the ambassador's stamp. With curiosity piqued, he questioned us.

"Where is the older gentleman who was with you yesterday?"

"Oh, he had business to do and left without us."

In our minds, we believe the customs gentleman may have been eager to check out all the luggage. However, Dad Saint had wisely left the outpost before the official and the other agents inspected our treasures.

Finally, we made it into Argentina, albeit by just a few feet. Our subsequent task was to find a ride to the next town. A taxi sat waiting close by, across from the immigration/tent/lean-to. We prevailed upon the driver to take us to the neighboring town for a few American silver dollars, as we had no Argentine pesos. He readily agreed to the arrangement. After traveling five to ten kilometers, and then entering the town, we caught sight of Jim's dad. He had taken advantage of the wait by indulging in a little siesta on top of a foot-wide, three-foot-high, block fence. On our arrival, he instantly woke up, rolled off the fence and motioned for us to get into the car. Once again, we boarded the Ford Falcon station wagon and headed for Córdoba, eighteen hours away, two hours shy of the entire flight time.

After journeying on a rustic and bumpy road for an hour, another obstacle loomed before us. We came to a place on the road where the presence of machine-gun-armed government militia blocked clear passage. In front of us, a busload of passengers milled around as soldiers carefully rifled through every piece of luggage. Dad directed us to pray in earnest. I'm not sure how we'd been praying before, but this time the need presented graver consequences. Feeling faith drain from my reserves, I visualized months of careful and constant shopping evaporate. I silently cried a desperate prayer, *Dear Lord, these items are for our family. We have sacrificed to find them and buy them. Please protect these goods.* God heard our nervous and urgent pleas. The commandant courteously waved us on by without even looking at our passports. Had he realized we were North Americans, we stood a real chance of having to surrender most, if not all, our belongings with no recourse.

We continued driving throughout that entire day and night. To say we were at the point of exhaustion begs the quality of our own fortitude. Jim's father possessed remarkable stamina, unmatched by anyone I know. Jim did most of the driving, as he trusted himself behind the wheel. Dad Saint insisted we persevere. Enormous ruts gouged much of the road because of recent, severe flooding in northern Argentina. Besides these mini road craters and the militia, who appeared with guns drawn sporadically, another danger involved wandering livestock. Cattle, horses, donkeys, sheep and goats enjoyed free range over the countryside, without fencing or barricades to impede their travels. No streetlights brightened our way through this remote area, which meant we seriously needed every shred of light from the headlights. By 2:00 a.m., the car's headlamps didn't look all that radiant as we drove through the dust in the darkness.

Home in Córdoba

Eighteen hours of road travel left our nerves frayed and jangled. We beleaguered travelers arrived at the Saint home in Córdoba. Jim's mom had waited to serve supper for us the night before, with no idea as to our delay. When I had asked my father-in-law about calling to let her know what was happening, Dad Saint's reply was, "Oh, she's used to it. She knows we'll get home eventually." I am not sure she was *used to it* and suspect she must have spent more than her share of spare time in prayer for our safety and well-being. As a seasoned missionary wife, she had grown accustomed to putting aside her agenda and looking to the Lord for His. Mom Saint's trust in His protection was tried over many years.

We gladly collapsed into bed for a siesta a few hours later. Ben had a crib waiting for him. He indignantly voiced his disgust at being treated like a baby. On many nights, we welcomed a little visitor crawling into our cramped double bed. The temperatures during the days stayed in the humid 90s and did not drop low enough during the evening hours to cool off our room. In the Southern Hemisphere, December signals the start of summer. We caught the signal as we sweltered.

Glimmers of sunshine and rainbows through the mist

I am still amazed to think about the suitcase that burst at the seams as it popped onto the conveyor belt. God's care over those items started at home and extended to the various flights and the Asunción arrival. Then we faced the militia, who never even looked at it. What we were bringing down blessed many who would enjoy the items through gifting and through hospitality. We could see that God intended to encourage the recipients of our efforts.

Gathering grace gems from the bubbling waters

- Do you remember taking flights in which you needed to transfer luggage at each stop? How did you tackle the challenge?
- Our landing in Asunción filled us with apprehension and many what ifs. Jim's dad, however, expressed confidence that we would meet him the next day in the neighboring town. Has anyone's faith and confidence buoyed you when the situation looked bleak?
- Do you recall a time when someone appeared for you when you had a specific need? What was the need and how was it met?

I Heard the Wedding Bells on Christmas Day

They drink their fill of the abundance of Your house;
And You give them to drink of the river of Your delights.
For with You is the fountain of life;
In Your light we see light
(Psalm 36:8-9 NASB).

For the sake of Your name, do not despise us; do not disgrace Your glorious throne. Remember Your covenant with us; do not break it. Can the worthless idols of the nations bring rain? Do the skies alone send showers? Is this not by You, O LORD our God? So we put our hope in You, for You have done all these things
(Jeremiah 14:21-22 BSB).

The day after our arrival in Córdoba, we jumped into preparations for the upcoming ceremony. This meant purchasing and ordering food for the reception, buying flowers for floral arrangements, sewing last minute tucks into bridal outfits. Evelyn invested a major effort to make this wedding one she and her family would fondly remember. We remember!

Come, celebrate

Rather than mail out invitations in Argentina, people hand-deliver wedding cards. Mom invited me to accompany her, giving me a chance to renew former acquaintances and to make new ones. It takes time to hand out invitations, especially when one must drive long distances to share them, and then visit briefly, which often includes a time of drinking mate. However, the personal touch keeps people connected.

Common in many cultures are goodbyes to single life. Argentine culture is no exception. In the large garage/movie studio next door, friends and family gathered for a *despedida a los novios* (farewell to the bride and groom). The youth from their church held a roast for Eve and Humberto. They wrote and performed a satire with youth group actors playing the roles of those who participated in the *noviazgo* (courtship). The participants gave the actual Eve and Humberto black and white prison garb with significant dates, including the dates of rejection, written on paper signs hung around their necks. The actors had names inscribed on their clothing, designating whom they represented. The activity created a delightful interlude before the official and somewhat hectic week of final arrangements.

Eve and I stopped at a florist to see about purchasing flowers. With a Stateside mentality, I thought we'd simply order bouquets and boutonnieres. No. We ordered flowers, tulle and other accessories so that we could put floral arrangements together ourselves on the day of or the day prior to the wedding. Seriously? Insisting I knew nothing about how to make corsages or arrange flowers did nothing to dissuade Evelyn, as she possessed great faith in our abilities to pull this off. We had to. After all, it was her wedding. In the end, the flowers looked splendid.

On the home front, guests in various shapes and sizes came to the door frequently, all day and half the night. They also came ready to eat. Some of them were curious about us. Many came because of the wedding, wanting to know about the plans in place for the occasion. One time, while seeking a moment of quiet inside the house, I ran into a man whom I had not previously met. Happy to see me, he extended his good wishes and greetings. I never did figure out how he entered.

Humberto's mother, Doña Elsa, arrived from Peru a few days before the nuptials, accompanied by a surprise couple. Therefore, it was Mom Ruth's responsibility to find a spot for them and to include them in all the festivities. Her "instant in and out of season" [4] never ceased to amaze me.

To treat the family during this visit, Doña Elsa, who owned her own restaurant, prepared a special Peruvian dish with fermented potatoes and pork she had hand carried from her home. The potatoes were black, as I recall. I am not sure if that was the original color or the result of the fermentation process. Mom rarely, if ever, welcomed another cook into her sacrosanct kitchen. It must have required incredible grace for her to turn a blind eye to someone else fixing food and using virtually all her kitchen equipment—pots, pans, bowls and serving pieces.

After that dinner, we returned to prepare for more gatherings to come. To celebrate the civil marriage ceremony a few days later, we set up the film studio for dinner guests. The studio, where Jim's dad had filmed evangelistic movies, easily fit about five or six cars, with room to spare. We weren't packing in cars, but people. Men arranged wooden planks and sawhorses into tables for at least fifty guests. Folding chairs and dining room chairs graced each side of the massive, improvised tables. I have no memory of the food prepared. However, Mom served cake for dessert. After she had baked and frosted it, she handed me some cake decorating tools, a frosting bag and floral tips, directing me to put on some flourishes. Children's birthday cakes kept me occupied for young family members, but a cake for a bridal feast? I couldn't do that! But I did. Without food coloring, we used beet juice to rosy up the frosting. Mom kindly raved about how wonderful it looked. I cringed. Later, fresh flowers graced the cake, successfully masking the flourishes.

New ways to enjoy and remember Christmas

Christmas Eve included Jim's family members and the groom's mother, Doña Elsa and the guest couple. As usual, Mom prepared an exquisite meal. She set out her good plates plus whatever extra plates were needed. We washed a veritable mountain of dishes after supper and then gathered in the living room.

At midnight the assembly exchanged gifts, a late-night tradition we have not repeated here in the States. Earlier, one of the children had knocked over the Christmas tree, which disrupted some festivities for a brief interlude, but the tree was none the worse for wear. That plastic tree had arrived on a cargo ship with the family years earlier. Its balding, sparsely needled branches, accented with carefully saved lights and colored balls, would have given Charlie Brown reason to rejoice.

On Christmas Day, wedding day, my husband, the resident truck driver, made last-minute runs for the reception. Jim brought food items from the restaurant, the bakery and the warehouse. He had to remember maps in his head to find the best routes. Cost-wise, disposable plates, plastic eating utensils, plastic goblets and paper napkins were either not affordable or nearly impossible to locate. The family rented glassware, tableware, porcelain plates and cloth napkins from a local business. Somebody made a lot of trips, before and after the events. Jim was that somebody.

At 9:00 in the evening, we arrived at a beautiful old church for the marriage ceremony. The service started between 9:30 p.m. and 10:00 p.m., fashionably late for a 9:00 p.m. event. Invitees filled the church chairs. More people jammed the aisles. Others gathered outside on the sidewalk. Once the hour-long ceremony concluded, attendees rode by car or taxi to another location for photo sessions before midnight. Then the reception welcomed visitors at still another venue. The party lasted all night long. However, Benjy and I surrendered to exhaustion and sleep around 2:00 a.m.

After Christmas and the wedding festivities, Dad Saint drove us to Valle del Lago, about three hours away. We spent a few hours at the camp; the caretakers welcomed us into their home. Farm animals, including chickens, roamed around inside and outside the house. Much to my dismay, we had chicken dinner provided by a hen, which was sacrificed merely an hour before eating it. Not much of a farm girl, I had a hard time consuming the creature, not sure if it was warm from the oven or warm from its recently ended life.

Our visit ends with some surprises

Our time in Argentina ended in early January. The American travel agent had told us to make sure we verified our tickets for our return trip by phoning the airlines and securing our reservation. We engaged the services of a local travel agent who accessed his professional account to make this confirmation.

We tearfully bid goodbye to friends and family and then boarded a bus to travel the long stretch before catching our return flight out of Asunción. Prior to the trip, Jim's dad assured us we would ride on a luxury coach with air conditioning and all the amenities. We soon discovered he had once again used evangelistic hyperbole. At least the windows opened, giving us plenty of outside air. Our return trip on the bus to Paraguay happened without incident and gave us a more relaxing time than our previous harrowing ride down to Córdoba.

Upon alighting from the bus at the airport, we located the ticket agent for the designated airline to leave the country. Much to our dismay, the agent found no record of our tickets.

"They must have been canceled."

"What? They have been confirmed."

"No. They needed to be confirmed by phone. Did you call?"

"No. We had someone confirm through a special agent ticketing system."

"Sorry. There are no tickets in your name."

I cried. Not again! Jim's mom had given us money, just as we were leaving their home, to help cover the cost of our plane tickets. However, even with that amount, we could not pay for return tickets at the last minute. We didn't even own a credit card. Our arrival had required some heavy-duty prayers. Now our departure required some intervention from divine realms as well. All we could humanly do depended on the kindness and mercy of the airlines, the agents on hand—and God.

Our tickets, although confirmed electronically, had been canceled manually. A young woman put in many calls and worked diligently for several hours. Meanwhile, we uttered a few more frantic pleadings heavenward. Finally our ticket agent motioned for us to come to the desk. She beamed as she announced the airline's decision to reinstate our tickets.

After hours of desperate praying, nail biting, nervous waiting and anxious pacing, we boarded a late-night flight headed for Rio de Janeiro, Brazil, thanks to our agent's work in obtaining our passage home. At last I could look down on Rio and see the lit statue of Jesus holding His arms above the city. We leisurely explored the airport before the last leg of our journey toward home.

Glimmers of sunshine and rainbows through the mist

The trip included several surprising events. I learned to adapt in more ways than I thought. In looking back, I can see how God intervened on our behalf, giving me more history to share of His faithfulness, even when I couldn't see it in the swirling current.

Gathering grace gems from the bubbling waters

- Have you ever felt plunged into an apparently impossible situation that worked out? What did you do in the darkness when you could barely see the light of day?
- Weddings are joyous occasions, mostly. Can you remember assisting with a wedding? What was required? How did you react?
- Do you have family or close friends who live long distances away? Do you ever visit them? How do you stay in contact?
- Can you think of a time when someone performed above and beyond the call of duty for you? The ticket agent worked tirelessly for hours on our behalf. Too many years have passed. I would love to thank her and acknowledge her, but I do not even remember the name of the airline we took. How might I sow the kindness?

Deep and Bubbling Waters

The words of a man's mouth are deep waters;
The fountain of wisdom is a bubbling brook
(Proverbs 18:4 NASB).

Our house expanded with a few feet and arms poking out as Joe, Susy and their three children, Martin (6), Mika (3 ½) and Becky (9 months) joined us temporarily when Joe's job ended. Because his previous work included housing, they needed a place to live. Jim, Benjy and I stayed in the master bedroom. Joe, Susy and their three occupied the other two bedrooms for their family. With four children and four adults, life held its challenges. For those months, Jim bore the responsibility of supporting all of us, which increased stress for him.

On the plus side, Benjy had two playmates always on call. Because we lived in Phoenix, Arizona, we had an advantage because the children could play outside for hours on most days. Our friends, the Lunns, also lived across the street with their young boys; their home served as an extra neighborhood playground. Sometimes we moms needed breaks from all the fun activities... truly.

Another baby on the way...

Within a month of growing our household, my mother called me with news about a possible baby for us. She had received information from Duane at church choir practice. He had told her there was an expectant mother who had gone to Dr. K's office, looking for a family willing to adopt her baby. Initially, this sounded like a great opportunity, as we had been wanting to expand our family with another child.

There were some extenuating circumstances which could not be easily resolved. First, because the doctor was not considered *"politically correct"* in his dealings with the medical community in northern Arizona, he was scheduled for a license hearing in which he would probably lose his authorization to practice medicine. This baby would be his last placement with a family. Second, and more important, friends from church were also in line to adopt. Because of their age, perhaps they had lost interest. At least that was presented to us as a possibility. There were several best-case scenarios that gave us a sense it might be in our best interest to take the baby. However, we perceived that perhaps this was not the ideal way to move forward, as much as we wanted another child.

Jim and I wrangled through the evening. Perhaps the other couple truly had lost interest in having a child. Maybe they realized they were getting too old to handle a newborn. We could switch churches. This must be a baby God wanted us to have because we were given this option. The thoughts of another child were so tempting and the lure of expanding our family was so overwhelming.

I cried and argued with God all night long, sure that He should see my side of the situation. The more I considered this baby, the less peace I felt. I prayed, reminding God how desperately we wanted another child. Maybe He didn't understand how important this was to us. As Jim left for work, he told me he would support whatever decision I made. At least there was a consensus, but I still had to make the call.

Later that morning, I spoke to Duane to let him know our conclusion and how we felt God was directing. I told him God had given me two sections of Scripture. *"Take the baby and run"* was not one of them. In fact, there wasn't one Bible verse that remotely sanctioned that option.

The first story impressed on me was of Lot and Abraham. The biblical rendering explains the dilemma they faced:

> *Lot, who was traveling with Abram, also had flocks of sheep, herds, and tents. But the land could not support them living together, because they had so much livestock. There was strife between the herdsmen in charge of Abram's livestock and the herdsmen in charge of Lot's livestock... So, Abram told Lot, "Please, let's not have strife between you and me, or between your herdsmen and my herdsmen, since we are relatives. Isn't the whole land available to you? Let's separate: If you go to the left, then I will go to the right; if you go to the right, then I will go to the left." Lot looked around and noticed that the whole Jordan plain as far as Zoar was well-watered like the garden of the LORD or like the land of Egypt* (Genesis 13:5-10 ISV).

After reviewing that story, I wondered, *Do I want to leave someone else in barrenness while I bask in the fertile, green fields?* Also included in the Scripture was the promise that God would direct with a right or left, as I had received His promise when baptized in Paraguay and when the church prayed for Jeremy. *[Love] does not insist on its own way*[5] gnawed at my heart. God questioned me, "What is the path of love and how will you show it?"

In talking this over with Duane and sharing the Scriptures, he graciously stated, "I knew that is how you would decide."

"God is ultimately our only Source," I explained. "As much as we value you and your willingness to help in our family expansion, you aren't our source. Dr. K. is not our source. The birth mother is not our source. We have only one Source."

After apparently cutting off our provision for another child, Duane kindly reassured me, "We'll see about getting Benjy another brother or sister."

Moved to respond, I had made a declaration out of a conviction of God's ability, not necessarily a willingness to relinquish my hopes and dreams for something that might end with no additional child in the future. Because of His words to me, the true Provider assured me of my need to trust Him, even when I didn't perceive any changes on the horizon.

Although he wanted to speak positively, Duane did not know how his words would come to pass. He didn't know where to find another baby. The quiet in the office enveloped him. After hanging up from our conversation, Duane's secretary buzzed in to say he had another call on the line. He answered it.

"Hello, Duane, this is Pat. Our 16-year-old daughter, Kim, is expecting a baby, and we are looking for a Christian family who could adopt this child. Would you be able to find one for us?" Dumbfounded by God's timing, Duane explained what had just occurred. Pat was waiting on the other line while he and I were ending our conversation.

Duane and I connected by phone later in the afternoon. He told me what had happened and how amazed he was that the timing was so precise.

Two babies

A couple of weeks later, we had dinner with our friends who were scheduled to receive the original baby. Duane had given us permission to announce their blessed event to them. So, over our meal, we revealed their news. They were expecting a baby! Their baby was due in December and ours at the beginning of January.

The months passed slowly and quickly. We made it through December without either baby showing up. Then, early in January, our daughter was born. The other baby did not arrive until the middle of February. In questioning the birth mother later, Duane learned her dates were off, and she did not know the baby would be born two months beyond her speculations. Duane also asked the doctor about this calculation error. After the obstetrician had examined the birth mom, it appeared to him the baby was due earlier than she was. She had gone to his office, seeking an abortion. However, because the doctor believed she was due to deliver much earlier, he refused to perform an abortion on a late-term baby. Both couples heard the intermingled stories at Duane's and my parents' home church for the first time in March. We sobbed as we each recognized God's hand in creating and preserving the lives of our daughters.

What's in a name?

Before our daughter was born, we had some serious discussions/ altercations about her name. Jim and I had babysat a little girl named Chelann. She delighted us so much that we decided we would name our first daughter Chelann. However, after three sons and holding that name in reserve, I decided we should find a name with more meaning as all we knew was that the child was named after a body of water in Washington, Lake Chelan, with an extra *"n"* in her name.

Our pastor's wife had called a few weeks before her birth.

"Have you decided on a name for the new baby?" Marge asked.

"I need you to pray for Jim. He doesn't agree with any of the names I've chosen." I whined.

My rant continued, "The name he wants doesn't have any meaning. We know nothing about the significance of the name." I was sure this would pound the nail into the coffin for his name choices because his reasoning did not meet my lofty expectations.

"The answer is simple," she replied. "Decide to submit to your husband's wishes. The meaning of her name can mean 'submission.'"

I wasn't terribly wild about her response nor her explanation. However, to prevent further issues at home, I opted to submit by giving the name we had held for years. I was still hoping for something fulfilling and meaningful.

A second grafting onto our family tree

When Chelann arrived in midwinter, we met at the hospital, three days after her birth. Benjy, the new big brother, took the trip with us. After several delays and waits, we saw Duane with the nurse who was carrying the new baby. The first one to recognize the three, Benjy jumped up and down in the back seat of the car as he yelled, "Our baby's coming! Our baby's coming!" Sure enough, we were soon handed our new baby girl to take home and to love.

I also wrote a letter to our second birth mom:

Dear Precious Young Lady,

How much I wish I could wrap you in my arms and cry with you. Please know that many tears are being shed for you, even now. Our joy comes with suffering as we try to comprehend the deep hurt in your heart.

The New Testament holds a verse, "Greater love has no man than this than to give up his life for another." For a long time, I have felt that this verse applies, too, to birth mothers. Surely the love a birth mother feels is so great for her own child that she releases this life into the hands of another.

As Duane has explained to you, we are sublimely happy with the dear son God gave us after the deaths of our first two babies. Our three-year-old has been asking for a new baby for over a year now. We could not imagine that it would be possible to grant him his request while he was still young enough to enjoy a new sibling!

We have been praying for you for as long as we have known about the hope of having your little one to nurture in our home. We pray, not only for your physical, emotional and spiritual well-being but also that through this, God may recompense you in a way you never thought possible.

At the funeral of our second little boy, a lady approached us and shared from her prayer time what she heard: the days ahead would be hard, but God would provide a double blessing as we stayed obedient. Our double blessing has now been realized: two precious, adorable children... a son and a daughter!

I am enclosing a letter which we wrote for our first birth mother. What is expressed in that letter is meant for you to read, too.

One will never know how many times we have prayed for our first birth mother. I thank God for her every single day. Each time I stop and observe our son developing and growing, learning and living, a prayer of thanksgiving is breathed.

We know that having a child is a great privilege and responsibility. We also know that being able to adopt requires, for us, divine intervention. We don't know why God has seen fit to bless us when so many must wait. It is humbling to recognize His gentle, loving hand in our lives.

Dear one, we understand that your parents have been with you through much of this. They are in our prayers. For surely this baby has touched their lives as she developed in your womb... and through the hours of labor... and in those precious few days with her.

This little girl affects the course of the life of the birth father as well. We pray God will give him new insights and increased understanding.

For all those who love you, dear one, and especially for you, we pray for peace... peace in mind and heart.

Shortly after Chelann's birth, we signed the required legal papers to verify we were agreeing to adopt this baby. The last name of the birth mom was listed as the baby's last name. Because I had worked at the family's home church a few years previous, I recognized the surname as belonging to Pat's two daughters. Something similar happened to them as they had spied our name on a folder. For 22 years, both parties knew about Chelann's family of origin and her family of destination. After two decades, we had a reunion here at our home with Pat, Kim, Jim, Chelann and me. We tried to capture some of the lost seasons as we laughed and cried together. A lot of pieces have been placed into the puzzle. Some pieces may never come to complete the picture, but we have more awareness now.

The name *Chelann* holds a wealth of meanings. The Native American name, *Tsillan*, means "deep waters." It has also been interpreted as "bubbling waters." My friend, Sarah, the Hebrew professor who had researched the meaning of *Benoni*, the name given by the biblical Rachel for Benjamin, called me to ask about the baby's name meaning after she was born.

"I know you like to use biblical names. Where did you find *Chelann*?"

"I don't think it has any biblical interpretation," I admitted weakly.

She then explained, "I thought of the phrase Shalah tech from the story of Hannah pleading with God for a child. When Eli heard her story, he responded, *Shalah tech*, which basically means, 'The Lord will answer your prayer.'"

"Actually, I was thinking of *shalom* because it sounds like 'Chelann.'"

"You are correct!" she exclaimed. "Because biblical Hebrew has no distinguishing vowels and because the 'm' and the 'n' can be interchangeable, 'shalom' is a perfect way to interpret and understand 'Chelann.'"

Chelann's name possesses far more significance than I could have dreamed. The meanings offered a rich treasure that God had been storing to give me reassurance. *Shalom*[6] is one word I used freely in my prayers for her as she grew up. Calling on God's peace became my heart's cry. *Thank you, Lord, for peace. Thank you. I submitted, and you gave truer peace than I could have hoped for.*

Glimmers of sunshine and rainbows through the mist

The synchronicity of God, His unbelievable timing, has fascinated me, especially when reviewing events over the past decades. As tempting as it was, I am so grateful I listened to the Lord's heeding and didn't *"take the baby and run."* God prevented me from acting rashly by removing my peace. Honestly, even though Duane sounded positive, I wasn't so sure. That very day, right after I had spoken with Duane, God intervened. What joy He was carefully guarding for us, in the matter of minutes and a few hours.

Gathering grace gems from the bubbling waters

- Have you ever experienced the offering of something that you knew wasn't intended for you? How did you emerge from violation to victory?
- Has the Lord given you clear direction about taking a path you weren't sure of? Then later, you saw Him work it all out, without your help. What welled up within you? Gratitude? Incredulity? Joy?
- Have you ever received something that cost someone else more than you can repay?
- What has God given that you can never repay? What is your response to His gifts?

Footnotes

1. This refers to the Old Testament teaching of placing a sacrifice on the altar (lamb, goat or ox) for the Lord. Many use this as an example, in a figurative sense, of handing a situation over to God. It may be possessions, hopes, dreams, feelings. It is difficult to trust God to take care of those areas I long for so intensely. The trouble with living sacrifices, a somewhat humorous quotation claims, is that they keep crawling off the altar. Too often, I have placed myself onto the altar of submission and relinquishment only to find myself crawling off. "Therefore, I urge you, brothers and sisters, in view of God's mercy, to offer your bodies as a living sacrifice." (Romans 12:1a, b NIV)
2. The name *Benjamin* means "son of the right hand," implying a person of indispensable worth. The name given Benjamin in the Bible, by his mother Rachael, was *Benoni.* In most texts, it is translated as "son of my sorrow." A friend from Israel, also a professor of Hebrew, researched the meaning in Hebrew and noted the term may more accurately imply "son of my strength" as it was Rachael's last strength to give Benjamin birth. Sorrow and strength link together.
3. "Beloved, let us love one another: for love is of God; and everyone that loveth is born of God, and knoweth God. He that loveth not knoweth not God; for God is love" (1 John 4:7,8 KJV).
4. Reference to 2 Timothy 4:2 (NIV) "Preach the word; be prepared in season and out of season; correct, rebuke and encourage—with great patience and careful instruction."

5. I Corinthians 13:5 (ESV)

6. (Soroski). According to Crosswalk, *shalom* holds much more meaning. "Beyond being just a simple wish for peace and happiness, the word suggests a state of fullness and perfection; overflowing inner and outer joy and peaceful serenity."

Section 4. Setting Sail in Storm Clouds with Silver Linings:

Northwest Passage

A time to be born, and a time to die; a time to plant, and a time to uproot what was planted
(Ecclesiastes 3:2 NET).

Farewell to Family and the Familiar

If I ride the wings of the morning, if I dwell by the farthest oceans, even there your hand will guide me, and your strength will support me
(Psalm 139:9,10 NLT).

Transitions and changes dominate our lives. A stagnant life cannot grow. Our family learned to grow through new and unanticipated events. Sometimes changes are more subtle. One doesn't see the oak tree make rapid adjustments in its early growth from an acorn. Other changes take a relatively short time. Vegetable plants can change from seed to fruit in weeks or months. Radish seeds are a favorite. Who doesn't glory in a crop of radishes? Within a couple of weeks after planting, they are ready.

Letting go

Every fall, our neighbors' church held a harvest party. Jim and Connie invited our family to attend and told us that a major highlight of that evening was a pet show. We searched desperately for an animal to exhibit. Our key problem was that we didn't own any pets, either conventional or unconventional. To our delight, we found a caterpillar on dill weed growing in the abandoned vegetable garden. Benj carefully placed his new pet into a decorated shoe box and carted it off to the gathering. The caterpillar won two blue ribbons at this gala affair—one for being the smallest pet and the other for being the fiercest.

We nurtured that concealed insect for weeks as it gorged itself on all the weeds we could give it. Eventually it cloistered itself within a translucent, blue-green chrysalis. The following year, on May 9th, we discovered a butterfly in the large glass jar.

Our transformed caterpillar emerged from his chrysalis today. The caterpillar had the colors of a tiger—orange, black and white. The large butterfly that came forth was black, beautifully, velvety black with fluorescent blue dots on its back. Orange and white patterning in a small patch on its underside gave the only indication of its former colors.

For weeks we had seen no sign of life. The blue-green casing stayed glued to the branch with no hint of change or activity. Then, as if by a miracle, a butterfly appeared in the jar where earlier a chrysalis-encased caterpillar rested on a twig.

We watched sadly as it frantically beat its wings against the glass. Benjy and I knew it was time to let it go. Our flying flower seemed to understand its home was outside and wasted little time in making an escape. When we walked to the garden in the sunshine, our stunning, ebony-winged butterfly rose quickly out of the jar, ascending high and soaring far away. Back inside the house, Benjy soberly observed, "That was hard, wasn't it?"

"Lord, when there is some creepy, crawly thing which dies within me, give me the grace to let it go. Maybe it is something You want to transform." That caterpillar raised its horns and emitted a horrible smell when touched. As it "died," it lost its ability to protect itself. However, when it was renewed—the same basic substance with nothing new added—a living creature of incredible beauty emerged.

That which harms me or hurts me can be transformed, by the Lord's gracious hand, into a velvety beauty. It can be released, freed from crawling on the ground, ready to soar in the heavens. I have a choice of crushing that which I find offensive or of letting it undergo change and renewal by Him as I accept my lot. When I liberate what would do me harm—when it "dies" and is rendered harmless—God can intervene and, in His exceptional creativity, bring forth His glory, a testimony to Himself. Even in that, I cannot glory in myself because that which is beautiful, if not set free, will fade, will break and will die. Each aspect of my life needs freedom from bondage.

Leaving for Argentina—not our trip

Once Joe started working at a new job, their family moved to an apartment complex within a few blocks of our home. We kept in close contact, seeing one another every few days. By this time, they were seriously considering a return to Argentina. When we came back from Evelyn's wedding, the call to South America remained strong for us. However, Joe and Susy were the ones who eventually heeded the call.

Over the next months, Joe and Susy disposed of some of their belongings. However, their plans changed. Joe packaged his household goods and loaded them onto a cargo ship, something his parents had done 30 years earlier. This prompted them to consider what they might keep instead of unloading most personal effects.

My mother hosted the equivalent of a wedding shower for Susy with about two dozen friends and others from the church family at Mom's home. I must have interpreted towels and toys as a major need, and that is all I recall in the gift area. They ended up with more than enough towels to pack and use for bathing—for years.

Joe, Susy, Martin, Mika and Becky left early in November 1984. After living together for seven years with endless shared experiences, we felt a cloud of sadness darken our spirits. Jim and Benjy drove them to the airport in our van. I stayed home to care for Chelann and cried that day as our loss encompassed me. The three of us spent quite a few days, thereafter, in tears.

Portland trailblazer

I am not uprooting you but transplanting you. Personal Diary.

In the fall of 1985, we started looking at ways to either enlarge our house or move to another, larger place. On October 3rd of that year, I wrote in my journal:

Keep your eyes on Me. Be at peace in Me and in My plans for your lives. Do not be surprised at the new life I am giving you.

I will stablish you and place you on hard rock. My foundations do not crumble.

Let Me work a peace in your heart as you see all things are in My control. I am working in the hearts of men, tilling the soil, preparing it for new seeds and new plantings.

Do not regard being uprooted... but being transplanted. Be ready to discard the old, the weighty, the burdensome. What are your needs? Know that I shall provide for your needs and give you your heart's desires.

You are anxious. Trust in Me. Wait on Me. I am doing a work. The little seeds you have planted shall germinate, root, grow and flourish. I am the Master Farmer. You are a caretaker.

After reading a book that encouraged me to consider bearing another child, I presented the idea to Jim; we discussed this for several months. Then we both concluded God was moving us in this direction. Many indications through Scripture and circumstance appeared to direct us down this previously traveled road. Within a short time, we were again expecting a baby, due exactly one year after the journal entry.

Feeling awkward, I tried to make sure our close acquaintances and family approved. I sent a letter out to many individuals, detailing all the reasons we were having another child and how God had confirmed this through Scripture, radio messages and other avenues. I wanted to guarantee this baby's health. The more I informed people, the less God would let anything happen, right? After all, wasn't His reputation at stake? Desperate to see a dream realized, sometimes one resorts to extreme means. I know I did.

We considered increasing the physical size of our home to provide more room for our growing family. Jim and I attended a house auction, hoping to seize a good deal. When we realized those houses cost more than we could afford, we looked at hiring a contractor to expand our dwelling. Several remodelers came over, explaining what we would need to enlarge the space. We almost signed papers with a contractor when a different opportunity appeared.

Jim's company started opening several hubs in different areas of the country—Seattle, Denver and Portland. At 12 years of age, I had visited Portland for my aunt and uncle's wedding. From then on, that area drew me, and I hoped to live there one day. I still remembered that August summer in Portland when air conditioning was superfluous. For someone who had endured swamp cooler summers for much of her life, while wilting from the dry, desert heat, Portland represented paradise. Besides the cooler air in the summer, greenery filled the landscape. The grass was greener on the other side of the Cascade Range. Portland got my vote. One day in the spring, Jim came home from work and announced his transfer to Oregon had been accepted. The siren call of mountains, trees and nearby ocean breezes filled my days as we started preparing for our own move.

My husband planned to leave Phoenix close to the Fourth of July. A giant, gray shadow of responsibilities and obligations towered over me—packing up household goods, selling the house, caring for the children, dealing with another pregnancy. How could I handle all this? What if the house didn't sell? How was I going to pack everything by myself? With their dad away, how were the kids going to handle their days? While fretting and worrying during my private devotions, the following words calmed me:

Let your heart be at peace in Me and in Me alone. You and yours are chosen vessels for My work. Look to Me for direction and guidance. See Me in all events.

Accept the interruptions as My working in your life. Are you able to respond with love, patience and kindness? Or do you recoil in anger, railing against that which I have allowed and sent to mature you and increase your dependence on Me?

I am making a well-worn path for you to follow. Even if no one had ever or has ever walked it, I have gone on ahead, cutting out the weeds and obstacles in your way. My footsteps are enough for you to follow.

Do today what I am commanding. Do not take on tomorrow's work—that is not in My provision for you. You have strength for today's problems, but I have not given you any for tomorrow's difficulties. Do not draw on tomorrow's strength. You will go bankrupt, overdrawing on what is not yet invested. Look to Me for today!

Look to Me today to complete unfinished tasks in your life. Are you perfect in all areas of your life? Of course not! I have started new construction—an additional work in your heart and soul. You will see more evidence of this work in the days ahead.

As I am Lord of your spiritual life, so I am Lord of the world outside and around you. Rejoice in how I am moving. Do you not see My steadying hand in all areas of your life? Rejoice in My goodness to you. I love you and want you to rest in My provisions in each area.

In May, our house sold a few hours after the realtors' walkthrough, before officially listing the house. In the counter offer we made, the buyers even agreed to take our dog, a promise written into the final contract. We didn't know how to find someone to take Chelsea, our canine companion. The contract proviso meant one less concern in moving. Lest one believes this sale transpired with no glitches, it did not. The young couple eventually gained possession of the house, but there were many delays and interruptions due to incomplete paperwork, foot dragging, etc.

Although the temperature in Phoenix reached 110 degrees that July day, it still felt gloomy when Jim took off in our light blue Maverick for Portland, Oregon. Watching his dad drive away devastated Benjy, as the two had forged a tight bond. Back inside the house, Benjy and his bud, Justin Lunn, stood together in our kitchen when Benj turned to his friend and fell, sobbing into his arms. Justin hugged Ben as he kept repeating, "It's okay, Bud." Dear little six-year-olds shared their tender hearts.

Week after week dragged by with little change or movement in finalizing the sale of the house. Because the sale was relatively uncomplicated, closing should have happened before the end of June. Once he left town for the Northwest, Jim called every few days, specifically asking about the house. With every conversation, I told him there was no news. No news—not our good news.

Three months from the initial sale, near the end of August, the realtor called to report the paperwork's completion. Jim flew back to Phoenix within days of learning about the house closure. His arrival at the airport lifted a great load from my shoulders. What I didn't know, until the next day, was that he almost missed his flight out of San Francisco as the first plane had been delayed leaving from Portland. As Jim watched the yard goat pushing the Phoenix-bound plane away from the gate, he ran to the door of the departure gate and threatened to run out onto the tarmac to flag down the plane. The other 15 passengers lauded his bravado as they were also headed towards Phoenix and risked losing that flight themselves. The plane returned. Thankfully, we had not waited all those anxious hours needlessly inside the airport. After our extended wait, we saw Jim emerge from the passageway. Dad's home! Relief.

For weeks, exhaustion and physical pain persisted from much lifting and packing during the last trimester of pregnancy. Propping myself up in a recliner, I lost three nights' rest immediately prior to Jim's arrival. Now that he was home, he could hoist and pack. I fell into a welcome, relaxed sleep in the early morning hours.

By the time we left Arizona, I calculated three and a half weeks before the baby's due date. I had to see an OB-GYN right away. Fortunately, my Phoenix obstetrician gave me several reliable recommendations of physicians in the Portland area, allowing me to call and schedule an appointment from our Phoenix home with a respected doctor in our new city.

Glimmers of sunshine and rainbows through the mist

I have often returned to those months of watching the caterpillar and the chrysalis to the ultimate day of releasing the winged beauty. Letting go, as Benjy affirmed, was hard. In fact, my friend Lisa, who heard the story, gifted me a plate with the picture of a young, towheaded boy gazing delightedly at a butterfly. The child's likeness resembles our own Ben when he was a preschooler. Whenever seeing the plate, I am reminded of the lessons in those butterfly months.

Often, analogies between creatures and humans fall short, but similarities can be found. Sometimes aggressive creatures, even humans, when given the chance to change and grow in the right environment, can become a vision of delight and beauty. Transformations take time. When the transformation occurs, new life and freedom of expression are released.

When we said goodbye to Joe and Susy, there were several areas in which God comforted us. By the time we left Phoenix, Joe and Susy had already departed for Argentina. God gave us a passage to begin a fresh start in Oregon.

My learning to wait on God stretched me those last few months in Phoenix. Although handling the children was effortless, fussing over the unfinished paperwork, managing the packing and dealing with the pregnancy proved more challenging.

Gathering grace gems from the bubbling waters

- What have you released that experienced freedom when you could let it go?
- In bidding farewell to loved ones, what have you learned? What helped you release them?
- Have you ever had to leave the familiar to start anew? How did you respond? What gave you encouragement to adjust to a new locale? A new job? New relationships?
- Expectation is the key. The new location and its attendant intricacies have not yet appeared. In some ways, we all move from one expectant and pregnant moment to another. What gives you the drive and the encouragement to embrace a future full of hope?

God's Joy is My Strength

Then those who sing as well as those who play the flutes shall say,
"All my springs of joy are in you"
(Psalm 87:7 NASB).

With the help of my dad and some friends, Jim loaded the trailer to be railed north to Portland. Soon we said goodbye to dear friends and my folks. We excitedly boarded the bright yellow van and took off for the Pacific Northwest. Two and a half days of driving passed quickly as we looked forward to cool breezes. On arriving in Portland, we quickly found a hotel, a joy for the kids, as it had a swimming pool and a TV set with a video player. The hotel didn't supply a great selection of movies. "The Adventures of Robin Hood" offered us hours of repetitious entertainment.

Hotel or rental home

Locating a rental house presented our next hurdle. The market in the Portland area was very depressed—for the seller. Buyers had their pick of the finest homes for reasonable prices. However, this area was not a renter's paradise. Naïvely, we thought the abundance of houses for sale would reflect an abundance of rentals.

While Jim worked, the kids and I drove through neighborhoods, searching—in futility. Prospects appeared bleak. I was wondering if I would give birth at the hospital and then return to the second-floor hotel room. We prayed individually and as a family. God showed us His merciful compassion. We moved into a rental home one and a half weeks before the scheduled C-section.

We met a young couple, property managers of our future rental home. In a short time, we learned we had connections with this husband and wife. The wife's parents attended the same church as my mother's good friend, also from Portland. The husband's father had attended Wheaton College with Jim's dad.

Our move into the neighborhood filled us with delight as we watched many children, and potential friends, romp through the yard littered with our boxes and furnishings. However, atypical of Benj, he dragged himself around with little energy and a dour look on his face. We took him to the emergency room of a nearby hospital for throat cultures, etc. Besides cutting new molars, he had a mouth full of canker sores and a throat infected with strep. He started out in the new place with a fresh dose of antibiotics and whatever else would bring him some comfort.

Fall baby

The following week, we welcomed a new baby into the Saint home: Alyssa Kara Ruth. Alyssa smiled at a week of age. She was strong and healthy. My mother stayed with us for two weeks following Alyssa's birth, to help me and to care for Benj and Chelann. She read to them. They took long walks together, gathering wildflowers from the nearby field and collecting fall blackberries. We made an excursion as a family in the van—a breathtakingly beautiful drive around Mt. Hood, fall colors blazing through the trees.

Alyssa's health held on for a short duration. When she was three weeks old, I noticed her muscle tone did not seem to match what it had been earlier. I asked the pediatrician about her physical responses, but she answered positively, noting her initial strengths at birth. However, she advised us to get the opinion of a pediatric neurologist, just to put our minds at ease.

For the appointment, Jim took off work to free us for a consultation with the specialist. All five of us visited the medical center on the hill. Because this was a teaching hospital, the doctor who came into the little cubicle where we were waiting also had a student accompanying him. As he examined Alyssa, he pointed out the problems as he observed them. It is unnerving to watch one's precious child treated as a medical project and oddity. The physician finally explained to us that our new baby also appeared to have the same muscular disease as her two brothers.

The news, though somewhat expected, crushed me deeply. *But God, this is the child you promised!* For three days, I sank into a profound sadness, doing little more than barely tending to the needs of Benjy, Chelann and Alyssa. Through the prayers and counsel of dear friends, the light broke through. I could look to the Lord for His presence and grace to invade the situation. Somehow, joy flowed in and saturated my heart once again.

Benjy cared for his baby sister with tender kindness. He often held her and helped get her diapers. She remained calm in his arms and smiled easily whenever he talked to her.

One pastor from the church we were attending contacted me by phone and asked how the church body could stand in prayer with us. I requested, "I want us to faithfully hold up her arms as Aaron and Hur did for Moses while the battle raged below them."[1]

While we prayed intensely for Alyssa's health, we tried to speak of healing all the time and not allow any room for doubt. The one who posited the question, "What if…" was Benjy. "Mom, what if God doesn't heal Alyssa?" In retrospect, I cringe at my glib answer. "We're believing God for healing, and that's all we are going to do for now." As hindsight enables magnification and clarification, if I could return to that conversation, I would respond with careful, thought-filled words. "Yes, we are praying and believing God for healing. However, God is a sovereign God. We need to understand that because His ways are beyond finding out. Sometimes the answer we so desperately want is not the answer we get. It does not mean God does not love us or care about us. It simply reveals that He is working in our hearts and lives in ways we cannot yet understand."

Benjy and Chelann petitioned God for their little sister throughout each day. We anointed her head with oil and prayed. Chelann enjoyed anointing the baby's head, causing Alyssa to glisten from the many times Chelann "oiled" and prayed for her.

Choosing joy

During those weeks, I practiced responding with joy. It was a discipline to cultivate a joyful heart, but it was one I earnestly sought. I chose joy. A song formed in my mind as we continued our prayer journey.

Have not I commanded you?
Be strong and of good courage.
Be not afraid.
Neither be thou dismayed.
For I, the Lord, am with you wherever you go. [2]

At the very end of November, Alyssa caught a cold which rapidly developed into pneumonia (an expected complication of this illness from the paralysis of major muscle systems, including the diaphragm). I rode in the ambulance as she was taken to the hospital late on Tuesday night. One paramedic, a tough-appearing lady with bleached blond hair and a raspy voice, encouraged me to not give up hope and to stay firm in my faith. She touched me where I needed a fresh word and extra support. Her presence became God's whisper to my aching heart.

I remained with Alyssa throughout the night. The next morning, Jim brought Benj and Chelann to the hospital floor to stay with me so he could go into work. New in town, we did not have many options regarding childcare. A nursing student, training at the hospital, showed great kindness and compassion as she entertained the children for most of that day.

That evening, a gentleman from church prayed with us. He strongly admonished us to have faith, and not to doubt God's Word on healing. We wanted to see Alyssa's body restored. We believed and still strongly believe in God's power and will to heal, as we have both seen and experienced evidence of His healing work in our own and in others' lives. But sometimes, He does not bring the healing we are seeking. Dr. Billheimer offers tremendous encouragement in his book on this subject:

> Until recently, during all my lengthy ministry, I have been under the solid impression that supernatural healing and deliverance here and now always brings more glory to God and more eternal profit to the individual than continued suffering. For those who are not healed, may it

> not be otherwise? There is something to be said about this viewpoint. If the goal of the universe is character—that is, a disposition of agape love—and if character cannot be created without tribulation, then may not the discipline of tribulation produce in both time and eternity as desirable a result, if not a better one? The answer lies in our reaction to the discipline. Resentment and rebellion only waste one's sorrows, whereas humble acceptance and brokenness allow the creation of an "eternal weight of glory." [3]

I went home to rest on Wednesday night and returned with Benjy and Chelann on Thursday afternoon, having called the hospital to assess how Alyssa was doing. Theo Johnson, a pastor from our church, joined me later to wait until Jim arrived from work. His foundational and balanced counsel buoyed my flagging spirits. He gently encouraged us to remain standing for healing. "As long as there is life," he affirmed, "continue to believe God for His intervention." Because I was riddled with questions about what might be asked of us and what the medical teams might try to attempt, the verse he stressed declared, "Casting down imaginations, and every high thing that exalteth itself against the knowledge of God, and bringing into captivity every thought to the obedience of Christ…" [4] A trusting heart does not entertain *what ifs*. As I cling to Him, I must maintain an attitude of complete trust in an omniscient God. He knows what He is doing. Stand on the word He has given.

Jim reached the hospital right after work. He and I stayed with Alyssa for several hours. At 9:00 p.m., it became clear she had little time to live. She had slept most of the day. Jim and I stood on either side of her bed, each of us holding one of her hands, talking to her. We told her how precious she was to us, that we loved her dearly, and to be sure to greet Jeremy and Nathaniel when she got to heaven. Just before dying, she opened her eyes wide, looked to first one and then to the other, as if to say "Goodbye, Daddy. Goodbye, Mommy." Then she closed her eyes and left. Two nurses stood by and softly wept at her passing. They brought comfort in ministering God's love to Alyssa and to us. (Later, in reflecting on this deathbed farewell, we realized God had indeed allowed us to hold up Alyssa's arms during her last battle, just as Aaron and Hur had done for Moses. He had answered that prayer.)

Benjy and Chelann had entertained themselves outside the hospital room for most of those hours. They had watched a few shows on a television and had played games set up for them in an adjacent, empty room. We called Benjy in to see the body of his little sister. We explained she had gone to be with the Lord. He stood, uncrying, head bent down, holding a Rubik's cube, determinedly and helplessly twisting it over and over in his hands.

A couple, who had also lost a one-year-old son in a tragic accident, came that evening to lend us their comfort and consolation. (Jim had stayed with them for two months when he first arrived in Portland.) Theo returned from his home to minister to us, too. The Bible verse he gave us was one which had encouraged him when his own mother died: "The righteous perish and no man layeth it to heart: and merciful men are taken away, none considering that the righteous is taken away from the evil to come."[5]

Glimmers of sunshine and rainbows through the mist

A valuable lesson God walked me through during Alyssa's life was that joy is a choice. I had to make a concerted effort to walk in joy. In that season, I only walked for two short months while Alyssa lived. However, for later life lessons, I realized I had to keep on choosing. For me, God graced me with a sweet sense of His control, of His care and of His comfort. Alyssa's life here on earth taught me joy.

Gathering grace gems from the bubbling waters

- In similar situations, how has the Lord talked with you? How did God encourage you? For example, did He use Scripture, others, prayer, memories?
- Do you recall times when you wanted to encourage someone else's faith? What are words of encouragement which touched that person's heart?
- Are there any Scriptures that have been meaningful to you when you have needed comfort and solace?
- What does joy mean to you? Where does it reside in your heart?

Wastewater to Living Waters

And in that day
The mountains will drip with sweet wine,
And the hills will flow with milk,
And all the brooks of Judah will flow with water;
And a spring will go out from the house of the Lord
To water the valley of Shittim (Acacia)
(Joel 3:18 NASB).

We made plans to return to Arizona for Alyssa's memorial and burial service and to spend time with my parents and close friends. Prior to our leaving for the airport, my mother's friend called to express condolences. Her words were an unusual way to console someone who was grieving, but they stayed with me. Lucille told me she had never understood why Jesus had cried out to God on the cross, *"My God, My God, why have you forsaken Me?"* [6] Her comments left me pondering and asking God for an answer that would satisfy her heart and my own.

Our Arizona pastor and his wife helped plan for the Sunday of Alyssa's burial and memorial service. During the regular church service, Pastor Zollner invited Jim and me to share some of our thoughts.

Never forsaken

I stood before the congregation, unsure about what to say except I felt impressed to share Lucille's question. Desperately, I asked the Lord to give me words. While in front of the gathering, the answer arrived. Jesus knew what it was like to be forsaken. One of those reasons was so that we would never have to endure the pain of abandonment. Everything He endured became a substitution for us. In Hebrews 13:5, it states that God will never forsake us.[7]

While presenting a brief explanation of our story, I watched a friend, in tears, standing at the back of the church. Dani and I talked together after the service. She could hardly speak as her voice shook with emotion. At that time in her life, she was childless and had earnestly sought God for a baby, a child of her own. Her husband, the youngest of several children, had been adopted at a young age by family members because of the deaths of both his parents. Their search for a family was real and painful. She shared how hard she had prayed for us and how devastated she felt when we lost a birth child for the third time. Her hopes of having a child were somehow tied to my ability to bear a healthy child. Alyssa's death crushed her hopes. We prayed together. God gives consolation during the time of heartache; I found Dani's tears a further cleansing ministry for my soul. Four years after our conversation, they adopted a little girl. Then four years after her adoption, they had a birth son of their own. When they became a family themselves, God answered another one of my aching prayers.

After the service, we ran into a six-year-old girl who was playing outside. Rachel seemed quite animated, so I asked her how she was doing. She brightly exclaimed, "We're going to a funeral today!" I doubt Rachel fully understood what a funeral was, but she was looking forward to the event. Her parents must have made sure she would not fear the idea of people going to heaven, even babies.

We held a graveside service that afternoon. Friends and family, old and young, stood by us. Quiet and thoughtful, six-year-old Benjy stayed with us during the service. Meanwhile, a short distance away, Chelann busily played with her 2 ½-year-old friend. Unbeknownst to us, the two girls had smeared mud on a few gravestones in another area. We had some cleaning up to do later. The incident reminded me that life goes on. Children continue embracing life and their calling, as they do what children do.

What's a waste?

During the week, we had opportunities to meet with friends. Rachel's parents nvited us for a meal. During supper, Mike brought up an intriguing dilemma. He talked about wasted lives. When is a life a waste? At what point do we decide that a life has had no value? Is it because the child is young? How young? What about someone who has reached old age and has not contributed significantly, in our eyes, to the world? Is that person's life a waste? How do we judge a wasted life?

Mike's questions left me searching for something deeper and more meaningful. Scriptures gave me some valuable insights. "But beloved, do not let this one thing be hidden from you, that with the Lord one day is like a thousand years, and a thousand years like one day." [8] The value God places on time is not the same as ours. Who, but God, knows how eternity will hold each life that has been conceived by His divine ordinance? His plans exist from the foundation of the world. "For he chose us in him, before the foundation of the world, to be holy and blameless in love before him."[9]

The Bible reveals many examples of what most of us humans would consider wasted lives. If the same things were to happen to us as happened to the saints of old, we would, more than likely, consider those efforts and all that time a total waste. Often I will, out of frustration regarding incomplete goals, comment, "Well, that was a waste of time." Think of the years Abraham and Sarah spent without enjoying children. Certainly Joseph spent wasted years in prison before he was finally exalted to one of the highest positions in Egypt. David spent years with sheep and then he spent years running from Saul. Moving past many prophets, including Daniel, our greatest example is Jesus. We know relatively little about His life before starting His ministry. How many years did He construct and build items which were not saved for posterity? Didn't He, of all people, realize He had a greater destiny? Did God look at His life as mundane and meaningless? What is the key to understanding *waste?*

Decades ago, Elisabeth Elliot shared her feelings about waste and our definition of what makes up waste:

> The older I get, the more clearly that rings true to me. I absolutely believe that it doesn't matter whether I'm cleaning the bathroom or sitting at the computer and writing a book or standing in front of a crowd of ladies—as long as it's offered to God, it doesn't make any difference. We're prone to take it for granted that there are certain things in life that are very important and other things that are just trivial. But as a Christian, I want to follow in the steps of Jesus. I can't imagine that Jesus thought of anything in His life as trivial. Presumably, He worked for the first 30 years or so in a carpentry shop, learning to use a saw and a hammer. Was that a waste? Or do you suppose it was offered to His Father in heaven?[10]

Brother Lawrence, a monk from the 1600s, had almost died from an injury to his sciatic nerve during the Thirty Years' War in Europe. Although the injury left him crippled with chronic pain for the rest of his life, he never alluded to it in his conversations or letters. The small booklet, *The Practice of the Presence of God,* collects his thoughts, compiled by someone who knew him. Perhaps his references to dealing with life's pains and how he used them to draw closer to God may be how he viewed pain as a tool in the hands of God, tools for refining him in the process of his own purification. He asserted that God will use any means to reveal His grace and kindnesses to him.[11]

Cannot pass by

During the 1988 Easter season, former neighbors from Troutdale invited us to their home for a Passover celebration. After the meal, Beth showed me some of the musical pieces she had composed. As she was leafing through her scores, I glanced at the title of a composition entitled "For Alyssa." I was taken aback and asked her about the arrangement which she had tried to brush past. She explained, "I wrote it after Alyssa died." Her thoughtfulness touched me deeply, in part, because I didn't realize how she had been moved by our experiences. Months later, she sent me a cassette of the composition with her playing the music on the piano.

It didn't dawn on me how much that piece affected me until I tried to tell others about it. Each time I referred to her musical score, my throat tightened, and I would burst into tears. It didn't matter the situation—over the phone or in person. My reaction stayed the same, and it didn't matter to whom I was talking, be it a close family member or a friend. I simply could not talk about the music.

The week following the Passover dinner, other friends invited us to their home for a meal. During the evening's conversation, "For Alyssa" was mentioned. In explaining about the composition, I started crying. The husband later told his wife he thought I had some areas which had not been healed. She shared those reflections with me. Surprised and somewhat bemused, I insisted, "But, I am fine!" Over the next few days, the more I deliberated, the more the truth pressed in on me. *Lord, I am not fine. What is my problem?*

Initially, following Alyssa's death, my response revealed a deep confidence in God's eternal plans. Gradually, I withdrew certain areas from Him because of my pain. In essence, I declared, *God, I will rely on You in other places of my life but not with my children.* After this time of meditation and soul-searching, I confessed and prayed, *God, I have not trusted you. Please forgive me for withholding my children from You. Help me trust You to watch over them. Help me see that whatever happens, it first must pass through Your hand.* That prayer released something from within me. My children's welfare, though important to me, no longer weighed me down. Truthfully, we know there is little we can do to keep anything from happening. Due vigilance may be required, but ultimately, God is the Strong Tower, the Protector, the Guide. I learned to trust God once more.

Glimmers of sunshine and rainbows through the mist

Feeling responsible for our loved ones seems to be something that causes us to experience anxious moments, more anxious than we truly need to live out. It was hard for me to release my children's welfare into God's hand. The changes were so subtle; I didn't realize how I was distancing myself from Him. Hannah Whitall Smith[12] rightly encouraged her readers as she acknowledged the necessity of bringing her children to the Strong Tower. Worrying about them had the same effect as preventing them from coming within the protecting Tower. It's sobering to realize I can rest for myself in the Tower while my children have been locked out through my unwillingness to trust God.

Gathering grace gems from the bubbling waters

- Have you ever looked at someone and felt their life was a waste? Does it look like a waste while they are alive? How can you pray for that person to instill life and wholeness?
- What do cleansing, healing tears look like for you? Are they your own? Someone else's?
- Have you tied your prayers to someone else's and then endured hopelessness if theirs are not answered in the way you prayed? Has that made you depressed? How can you view your situation differently, apart from theirs?
- Are there any checks in your heart about past incidents? Are there any reminders that cause you deep, insurmountable pain? What can you do to come to healing?

A House on the Hill

He makes me lie down in green pastures. He leads me beside still waters.
(Psalm 23:2 ESV)

You shall teach them diligently to your children [impressing God's precepts on their minds and penetrating their hearts with His truths] and shall speak of them when you sit in your house and when you walk on the road and when you lie down and when you get up.

(Deuteronomy 6:6 AMP).

At our rental home in Troutdale, we tried to get a grip on the tasks set before us. Benjy and Chelann needed nurture and care. We looked for areas in which to engage them with social and academic activities.

Because we homeschooled, we attended a church with several dozen homeschool families. Through that contact, we joined a group of home educators, which had a broad base of members. In those pioneer days of homeschooling, parents, by necessity, endured more intense scrutiny by the lack of legislation protecting this method of education. Now, each state in the Union has laws relating to homeschooling.

Same passion, new generation

Athletic and competitive by nature, Jim tried to nurture these same qualities in our children. Fortunately, Benjy adored playing soccer, which had been the passion of Jim's life during his growing-up years in Argentina. Ben started his soccer career at 6 ½ years on an indoor soccer team in Troutdale. The team held a roster of powerful players and culminated in a top season, as they claimed victories in all but one game. With this lofty introduction to the sport, the "*soccer bug*" bit and infected Benjy.

Finding a nest

When our days were devoted to caring for Alyssa, we put our search for a home on hold. Knowing the profits from the sale of our Arizona house would expire eventually, we embarked on a diligent search for a more permanent home after Alyssa's death. On a cool and rainy February day, we discovered the quintessential place on a Gresham hillside.

Finding the property was the first action; buying it was the next. We presented an offer to Mrs. G. In fact, we submitted two separate proposals. Another couple also expressed an interest in the home. Their offer would have initially given Mrs. G. more funds. I fasted and prayed the day she was to decide. That night the real estate agent called, considerably amazed at the succession of events. She disclosed what had transpired. Mrs. G. had refused both our offers. With pen raised and her hand at the "acceptance" line, Mrs. G. readied herself to confirm the other contract. Mrs. G. abruptly signed "refused." She then crossed out her name on the "refused" line of one of our agreements and accepted our proposal.

All was solved, or so we believed. We had received our acceptance to buy the house. However, we had more hoops to jump through to receive a VA loan. Wherever we turned, the bank or loan agency would not accept our application. It looked as though the house deal would go no further than the acceptance of the original contract. One bank officer told me she had seen no one with such good credit have such a hard time securing a loan. The wait was nerve-wracking. This was another case in which I had to recognize the divine Controller. My stomach churned as I considered all the what ifs. After days of fussing over the likely outcomes, a word from the Bible spoke strongly to me, "In the midst of the battle, Shammah stood his ground." *Okay, Lord, the difficulties of each day will not affect me. Whatever You want regarding this house, I will trust that You know what You are doing. I will stand firm.* I must admit that as I mulled this over, sometimes my thoughts blocked me from staying hopeful. *Maybe that house isn't so great after all.* Sour grapes crept in, not the best way to overcome disappointment.

Even though the house paperwork should have closed by the end of April, the VA loan never materialized. Mrs. G. and our realtor suggested a second option. Mrs. G. would hold a contract on the house while we paid off what she was paying on her mortgage. Even though the house did not officially close until August, from then on the paperwork proceeded smoothly for us. The final agreement benefitted us and helped her, too.

Happy birthday, happy home day

On Benjy's birthday, May 31, 1987, we moved into our new home. On a 2/3-acre lot the home itself was twice the size of our home in Phoenix. The house was indeed a dream come true… in a rural area, yet only a mile from the center of town. Eight years earlier, at Jeremy's memorial service, a lady from our church family had come to us with a word of comfort, "Two times the Lord has taken the first fruits of your love. As you have been faithful to surrender these precious lives to the Lord, He will give you a double blessing." After living in the house for three years, a verse astonished me with a similar message, *"Instead of shame, My people will have a double portion, and instead of humiliation, they will rejoice in their share; and so they will inherit a double portion in their land, and everlasting joy will be theirs."*

Before purchasing or even looking for a house, we had sat down as a family to make a list of all the things we wanted to see in our dream home. I coveted a place for a garden and more room, outside and inside. As a three-year-old, Chelann believed a house with stairs would give her more climbing action. Benj thought that a fireplace and woods close by fit his fancy. Jim wanted a double garage, a fireplace, a view of Mt. Hood, and a location close to work. Much later, after we found the house and the paperwork was completed, we realized this house matched the specifications we had talked about a year earlier. Receiving all these house extras should not be interpreted that we must get everything we want from God. However, God does delight in giving His children good things—not to be safely hoarded but things for sharing and enjoying with others. My maiden name, *"Hulstedt,"* means *"place on a hill."* From what I know, my dad's family has lived on flat farmland for over a century. God granted me a place to honor the name with which I was born. Another detail from His heart to mine.

Ben treasured our neighborhood. The woods held many locations in which to hike and explore. He often invited friends over to play. Outside, they competed in basketball, table tennis, soccer. They rode bikes and raced motorized go-carts.

Good Scouts

A homeschool Cub Scout troop met weekly at our home. The Scout handbook suggested ample activities for learning and exploring. We took hikes, collected rocks, made kites, created crafts, tied knots, learned songs, acted out plays. At the start of each summer, the boys and helper moms participated in week-long day camps at Scouters Mountain where they enjoyed magnified activities of crafting, singing and exercising.

An excellent undertaking boys enjoy during their Scouting career is the annual Pinewood Derby. This is a father/son project intended to bond these two and ultimately the entire family as they produce a home-made racing vehicle from a 3-inch x 5-inch block of soft pine wood. The structure and composition of the car need to meet definite specifications, all spelled out in the rule book. We pored over the rules, making certain that each step was followed carefully and precisely. Jim and Benj produced a flashy yellow sports car, replete with as many stickers as Ben could find room for on this creation. That car made it to the Scout-O-Rama in the district competition. This honor is qualified. Because our group was small, Benj was the only participant in his age bracket. This did not dampen his or our enthusiasm. On to the big time for us.

There are uninitiated fathers who do not know about the competition. Conversely, experienced fathers would stake their engineering degrees to win a Pinewood Derby race for their sons. Unfortunately, the Saints fell into the inexpert category. Ben's car lacked the added oomph to get over the finish line faster than the guy next to him, every time. With the years also came experience. Curiously, as father and son studied and developed their techniques, they could never duplicate the velocity of that first yellow, bestickered hotrod. The later model cars looked much better but somehow lacked a certain combination that would produce a lean, mean machine. We all bonded—male bonding, parent-child bonding, sibling bonding. Even Chelann had her own purple derby car that she raced, unofficially.

An opportunity for more social life came with a babysitting job, which opened through the Yoshiwaras, a family from Ben's soccer team. The family had lost their babysitter and needed a temporary back-up for the school year in the spring of 1988. The three youngsters joined us almost every day for several months. Our children and theirs quickly adjusted to each other, thus providing a perfect solution for extra friendship in our somewhat isolated area.

Glimmers of sunshine and rainbows through the mist

We have not moved often in over 45 years of marriage. Moving to Oregon offered us the promise of a new life with fresh opportunities. As most will attest, house hunting and house buying rank high on the stress scale. When the realtor called to tell us of Mrs. G's acceptance of our offer, I was amazed. Even more so after she told us the back story.

Finding the note about the dream house in my Bible, a year after the fact, showed me God's careful attention to the details. Not only did He answer the desires for the adults, but His heart included the children's longings. Each of us needed a home, a home that would embrace and include a seven-year-old and a three-year-old in the plans.

Gathering grace gems from the bubbling waters

- Have you ever needed a place to call home? What were your greatest needs?
- How specific are you when you pray? Sometimes, it is preferable to trust God with the results. However, when our hearts are crying out for something, how will we know God has answered unless we describe our needs?
- If you have family close by, what are activities you have found that bind you together with cords of love?

Pure Grace

For 'just as rain and snow fall from heaven and do not return without watering 'the earth, making it bud and sprout, and providing 'seed 'to sow and food 'to eat, so My word that proceeds from My mouth will not return to Me empty, but it will accomplish what I please, and it will prosper where I send it

Isaiah 55:10, 11 (BSB).

Once again, our home expanded to make room for a family of six for six weeks. Friends from our church in Arizona planned to make a location change in the fall of '88. Paul and Sharon Collins, with three sons and a daughter, were expecting another baby in December. They also homeschooled their children. We spent our mornings separately with instruction and study; then we joined forces at noon for meals. The children spent afternoons playing together. Sharon and I worked on supper later in the day. Our dinner table bulged with children and food.

Because the father of the family had encountered difficulties finding a pastry chef job close to Portland, he worked two hours away at the coast. Because of the distance, he came and visited with his family on his two days off. After six weeks, he found a job in the area, at which time the family moved to a rental home in Vancouver, Washington, across the river from Portland.

Family expansion

A week after the family moved in with us, Jim and I realized we were expecting a baby. Jim always showed ready support during my pregnancies. Despite his reassurance, I felt utterly overwhelmed. I had not prayed about having another baby in advance. This was a complete and total surprise. I prayed, *God, I do not think this is funny anymore.* A strong fear tormented me: *Can I handle losing another baby?* This pregnancy was something over which I had no control. After all, it had not been my idea. For some time, I failed to realize the other three babies, who were a part of my plan, had not survived. The question persisted, *How can I trust Him with this situation?*

Nineteenth-century author, Hannah Whitall Smith, captured my dilemma in a passage which succinctly described my agonizing time of searching for peace and resolution:

> A great deal of what is called "spiritual conflict" might far better be named "spiritual rebellion." God has told us to cease from our own efforts and to hand our battles over to Him, and we point blank refuse to obey Him. We fight. It is true, but it is not a fight of faith, but a fight of unbelief. Our spiritual "wrestling:" of which we are often so proud, is really a wrestling, not for God against His enemies, but against Him on the side of His enemies. We allow ourselves to indulge in doubts and fears, and consequently, we are plunged into darkness, and turmoil, and wrestlings of spirit. And then we call this "spiritual conflict," and look upon ourselves as an interesting and peculiar case. The single word that explains our "peculiar case" is the word unbelief, and the simple remedy is to be found in the word faith. If the God who created us is a good God, then everything must be all right for us, since a good God cannot ordain any but good things. The true ground for peace and comfort is only to be found in the sort of God we have.[15]

In short order, the evidence of my pregnancy assaulted me with a vengeance. Nausea stalked my mornings and most afternoons. Often I raced to the bathroom while fixing supper for our large family. Once relieved of my previous meal, I returned to fixing food for the next one. We never missed a supper.

After our extra family left in October, we returned to a life of the four of us, plus one on the way. Benjy played soccer, which meant that I drove him back and forth to games. I also continued as a Cub Scout leader and assisted a separate homeschool group.

Hearing from heaven

Meanwhile, I continued to struggle with expecting another baby. During those first four months, no definite words fell from heaven. No confirmation that this child would survive provided me with longed-for peace and assurance. I remember thinking that an abortion for someone in my place would have been an easy alternative. I also knew that choice would violate the life God had created. This was not an option for me. I firmly believed that God was in control. He is sovereign. After months of agonizing, I concluded that if this baby died, God recognized what I could handle because He knows me better than I do.

In mid-December, a song wafted through my thoughts. It became my theme for the rest of the pregnancy. While studying in Psalm 113, the words I read formed a melody. Two days later, while meditating on Psalm 115, the next words to the song were added:

He makes the barren woman to keep house
And be the joyful mother of children.
He makes the barren woman to keep house
And be the joyful mother of children.

"Praise ye the Lord. Praise ye the Lord.
From this time forth and forevermore.
Praise ye the LORD.

"The Lord shall increase you more and more,
You and your children.
The Lord shall increase you more and more.
You and your children.

Praise ye the Lord. Praise ye the Lord.
The Lord will bless you who fear His name.
Praise ye the LORD.

From then on, a deeper sense of peace rooted within my soul as I pondered our blessed event. I sang the song for our children and told them it was a song God had given me about them and the new baby. In the ensuing months, either Benj or Chelann would beg, "Mom, sing the song Jesus gave you."

At the end of January, I awoke in the early morning from a dream. I had received marks for classes I was taking, which were good. In my previous dreams from the past year, I was dropping courses and not finishing them. In this dream I was earning an A minus in English composition. That must mean I am following His direction.

Two weeks later, I wrote the words I believed God was telling me.

Seek Me. Seek Me. I can be found. Trust Me. Trust Me. I am faithful.

Persevere in well doing. Don't begrudge time spent reaching out. In blessing others, I will bless you. You are living in blessedness. Rejoice in My goodness to you. Let your joy overflow and spill out upon those whom you contact. Let your life be a waterfall of My blessings, spraying a cooling mist on those who draw near.

Sharing news - gulp

I dealt with a predicament in how to share our expected baby news with my folks. My mother, especially, had always expressed her feelings freely. I didn't want to face possible disapproval. In the previous fall, while talking on the phone, Mom had casually asked, "Who knows why people keep having babies who are going to die?" That remark kept me from saying anything for months. Perhaps she wasn't talking about my life, but the statement affected my thoughts. Worries about her reaction curtailed my freedom of expression. I asked the children to write to my parents, telling them about the new baby. Benjy wrote a carefully composed letter.

Dear Grandma and Grandpa,

I have good news for you. My mom is going to have a baby. I am really excited about it.

Love,

Benjy

Five-year-old Chelann had a lot to say. Originally she planned to write, "I sure hope this one doesn't die." I persuaded her to leave that statement out. The comment she included was that she planned to name the baby "Pretty Angel Saint." Fortunately, she forgot her first naming plan once her new sibling arrived.

Close to New Year's, we asked our former church in Arizona to please keep us in their prayers during this season as we needed the buoyancy of prayer support. Marge called to ask permission to include the expected event in the church newsletter. Thinking the newsletter was coming out much later, I told her there was no problem, as my parents would be informed beforehand.

Because we lived in Oregon and my parents and the church were close to each other in Arizona, the newsletter's arrival and our family letter's appearance did not mesh. One morning I answered the phone to hear Mom on the other end. Feeling cheerful, I answered her with a lilt in my voice. Her greeting appeared flat and stilted. A palpable reserve hung in the air as we talked.

"Hello, Lynn."

"How are you doing, Mom? Is everything OK?"

"We received a newsletter in the mail today."

"All right. Who was it from?"

"Calvary Church of the Valley."

After a few moments, the fog in my brain cleared, and I quickly tried to smooth things over. "Oh, you read about us. The kids just sent you the news a few days ago. You should get their letters by tomorrow at the latest." I felt sick to my stomach. *Why didn't I have the kids write sooner?* In truth, I finally had the kids write because my folks were planning to visit us, and we were obviously in the family way months before their arrival.

We worked out this grievance. Mom was more upset about not hearing sooner and not being the first to receive the news about the expected baby. God must have been talking to her because she offered incredible support. She started making plans for the baby and for all of us. As a seamstress, she sewed outfits and blankets for the newcomer. Chelann also benefited from Grandma's sewing skills and newfound inspiration.

Within a month of the announcement, my parents came to visit us. To add to the adventure, Mom sat next to a player named Vince from the Chicago Bulls team. All the Bulls' players were on the flight. Mom passed a slip of paper, asking the team members to sign, but no one signed their names; they passed it on to Michael Jordan, a basketball legend.

The Bulls exited the plane before the other passengers. Benjy, who was waiting with Chelann and me, noticed Michael Jordan and wanted to get his autograph. I was mortified. *How would he know Michael Jordan? Besides, who is Michael Jordan?* Ben stayed with me and didn't go traipsing off to talk to some basketball player I wasn't sure of.

Thankfully, Mother had more sense and boldness than I. She didn't know who Michael Jordan was either, but she trusted her seatmate Vince, who told her Jordan was a well-known and gifted basketball player. Hence, Ben received his autograph, treasuring both the paper and the story behind it.

We enjoyed a peaceful and rewarding time with both my parents. Dad was exhibiting more mental deterioration from Alzheimer's, but Mom was determined to let him experience as much of life as she could, which must have caused much strain, especially when taking him through airports, dealing with bathrooms, facing his confusion. During their two-week visit, Mom and I enjoyed meaningful talks. Repeatedly, she expressed her strong conviction that this baby was going to be healthy. Her support comforted my anxious thoughts.

Finally we approached the due date. The doctor wanted to perform a C-section at the beginning of May, but I requested a week's postponement so that my Cub Scouts could give their year-end performance. The show went on and the baby stayed put for another week.

On the morning of the surgery, Jim stayed with me to calm my jangled nerves. The epidural gave me the "shakes," adding to my tenseness. Our pastor joined us before surgery for prayer. Jim's heart cry for a healthy baby expressed a confident trust and a secure rest in God's dealing with us and in His provision. Within an hour, we rejoiced in the appearance of Katelyn Ann, a wiggly, red-skinned newborn.

Katelyn stayed strong and healthy. She exhibited an active startle reflex that lasted well over the usual time for most newborns. Our other three birth children didn't startle, owing to their illness. Katelyn startled for months, which added to my reassurance that she was healthy, even though the pediatrician expressed amazement at how long she had this response. Over the weeks, Katelyn exhibited normal growth and development. She was the first of our birth children to survive past six months of age.

Because we had trouble deciding on a girl's name, Jim and the children opted to call the baby "Katelyn." I wasn't so sure as I knew they were enamored with a television show, *Air Wolf*, which had a support character named Katelyn. No one voted for the names I had chosen. Three against one was no match for me, so I consented to keep the atmosphere kind and friendly.

The following year after her birth, I spoke at our women's meeting at church. "Seasons of Life" featured the luncheon theme. The ministry team had asked me to describe what I was learning during my summer season. My talk included sharing how God had helped us find significant names for our children. Although I knew our other children's name meanings, I had not studied Katelyn's name in depth, as I had resigned myself to the name before wrapping my arms around it. I was amazed to realize that "Katelyn" and "Ann" mean "pure grace."

Glimmers of sunshine and rainbows through the mist

When I first found out I was expecting our fourth birth child, I sensed the panic of an unexpected pregnancy. Although I was married, I recognized, in a small way, what a young woman might experience finding herself unmarried and pregnant. I even dreamed that I was not married and had to face people with my pregnancy. Because of our previous losses and because of open disapproval from people I knew, I lived with shame. How am I going to face people? How can I explain what happened? The questions implied a need to sink deeper into God's sovereign control. Ultimately realizing this, my life must be lived out to reflect Him. I am answerable to God for life events, especially the ones over which I have little to no control.

When working through an accusation, I must acknowledge the enemy as the accuser of the brethren. If I am wrongly accused, it is possible the author of the accusation is not a human source, but an evil one. If it is, I need to release the claim to the Father and allow Him to handle it. I don't have to absorb it or own it.

Gathering grace gems from the bubbling waters

- Has shame ever overwhelmed you in your experiences? If so, how did you resolve it? Have you ever found a resolution?
- When there is shame, what is the source of the shame?
- In what ways have you found comfort when facing God with your own trials and imponderable circumstances?

- How have you resolved sharing information in which you have needed reassurance but expected rejection?
- Has God given you original insight and a new revelation with an issue you could not accept? How did it change for you with the transformation?

Going Public

Land that drinks in the rain often falling on it and that produces a crop useful to those for whom it is farmed receives the blessing of God
(Hebrews 6:7 NIV).

Every man who strives in the games exercises self-control in all things
(1 Corinthians 9:25 WEB).

When Katelyn was a one-year-old, Joe returned from Argentina to investigate the possibilities of resettling with his family in the States. Because finding a job did not happen in an instant, he spent a lot of time at home with Benjy, Chelann and Katelyn. He even coached Chelann's soccer team, the one Jim had planned to manage.

Benjy and Tío Pepe (Uncle Joe) spent many hours together—much of it in competitive play, either at the basketball hoop or with the soccer ball. When Joe departed to reunite with his own family four months later, Benj expressed sadness and emptiness in losing the companionship of his beloved uncle.

Vroom. Vroom.

Undeterred by their Pinewood Derby challenges from the past, Jim and Ben embarked on another major vehicle project during Ben's middle-school years. Both loved cars and trucks. One of Benjy's favorite words, as a baby, was "*truck.*" Jim excels mechanically and involved Ben in the repair and maintenance tasks for our vehicles. Ben had saved money for many months. He spent weeks searching through ads from the newspaper, calling and checking. At last he located the perfect motorized conveyance. Father and son split the cost 50/50 to purchase a dilapidated-looking go-cart. They spent hours sanding, welding, painting, oiling. The Briggs and Stratton, five-horse-power rototiller engine needed complete rebuilding. Upon completion, this stock model go-cart looked and ran like a charm. Ben blew up the engine one afternoon, not realizing the amount of oil it required. Undaunted, the father and son duo managed, once again, to rebuild it and have it in running order within days. Several years later, when Ben tired of this hobby, he doubled the original investment by selling it.

Ben also had other quieter interests. He had learned to sew needlepoint Christmas gifts for family members when he was in primary grades. During our cool and rainy winters, he worked on projects to give away. He also fashioned beaded necklaces and bracelets for family members. One Christmas he worked with plaster cast angel figurines, painstakingly painting them for his grandmother and great aunt.

Sibling babysitter

For many years, Ben performed his duties as the main babysitter of the family. He had a way of commanding respect, even from his nearer sibling, Chelann. Katelyn simply loved spending time with him and basked in his presence.

We rarely left the children alone in the evening, but one night we attended a church function, so Ben was left in charge of his two younger sisters. We returned home before midnight, fearing the girls had not settled down without us. After walking upstairs into an unusually quiet house, we peeked into the dimly lit living room. Snuggled together on a chair, sound asleep, were Ben and his two-year-old sister. We questioned him later, "How were you able to convince Katelyn to go to sleep?" He good-naturedly divulged, "I asked her if she wanted to play a game with me. Whoever keeps their eyes closed the longest is the winner. She wanted to play."

With all the superlatives about Benjy, instead of painting a picture of a saint, there are some stories we didn't hear at the time of their occurrence. What we didn't know was that Ben taunted Chelann. From what she reported, years later, he sometimes dragged her down the stairs by her toes. The reason we never heard the story was because he had bribed her with hush money. He must have given her a generous amount of cash to keep her quiet for 20 years.

Getting a kick out of the game

Soccer remained a big sport in our family. Although Ben did not boast the height of some teammates, he conquered those challenges by running with ease, handling the ball with finesse and playing with determination. Jim worked with him for many hours through the years. Benj played in the fall league, the winter league and the spring league. Summer was our respite time until Benjy became involved in club soccer.

The East Gresham Football Club comprised teammates, practices and fields. Even though competitions could occur in various locations throughout the state, school playgrounds offered close locations for training. His good friend Grant had also joined the team, giving Ben an added impetus to sign up.

Practices took place several times a week with most games on Saturdays. The team performed well and offered stiff competition for any rivals. They played in the Portland metro-area, which sometimes meant traveling about 45 minutes to an hour away. Games in other parts of the state took hours to arrive. When we couldn't make extended trips, parents of the other boys volunteered to take Ben with them for the games. Although he loved the camaraderie, he remained quietly intense about his love for this sport.

An extremely difficult circumstance for Benj that first year was that he rarely played in regular games. The coach had promised that the boys who made it to practice and played consistently would compete. Regularly, Ben sat on the bench while a larger teammate took part. Rather than giving up and giving in, he increased his determination to succeed. Ben relentlessly pursued the perfecting of his skills. He ran uphill. He kicked the ball repeatedly. He worked with soccer balls in graduated sizes, steadily improving his footwork. He fulfilled the Apostle Paul's injunction: "But I discipline my body and bring it into subjection." [16] Ben disciplined himself intensely and lived by the Avis advertisement motto: "I may not be number one, but I try harder."

His team won the state championship when he was 12 years old. Parents and their soccer playing sons conducted fund raisers for a trip to play in regional competition in Denver, Colorado. All the team members flew to Denver. Although many parents accompanied their sons to Colorado, we could afford neither the time nor the money. Ben seemed content just to travel with his teammates and never once intimated any disappointment with our decision. The Yoshiwaras promised us they would look after Ben, and we know they did. He reported in daily.

The lowest point of his entire time of playing soccer probably occurred while he was in Denver. As a family, we had made financial sacrifices for Benjy to join the competition. But we were encouraged by the thought that he would have the opportunity to contend alongside his teammates. He played in only one game against a team that was a poor match against theirs. When we talked to him on the phone one evening, he was close to tears, an emotion he carefully guarded. It tore at us that we couldn't give him much consolation from so far away.

Courage, character and commitment

When Benj returned home, we held some serious discussions about his soccer future. In the end, he remained with the club and pursued the sport. He cared immensely for his teammates and wanted to maintain the close relationships. The decision to stay and persevere marked a major turning point. Several months later, when asked to write an English paper on personal courage, he related this episode. With the completion of the Denver games, a new coach, Mike, came on the scene. A young man in his 20s, Mike showed remarkable concern for every boy, not only as a soccer player, but as a human being. His goal was to produce competitors and gentlemen. Mike challenged the boys to do well in school and stipulated that they maintain strong grades. He taught them how to tip at restaurants. He lectured them on the need to love and respect their parents.

Mike looked beyond Ben's physical stature to see the character and desire within him. Ben played and started in every game from then on. He worked passionately to excel at the task at hand. Mike appointed him team captain after a competition in the state of Washington. Benjy, who was not into fanfare, never told us, but friends informed us later.

A supreme compliment Mike gave Ben, which delighted him, was that when Ben played, he was "meaner than a junkyard dog." That dog epithet didn't reflect Benj's manner, usually considerate, not prone to cruelty or viciousness. He had a compassionate heart for others, especially underdogs. (At 8 ½, he wrote about the things that annoyed him. Listed among bothersome traits were cruelty, loud noise, teasing and lying.) He liked little kids and tenderly cared for his baby sister, Katelyn. The junkyard dog moniker gave Ben a great inner sense of confidence and strength.

In the fall of '92, 12-year-old Ben entered public school. He left the confines of homeschool and started pursuing a life in the halls of Dexter McCarty Middle

School. Fortunately, he had friends from the neighborhood and soccer buddy Grant to show him the ropes. After the second day of classes in a strange setting, Ben came home to say that a boy who had been there the year before had asked him for directions to a certain classroom. Ben patiently explained the route the 7th grader needed to take. Deliberate about tasks, finding his way around a new school had been something he had assessed well ahead of time by studying the school map at home and then walking through the halls. Besides meticulous attention to detail, another trait was an innate sense of direction.

Ben earned high marks in his studies and gained the respect of teachers and classmates alike. As an incentive at the school, each teacher selected one student from all his or her classes (within the grade level) to recognize that individual's good behavior, etc. A student could only be chosen once in the year. In December, two teachers nominated Ben.

The church youth group held a snow camping experience in February. The youth pastor addressed their need to decide how they would use their lives. Steve later disclosed that two or three young people, out of 20, had stood up to declare that God was speaking to them personally, telling them He had a special mission for their lives. Ben was one of the two or three who rose. Guarding his heart scrupulously, even as a small child, rarely did Ben decide based on his feelings; logic overruled his choices. Thoroughly studying issues before determining any course of action, Ben's stand to follow God and accept His mission was birthed through a deep and earnest conviction.

Year 'round soccer competition kept us driving to games. When the weather prevented playing outside in the mud and rain, there were indoor soccer matches. Once, Ben ran into a wall and sprained his ankle, which kept him nursing it for several months. That spring, Ben's team competed in the state finals and again won the state championship. Ben's face beamed with pride and joy as he joined his fellow teammates, each one with a gold medal around his neck. Because age brackets for regional competition were selected every other year, the season ended with the state championship.

Glimmers of sunshine and rainbows through the mist

In thinking about and remembering the hard days when Ben was discouraged from playing because of his height, I am encouraged to keep on. What is it I am allowing to hinder me? Where do I come up short and allow that to define who I am? Many times I escape the difficult by making excuses for not trying what seems impossible. Truthfully, I try to avoid those things that stretch me. Why stress? However, what am I learning by not breaking out of my personal comfort zone?

Gathering grace gems from the bubbling waters

- What keeps you from persevering?
- How can you encourage yourself to strengthen your determination?
- Are there Scriptures that encourage and challenge you to reach toward the goal? Perhaps examples from the lives of others? Proverbs and axioms that encourage tenacity?

Footnotes

1. *Moses' arms soon became so tired he could no longer hold them up. So, Aaron and Hur found a stone for him to sit on. Then they stood on each side of Moses, holding up his hands. So, his hands held steady until sunset* (Exodus 17:12 NLT).
2. Joshua 1:9
3. Billheimer, p 55.
4. 2 Corinthians 10:5 (KJV)
5. Isaiah 57:1 (KJV)
6. Mark 15:34c (NKJV)
7. Harris. From the author of this explanation, he learned that when this verse was translated into English, it was not conveyed as strongly as the original Greek, because of double negatives and other grammatical rules regarding our language. In the Greek as in some other languages, two negatives intensify the meaning. When we read this verse in English, it says, "I will never leave thee nor forsake thee." That should be acceptable. It is important to realize that the actual rendering of the verse more likely states, "I will never, never leave thee, and I will never, never, never forsake thee."
8. 2 Peter 3:8 (BLB)
9. Ephesians 1:4 (CSB)
10. I have looked for the quote online and in a half dozen of her books. It is possible this was copied from her radio program many years ago. I am quite certain this is attributed to Elisabeth Elliot but have searched in vain for the source.

11. Lawrence 5657.

12. Smith, Hannah Whitall. *The God of All Comfort.* 1956 edition ed., Chicago, Moody Press, 1997, pp. 117-118.

The practical thing to do, therefore, in face of the fact that God is declared to be our fortress and our high tower, is, by a definite act of surrender and faith, to put ourselves and all our interests of every kind into this divine dwelling place, and then dismiss all care or anxiety about them from our minds. Since the Lord is our dwelling place, nothing can possibly come to any harm that is committed to His care. If we believe this, our affairs remain in His care; the moment we begin to doubt, we take our affairs into our own hands, and they are no longer in the divine fortress. Things cannot be in two places at once. If they are in our own care, they cannot be in God's care; and if they are in God's care, they cannot be in our own. This is as clear as daylight, and yet, for the want of a little common sense, people often get mixed up over it. They put their affairs into God's fortress, and at the same time put them into their own fortress as well, and then wonder why they are not taken care of. This is all folly. Either trust the Lord out and out, or else trust yourself out and out; but do not try to mix the two trusts, for they will not mix.

13. *But he took his stand in the midst of the plot, defended it, and struck the Philistines; and the LORD brought about a great victory* 2 Samuel 23:12 (ESV).

14. Isaiah 61:7 (BSB)

15. Smith.

16. 1 Corinthians 9:27 (NKJV)

Section 5. Stepping on Rocks Beneath the Current:

New Battle

O GOD the Lord, the strength of my salvation,
You have covered my head in the day of battle
(Psalm 140:7 BSB).

Soccer Days, School Days, Sick Days

O God, you are my God; I earnestly search for you. My soul thirsts for you; my whole body longs for you in this parched and weary land where there is no water
(Psalm 63:1 NLT).

'Fear not, stand firm, and see the salvation of the Lord, which he will work for you today'
(Exodus 14:13 ESV).

The LORD will guide you always;
he will satisfy your needs in a sun-scorched land
and will strengthen your frame.

You will be like a well-watered garden,
like a spring whose waters never fail
(Isaiah 58:11 NIV).

The start of school and a hectic sports schedule signaled the beginning of an active fall. During the autumn months of 1993, both Ben and Chelann played on soccer teams. He competed with the upper echelon of club soccer while his sister played with the YMCA, an organization that encourages participants, no matter the level of interest, skill or expertise.

Although Ben faithfully played and practiced, he did not seem to have the same drive, energy or stamina exhibited in previous years. His coach did not always start him. That did not sit well with Ben, but he never commented or complained about this at home.

Visiting Phoenix

Over Thanksgiving vacation, all five of us rode in our yellow van down to Arizona. Although not exceedingly picturesque, the Nevada high desert presented immensely better views in the cooler months than in the blistering summer ones. We experienced one narrow escape toward dusk one evening. Proceeding at speed limit through the northern Nevada hillsides, we rounded a bend. Immediately beyond the curve was a cow, slowly and calmly crossing the road. Had we been there a few minutes sooner, we would have had a serious wreck. We discussed how God had angels watching over us during that incident—or rather, the lack of one.

We spent our time in Phoenix with my folks and with friends. Ben made sure he stayed with his old buddy Justin as much as possible. They didn't know how to make or find marinara sauce. One day they made pizza for lunch using catsup, a never-to-be-repeated-afterwards culinary attempt.

While staying in Phoenix, apart from Katelyn, we all, my folks, Ben, Jim, Chelann and I, came down with severe flu-like symptoms. Ben was sick for just a day and then insisted on returning to spend time with his friends. We were too under the weather to argue. As we look back at pictures, he did not look vigorous; he must have been sick most of that vacation.

At the beginning of December, we drove back home and resumed our daily chores—at home, work and school. One day, while on Christmas vacation, Ben asked, "Mom, is it common to see blurry when you suddenly look up?" I explained that sometimes blood rushes to the head when one makes a sudden move and perhaps that was happening to him. I did not think about this conversation again until months later.

Feeling sick, visiting the doctor

The day after Christmas, Ben competed in an indoor soccer tournament. He returned very ill, with constant vomiting and considerable discomfort. He was sick for the next few days. Within a week, I took him for a doctor's visit. After listening to Benj describe his symptoms, the physician diagnosed an apparent virus. Another week and a half passed. Ben and I returned for another appointment and a battery of tests. The results of his blood work and other tests showed no abnormalities. The diagnosis remained "virus."

Knowing he was simply dealing with a virus did not change Ben's physical condition. He continued to vomit all morning until noon. His stomach could not tolerate any food (and we tried all we could think of) until he had been awake for at least three or four hours.

Obviously, medical science held no magic potions for viruses. *Perhaps natural herbs or vitamins could help Benj?* Ruminating on this possibility while out driving, I saw a bumper sticker with the name of a Christian radio station. I turned on the car radio and searched for KPDQ. Right after locating it, the announcer advertised a health food store. At home, I called Health Haus to ask if someone at the store could or would suggest a naturopathic physician. The individual was reluctant initially, but after my pleading, the gentleman relented and shared the name of a naturopath whom he respected.

Alternative treatment

We made an appointment with Dr. Abshier, the recommended naturopathic doctor, within a matter of days. Impressed by his diligence, I watched the doctor listen intently to everything either Ben or I said, recording every spoken word. He carefully explained his intentions and what herbal and homeopathic preparations he intended to give to Ben. He informed us that if Ben did not feel better within a week's time, he recommended either an MRI of his stomach or his head.

After the visit, we returned home, encouraged that at least Benj could take something that might help. We returned the following week to visit the naturopath. Ben claimed he experienced at least a 75% improvement from where he was previously. We had an appointment weekly. The doctor performed a urinalysis each time and sometimes recommended a change in the herbs or gave him a new formula to try.

Ben's vomiting never completely resolved. Occasionally, it would occur in the afternoon rather than immediately in the morning. He even experienced one or two free days without vomiting, but it always returned. After regurgitating, he often came upstairs with a smile on his face while licking his lips and making a joke.

A few weeks after starting with naturopathic medications, Ben showed up at soccer practice. He was determined to keep in shape for the soccer season and had decided this *"virus"* would not get the best of him. After dropping him off, I returned later to discover he had spent a good amount of time over by the trash cans, vomiting.

Winning out over our concerns, Ben also stayed a weekend overnight for a winter retreat with the church youth group. He found that chewing gum helped him handle his nausea, so he took an ample supply. Later he told us he had gone tubing in the snow at Mount Hood. Several youths had plowed into him and a friend at the base of the hill, knocking them on their heads in the hardened snow.

In February some verses crossed my path, which became rallying places for the months ahead. They also took the form of music:

But unto you that fear my name shall the Sun of righteousness arise with healing in His wings; and ye shall go forth and grow up (Malachi 4:2 KJV).

Then shall thy light break forth in the morning and thine health shall spring forth speedily; and thy righteousness shall go before thee; the glory of the Lord shall be thy reward (Isaiah 58:8 KJV). Two months later, our pastor's wife called and gave me this exact verse. She had asked God for direction for us, and that section is what He gave her.

And the LORD shall guide thee continually and satisfy thy soul in drought and make fat thy bones; and thou shalt be like a watered garden, and like a spring of water, whose waters fail not (Isaiah 58:11 KJV).

Heal me, O LORD, and I shall be healed, save me, and I shall be saved, for thou art my praise (Jeremiah 17:14 KJV).

Dr. Abshier left town the second week in March. That week Ben's condition worsened dramatically. Early Tuesday morning, I cried out to God for evidence of His presence with us and in this circumstance. Immediately the words, *Stand firm and see the salvation of the Lord,*[1] came to mind.

On Wednesday night, while lying on the couch upstairs, Ben's head throbbed in pain. He moaned, "Maybe if I could just go to the hospital and get some IVs, I would feel better." The next day, Ben returned to the office of the doctor who originally diagnosed his "virus." Ben's own doctor was not available, but a colleague examined him with a simple routine physical. While he was doing so, I calmly, but firmly, tried to explain about his vomiting and general physical deterioration. I also mentioned that his naturopath had suggested an MRI if his condition did not improve. Notwithstanding, the physician patted my hand as he advised, "You are just overreacting." After that, he prescribed a potent anti-nausea medication, Scopolamine.

I drove Ben home and then left to buy the prescription. The pharmacist expressed concern when he learned of Ben's size and age. He warned the drug was powerful. "A good course of action will be to cut the patch in half if it proves too strong."

Shortly after applying the patch on Ben's back, his vomiting ceased. Within an hour, however, he developed double vision. I called the doctor, who directed me to reduce the size of the patch. Ben still wanted to spend time with friends. That Friday night, he celebrated a friend's birthday with an overnight at Rocky's home. In hindsight, we question how he could have tried to ignore his body's signals to spend the night with a bunch of lively and bouncy 13-year-old boys. He returned from the party, pleased to spend time with his friends instead of staying cooped up at home. His eye condition had not improved, but he expressed relief the vomiting had ceased.

On Sunday we called the general practitioner about Ben's compromised eyesight. The doctor expressed that his response to the drug was highly irregular and advised us to make an appointment in the office the following day.

Back in town, Dr. Abshier called on Monday to see how Ben was doing. When he heard about the double vision, he feared the Scopolamine may have caused a glaucoma and insisted Ben see an ophthalmologist immediately before further damage could worsen his condition. I tried to beg off going, insisting he already had a medical exam scheduled that afternoon and was feeling too sick for another appointment. He countered, "All the more reason for him to see an ophthalmologist."

Thanks to the recommendation of friends from church, we found a respected ophthalmologist and scheduled to meet the physician early that same afternoon. The doctor spent 45 minutes observing Ben. During the exam, he had him do several eye exercises. I could tell Ben was near exhaustion upon completing the ordeal. Next the doctor called me into his office and explained, "Mrs. Saint, your son has a brain tumor. There is a major amount of swelling, and this is caused by pressure from the tumor. With your permission, I am calling a distinguished neurologist to make an immediate appointment to see him." I responded tearfully, "This can't be happening. We have already lost three children. Not another one." He further admonished me, "Please say nothing to Ben to upset him." Somehow I pulled myself together, crying out quietly to God, while the words "brain tumor" echoed loudly through my head.

I told Ben we would have to see another doctor. He was not too happy about it but had to accompany me in the car. On the way over, he kept asking, "Do I have to get glasses?" Then answering his own question, "I know I will have to get glasses." To comply with the eye doctor's wishes, I kept my answers vague.

Upon our arrival, a nurse quickly ushered us into the examination room. The neurologist looked at Ben carefully and gave his initial assessment. He explained to Ben that it appeared he had a brain tumor. Tests were needed. An MRI would reveal where this tumor was situated. Once the location was found, the course of medical action would be determined. I am uncertain why the ophthalmologist would not permit me to say anything to Ben when the neurosurgeon had no qualms about revealing his suspicions immediately, leaving little to the imagination.

We returned home that night, somber and subdued. Our pastor and his wife were flying back from a church convention and could not be reached for a few more hours. Many from our church began or continued to pray for Benjy and for us.

Early Tuesday morning, Jim and I took Ben in for an MRI. After a brief wait, the doctor explained the results to us. The neurologist showed us the tumor location on the brain stem and stated that he was referring us to Dr. Wells. He had contacted the specialist who was available, waiting for us. We left immediately for the other hospital.

Glimmers of sunshine and rainbows through the mist

Whirlpool is the only term to describe the days before Ben's tumor diagnosis. Things did not settle down. There was a continuous sense of discomfort and worry which took away our peace. Benjy never added fuel to the fire. He had an incredible acceptance of the way things are/were. He didn't fight. He rested. He taught me to rest.

Gathering grace gems from the bubbling waters

- When in a hard place, who do you look to for guidance and direction?
- How do you handle situations over which you have no control?
- Have you pushed on when in pain?

Do the Boy No Harm

The sick man answered Him, "Sir, I have no man to put me into the pool when the water is stirred up, but while I am coming, another steps down before me'"

(John 5:7 NASB).

"'Don't hurt the boy or harm him in any way!'"

(Genesis 22:12 CEV)

Upon arriving at the hospital, we faced the extensive admission process involving the paperwork, forms and insurance cards. A staff member directed the family to sit in the waiting area until a room was available. Our pastor and his wife came while we were sitting there. I hugged Betty and sobbed, which admittedly was not a mature or positive way to help Ben in all of this. I yearned to be his rock, but sometimes I caved in to my fears and emotions, ending up a pile of sand.

Soon a nurse arrived to transfer Ben to the Intensive Care Unit where he was placed in a bed. Ben's youth pastors came up afterwards. During their visit, a nurse came in to start his IV. She was brusque and rough. Most medical people use a pain killer first before trying to insert an IV, but not her. Ben turned white as she probed for his vein. Later, an IV therapist came up to assess Ben's needs. This same nurse gloated that she had done all the work herself. The therapist noted several areas the nurse had neglected. That IV site was the only one to become infected while at that hospital.

The IVs and the medications helped Ben's condition improve. He had to submit to test after test, however. More MRIs and CAT scans were ordered before surgery. He endured each ordeal with incredible patience, never questioning or protesting. For those who have never had an MRI, the person is placed onto a flat, hard surface which slides into a person-size, long narrow tube. While in the unit, a specialized camera and X-ray machine (and it is neither of those two items) takes picture slices of whatever is being examined. In Ben's case, his brain was undergoing precise scrutiny. While the machine is running, a constant pounding sound reverberates within and around the unit. People use earplugs to help them endure the machine's throbbing barrage. Many adults cannot deal with the process due to claustrophobia. Ben never outwardly expressed any fear or distress. He faced several procedures, and I do not recall him ever once complaining about needing to have them.

We spoke with Ben's neurosurgeon following his initial evaluation. He wanted Benjy to stabilize before taking him into surgery, which he hoped would occur toward the end of that week. He explained that Ben's tumor was on his brain stem, an area in which this physician specialized.

In the teaching hospital. Ben, on awakening early in the morning, met a barrage of medical students who would be informed, at length, about his condition. One doctor, who took the residents and interns on tours, asked Ben if he had any questions. When Ben answered, "No," the head resident responded, "Well, I have one for you. Do you think there is enough space for anybody else in this room?"

His neurosurgeon had left strict orders to keep Ben under constant surveillance on his first night in the hospital. His night nurse needed to awaken him hourly to ensure he did not slip into a coma. I spent the night at his bedside. Ben's nurse, a godly and caring young woman, gave me many gifts of encouragement. She assured me about his neurosurgeon and shared that she held him in highest regard. His nurse made a deal with Ben and told him that if he could answer her first question, she would not make him go through the other exercises she was supposed to perform with him. At about 3:00 a.m., Ben was again awakened.

"Ben. Ben. Are you awake?"

"Yes."

"What day is it today?"

"Wednesday."

"You're right!"

Out of ICU… for a while

Hours later, on Wednesday morning, the doctor gave permission for Ben's transfer to a regular room, away from ICU. Moving onto a main floor energized him. The glass walls in ICU had made us feel vulnerable and exposed. That evening all his soccer buddies came up to visit him. Even though they made a substantial commotion on the floor as they all trooped in, it was a thrill to see those young boys enter the room to cheer and support their friend and fellow athlete. Presumably the hospital personnel overlooked the clock on the wall as the teammates stayed past visiting hours. That time spent with his friends was one that encouraged Ben in the days ahead, to say nothing of what it did for his parents.

Aunt Carolyn offers to stay with us

We notified our immediate family when learning about Ben's diagnosis. My mom wanted to come to help, but she had her hands full caring for my dad, who was dealing with advanced Alzheimer's disease. Aunt Carolyn, Mom's sister, soon arrived from Upper Michigan to handle our chaotic household. She and I traded the duties of the household chores and care for the girls, Katelyn and Chelann, with staying at the hospital with Ben.

Aunt Carolyn, also a nurse, possessed strong medical knowledge and practical skills in many areas. Although she had never married or had biological children, she collected people to care for. Her eyes quickly filled, and her voice labored when she spoke or prayed about the needs of others. My aunt had cared for her own mother, an invalid for 10 plus years, while holding down a full-time job as the head nurse for 300 employees and their families at a manufacturing plant. Her support with Ben in the days prior to and following his surgery relieved our burdens immensely. She was a rock for us when we needed one more shoulder on which to lean or to cry. Aunt Carolyn was there, not condemning, just encouraging. She supported each course of action even though we didn't always make decisions that would have met with medical approval.

Additional behind-the-scenes help came from my brother, Doug, a pediatrician in Pasadena, California. He spoke with the neurosurgeon and learned about various aspects of Ben's condition which neither Jim nor I could understand. Doug became a blessed advocate for us as the months progressed.

The neurosurgeon consistently apprised Ben of every possible procedure. So much information was presented, I could barely take it all in. The day before his scheduled brain surgery, his doctor came in to speak with Benj, explaining what he planned to do in his brain. He also made it clear Ben would never be the same person again. He added, "You may not even wake up from this surgery." Ben received that news, also, with his typical, stilled acquiescence.

Brain surgery

Because we believed strongly that perhaps God would heal Ben before his brain surgery, the doctor gave permission for one more MRI. It did not, however, show any improvement in the tumor. Surgery was scheduled for Friday morning, March 18th. Jim and I stayed the night in his room. We spent one of those nights when, though our eyelids were shut on the outside, our eyes were wide open inside. Ben, however, had a restful night. That was one of his amazing traits. He remained calm and at rest despite tremendous turmoil.

During the night, I did not feel compelled to pray for Ben as much as for Dr. Wells who would do the surgery. In my mind's eye, I had a picture of Abraham raising the knife to sacrifice his son, Isaac. The angel of the Lord called out, *"Stop, do the boy no harm."*[2] Much later, I recounted this to the surgeon. He explained that during the surgery, on two occasions, he tried to remove the entire tumor. However, as he was attempting this, Ben's blood pressure dropped so dangerously low that cutting out the last piece would have killed him.

A stretcher arrived shortly after 9:00 a.m. We accompanied Benj to the pre-surgery section while the pre-op technicians prepped him for anesthesia. We prayed with him and encouraged him. His demeanor reflected incredible peace.

Waiting for hours

Then the waiting started. Our pastors willingly stood in the gap[3] with us while we endured hours of waiting. As the four of us walked over a glassed pedestrian overpass, we looked out over the city and into the sky. When a rainbow appeared, we clung to this sign as a promise of God's faithfulness for us and for Ben.

Thanks to the marvels of telephone hookups, a call would periodically come up from surgery to let us know the progress as we waited in the family waiting room. Ben's neighbor and friend, Jason, called us to inquire about the course of the surgery. Time dragged on. We opted for lunch in the lower floor cafeteria. As most know, food has little flavor or appeal when digesting weightier issues.

Finally, at 4:00 p.m., the neurosurgeon came up to tell us how the situation had progressed. The doctors had completed the surgery. His neurosurgeon advised that in viewing the tumor, it appeared to be an extremely aggressive type, a primitive neuroectodermal tumor. He was sending it to the lab for verification but assessed that this was one of the worst kinds. Jim responded with a phrase from Job, "Though He slay me, yet will I trust Him." My reaction echoed Jim's, "God will be God."

Back in ICU

The medical staff returned Ben to ICU at about 8:30 p.m. We spied him in the glassed room from the double doors of the hallway. He was moving his arms around and seemed to be talking. Someone came out and said we could see him. They allowed us in to visit, one at a time.

Half a dozen neighbors and friends stayed with us during the early evening, awaiting news about Ben. One neighbor kindly offered to drive Jim home that night so that Jim would not be alone. Dave's wife had cared for our girls and their three children as we kept watch at the hospital.

Aunt Carolyn and I stayed for an all-night vigil. The staff showed us a waiting room in which to rest. When Ben asked for me, I would remain with him. They had a chair and a cot for a bed on which I "rested" between visits from the doctors and nurses, who also kept an around-the-clock watch on him. They administered pain medication, monitored his heart rate and breathing, and dispensed the myriad of meds required following such a serious operation.

In the morning, he felt more comfortable. His friend Grant visited briefly with him in the ICU room, along with Grant's folks. By midmorning, they released Ben from Intensive Care and admitted him to a two-bed room on the pediatric floor. The orderly transported him from ICU in a wheelchair to his next bed site. Upon arriving at his room on the main floor, he stood up and crawled into bed on his own steam, less than 18 hours following brain surgery.

His soccer coach also came up to visit Benj. Mike expressed deep concern for Ben's welfare and made it a regular habit to check in on him. On one of his later visits, Coach Mike confided, "If I ever have a son, I would like him to possess the character qualities Ben has."

With all the visiting soon after surgery, Ben at one point turned to me, with a twinkle in his eye, and remarked, "I didn't think hospitals let you have any visitors until at least a day after your baby is born!" I laughed. "Ben, you are an exception."

Getting stronger

As each day passed, Ben's strength returned. Shortly, he was going on daily strolls. At first, he hesitated to exercise so vigorously. However, Aunt Carolyn encouraged him to persevere with the promise that the faster he improved, the sooner he could return home. By the following Thursday, he was home again, less than a week after surgery.

We also faced the usual barrage of decisions to make regarding follow-up treatment. His neurosurgeon advised us to consider a procedure by which chemotherapy drugs enter directly into the brain, bypassing the brain's natural protective barrier. With certainty, we proceeded until confronted by a radiation therapist who advised us of the deleterious effects from the disruption treatment, which included deafness. Furthermore, it was only successful 50 percent of the time. She urged us to use the intensive radiation method, which, according to her, produced better results, but also exacted a drop of 10 to 15 IQ points. Another side effect was that, with her treatment, he would stay at his same stature. For a person who was still not tall, this was also a consideration. A hint of the political nature of medical treatments, especially those involving cancer, created a new conundrum. A doctor vying for a new patient on whom to practice procedures caught us off guard and left us feeling vulnerable.

How do we continue? The radiation therapist's approach with her exasperated and sarcastic evaluation of Ben's physician failed to encourage us to accept her proposal. His neurosurgeon had acted judiciously and had indeed played a major part in saving Benjy's life. After prayer, we sensed Ben's surgeon was the person whom we should trust.

Glimmers of sunshine and rainbows through the mist

A vital lesson I learned from Ben's first hospitalization was the value of friends. People who cared enough to pour their hearts and their time into our lives kept us floating on this turbulent sea of treatment and diagnoses. Staff in the hospital gave us the courage to stay in the battle and fight on. I needed the encouragement. Each of us received help in diverse ways and from various individuals.

Gathering grace gems from the bubbling waters

- Have you ever received encouragement from someone else while in a dire situation? How did the person or people minister to you? What did they say? Did they say anything?
- When faced with making a major decision, what do you do? Do you pray? Do you read the Bible? Do you talk with others?
- How do you still yourself? What do you do to embrace a peaceful heart?

Post Brain Surgery—Port-a-Cath and Brain Disruption

Who covers the sky with clouds, who prepares rain for the earth, who makes grass to grow on the hills
(Psalm 147:8 NKJV).

We rejoice… in hope (Romans 5:2 NKJV).

Ben recuperated quickly. Within a week of returning home, he attempted to ride his bicycle, play basketball and kick soccer balls. He had to learn to walk normally again and found this challenging, but he maintained a relentless determination to recover.

Routine visits with his doctor occurred every 10 to 14 days. Prior to Ben's discharge from the hospital, I had asked his nurse if it would be possible to help enhance his immune system by giving him vitamins and/or herbs. Evidently, the physician had learned about my question. During the first post-surgical visit, he addressed me pointedly. "Mrs. Saint, I understand you want to give your son herbs or vitamins." To which I answered, "I asked if I could." He turned and came close, sternly admonishing, "While he is on my program, he is to receive no herbs or vitamins. Don't you give him anything, not so much as a vitamin C."

Our contacts with the medical community had only begun. Shortly, we were back at the hospital for a psychological evaluation, part of cooperating with the entire experimental program. The testing included mental and emotional assessments. This lasted for hours. Ben was weary and upset following the lengthy session. He told me in the car that the psychologist had probed him to find out about his family life, interactions at home, etc. In hindsight, blessed with 20/20 vision and now realizing how emotionally invasive these tests were, we would not have given approval to this further encroachment on his person. That he endured and lasted through those grueling hours, following on the heels of surgery, reveals his resiliency and stamina.

It's just a game

The neurosurgeon allowed Benj and Jim to attend a Phoenix Suns basketball game against the Portland Trail Blazers. Ben's hospital-appointed ophthalmologist gave him tickets for fourth row seats. Both Jim and Benj were wildly excited to attend the event, occurring two and a half weeks following brain surgery. A public relations man from the Portland Trail Blazers, who was also the eye doctor's patient, talked with us about the opportunity Jim and Benjy might have of venturing into the locker rooms to meet players before the game.

Upon arriving at the stadium on game night, Jim left Ben downstairs as he scouted for the contact gentleman. While Jim was searching, a delivery man saw Ben and offered to take him into the locker room area to meet one star from the team. Ben, with posters under his arm, willingly accompanied the worker. Meanwhile, Jim returned to the spot where he thought he had left Benj. He could not find the contact person, and now Ben was missing. Pacing, Jim waited in the lobby looking for somebody with answers. Soon Ben emerged from the locker area, face beaming as he showed his dad his two signed posters. They thoroughly enjoyed their almost front row seats. It didn't matter which team won. They rooted for both.

Port-a-cath

Within days, Ben returned to the hospital to undergo the installation of a port-a-cath (a special instrument for IVs to deliver chemotherapy intended to preserve the veins) inserted surgically into his chest. The doctor had initially suggested this operation take place at the same time as the first treatment. However, we were thankful Ben had time to recoup from this fresh assault when we realized the pain he endured to recover.

Following the port-a-cath surgery, Jim drove the girls to Hood River, Oregon, to meet with our former pastor's wife (who had driven from their home in Richland, Washington, two and a half hours further away). Jon and Candace had offered to house and care for the girls while Benjy received treatment at the hospital.

Meanwhile, Ben and I returned to the hospital for blood tests, an MRI and a three-day stay for the new treatment he was to receive. They assigned him to a medical ward with four beds. A nine-year-old boy had received all the brain barrier treatments the previous year. His tumor had swiftly recurred after a short remission. He could no longer receive the treatments but needed to endure the rounds of radiation therapy. Dariel had lost much of his hearing from the disruption treatment. His parents were doing all they knew to sustain and enhance his life, including juicing and supplementation. Like Jim, Dariel's father was also a missionary kid and had many family members praying for this young boy's healing.

Our first visitor from the hospital staff was the psychologist who came in to review the details of Ben's testing. She asked Ben if he wanted to hear the outcomes from his profile. Not knowing he had a choice, "Sure." She told us the good, the bad and the ugly. She only discussed his academic skills, never mentioning the psychological assessment. His verbal skills were at a college level. However, his math scores were two years behind. She did not preface her comments with, "This evaluation took place within two weeks of major brain surgery. Few people can perform at any level of competence with the assault on their body and brain." It certainly would have softened the blow, but she did not spare him. That visit left him feeling dispirited.

Our next encounter, an hour or two later, was with his physician's colleague, who came in to advise us about the ramifications of the chemotherapy treatment. This neurologist must not have taken any courses at Dale Carnegie. He aimed for the jugular in describing every area that could go wrong when Ben would receive the brain disruption, among which was the three percent chance of a stroke, the certainty of deafness, etc. By then, I was in a daze. Ben lay on the bed, quiet and pensive. Inside, my heart was crying out, God, is this what you want for him? We did not perceive any other options and believed we were committed to this course of intervention, no matter what might happen.

The next day, the staff came to take Ben to surgery for the procedure, which he received under general anesthesia. I sat alone in a waiting room for about three hours. Reports finally came that the treatment had met with success, and that they would return Ben to ICU, as they monitored his responses with constant attention.

The technique for administering chemo to the brain resembles a heart catheterization in which a thin tubing is inserted in the groin area and moved on up through the trunk of the body to the locale of the port-a-cath. An IV with chemotherapy solution is also administered through the port-a-cath in the chest. Ben handled the procedure with a positive attitude and encouraging physical results. The same action, entering through the other side, was repeated on the following day. Three days following admission, we returned home.

Once home, we learned new proficiencies. I had received instructions on how to give Ben daily shots of Neupogen for ten days to prevent his immune system from succumbing to other illnesses. Chemotherapy works at destroying cells indiscriminately throughout the entire body, and patients can be left in a seriously compromised state from the treatment. My nursing skills did not appear as a result of formal schooling but through experience. Ben had the dubious privilege of acting as my classroom for much of this training. The injections took a while to learn. The first time I gave him a shot, I forgot to stop pinching his skin, which made the injection more painful than it should have been. After days of giving him less than comfortable shots, I apologized to Ben for having to administer the injections. He reassured me, "That's okay, Mom. I could die if I didn't get them, so this is better."

4-H and trying to hear from God

Many people prayed for Ben following his surgery. During this time, I was impressed to petition God with what I called a 4-H prayer: Hair, Hearing, Healing and Heart. I asked:

1. That God would allow him to keep his hair and that it would not fall out from the chemotherapy.
2. For his hearing to stay strong so that he would not become deaf from the treatment.
3. That God would restore Ben and heal him.
4. For Ben to have a happy heart during the year of treatment.

Two weeks following the chemotherapy hospitalization, we returned to the large hospital unexpectedly early. The IV therapists from a local hospital here in Gresham could not access his port to do a blood test. Because there was a threat of an additional problem, we made the trip to the university hospital. The technicians easily accessed his port there. During our time at the clinic, without forethought, Ben and I elected to assess his hearing at the Veterans Administration clinic. This was a program of which his doctor had approved and in which Ben would be one of the first patients to undergo observation. Coincidentally, our pastor's daughter-in-law administered the auditory testing, putting us more at ease.

Ben tolerated the hour of sound discrimination exams. The results, however, were disturbing. He had received a similar test prior to the initial chemotherapy treatment so that the staff could monitor his auditory levels. To our dismay, his hearing had dropped in the higher ranges.

Glimmers of sunshine and rainbows through the mist

Walking through the brain disruption procedure was difficult. Not all doctors respect the patients or their family members. I recall removing the dressing from where they had performed the insertion for the disruption. While I was making Ben more comfortable, another doctor came in and demanded that the dressing stay on. I told him his own physician had directed me to remove the dressing at 3:00 in the afternoon, which it was. He stood resolute and repeated that he forbade me to take it off.

For me, an unsafe individual is one who cannot admit making a mistake. This doctor exercised authority over a situation that the directing physician had predetermined. His attitude has helped me understand caution with those who have authority. A humble presence allows for dialogue and agreement. Even God's Word invites us to reason with Him, *"Come now, let us reason together," says the Lord.*[4]

Despite medical family members, I never expected personal medical involvement with others, even though I had worked in a hospital for a summer after graduating from college. In caring for Benjy, I learned way more than I had ever considered about performing medical procedures and comprehending medical terminology.

During the weeks of dealing with Benjy's illness and his hospitalization, I learned to accept additional responsibilities. I also learned about those who are in the medical field. A few are so exemplary as to act as role models. There are others who caused me alarm in how they treated both Benjy and me. Healing and wellbeing are not always the goals of every medical professional. Sometimes experimentation and information gathering are more important than the welfare of the patient. Because of this, the vulnerability of patients and their families, when facing fragile medical conditions, deeply concerns and saddens me.

Gathering grace gems from the bubbling waters

- Do you have specific prayers for which you are petitioning God?
- How do you expect to see them realized?
- Have you recruited others to join you in your pleas?
- How do you embrace a peaceful heart?

Withdrawal from Treatment

Deep calleth unto deep at the noise of thy waterspouts:
all thy waves and thy billows are gone over me
(Psalm 42:7 KJV).

The hearing loss did not reflect my prayers. It was not my prayer alone, but that of others, as we asked God to protect Ben from the harmful effects of the drugs. The day we received the update on his hearing, I found our pastor and wife at church. We asked them to pray if they sensed any godly direction about the continuance of this treatment.

I started a three-day fast, asking God what He was telling us. Until this point, I willingly walked through all the treatment with Ben. However, a disturbing red flag appeared, waving in my face. Many were standing with us, praying the 4-H prayer. Scripture specifies that where two agree on any one thing, God will perform that which is in His will.[5] Could this treatment rest outside God's will for Ben?

On Tuesday, the next day, our pastor, his wife and the church elders met together for prayer. Each heard a distinct word for us and for Ben. Pastor Bruce had requested that each one ask God if we should continue chemotherapy, yes or no. One elder prayed in his prayer language and clearly heard the word, *No.* For the others, there was a powerful impression God would not use this means to bring healing and tentatively sensed God intended to restore Ben.

That night, Ben's youth pastors came over for supper. After sharing our predicament, Steve asked if there were any Scriptures which had affected one of us. I replied that while praying during the day, a verse kept repeating in my thoughts, *"Some trust in chariots and others in horses, but we trust in the name of the LORD our God."* [6] Steve looked at me strangely and then exclaimed, "That is exactly the Scripture which has been running over in my mind, too! Only I heard it as, 'Some men trust in doctors, some in medicine, but I will trust in the name of the Lord, my God.'"

All that week, not one individual made any negative comment to us about withdrawing from the program. We were willing to stay with the program if we were to take that path. Removing Ben from this treatment was farthest from my mind until then. However, situations were not improving, but worsening. Ben's emotional state was low. He was losing his hair. His hearing, gradually, might go, too. Was he experiencing a healing?

First letter to Dr. Wells

My fast ended on Wednesday night. I did not feel any definite answer. That evening, I prayed, *God, if You want us to withdraw from this, will You make this very clear to me? I cannot do this without Your presence. I don't see how You are going to move, but You are welcome to do something.* On Thursday morning, while standing in the kitchen, there was a voice which appeared to come from behind me (yet not audible), distinctly and gently declaring, *"This is the way, now walk in it."* It was so definite. I knew this must be the next course of action. With that directive came the thought that we should let the doctor know our position, prompting the following letter:

Dear Dr. Wells,

You have exemplified professional courtesy and concern for Benjamin, Jim and me. We know you helped save Ben's life. We will always be grateful to you and recognize you provided the highest caliber of care which modern medicine could afford. The course of arriving at your door was outside our hands. I took Ben to an ophthalmologist we did not know who sent us to an unknown (to us) neurologist who sent us to you. We knew you were the man God chose to treat Ben medically. We could not imagine there being a finer doctor to oversee just this situation.

Having had four C-sections, I am aware of how one can feel like another body. I have observed extra ways you have moved to ensure Benj did not feel like a "piece of meat." He has told me that if he ever had to go through any of this again, he would want you to be his doctor. It is impossible to express to you how grateful we are, not only for your high expertise and knowledge, but also for your kindness and compassion.

Last Monday we had to travel back to the hospital for another blood draw, due in part because the IV therapy nurse here in Gresham could neither take anything out nor put anything into Ben's port-a-cath—and she tried three times. Since we were at the hospital for his port access, we entered the VA audiology department for a hearing check on a spur-of-the-moment whim. My assumption was that Benj would show the same results he had two weeks previous, since his normal audition appears better than anyone else's here at home. However, that was not the case. We could compare the results of the first test, which were much better than the second. His right ear showed a dramatic drop at higher frequencies.

My heart sank, and Ben expressed his disappointment. From the start, he had informed us he would never want to wear hearing aids. So, what do we do now?

That afternoon I met with our pastor and his wife. I shared with them the situation we were facing. He prayed that when we submitted this to others, who would also pray, there would be a unanimous agreement of the individuals involved in interceding on Ben's behalf. No one heard anyone else's impressions. Each person who has committed himself to pray about this came back with the same conviction: we are not to continue with chemotherapy at this time.

We know withdrawing from the program is as much hassle as initially entering it. Until last Monday, I had no reservations about the program, except for seeing it as a necessary evil. I have had many encouraging words from parents and nurses. Jim has been more cautious in this as the course we should take. Benjy has not wanted to go through the treatment and has recognized the sword of Damocles hanging over his head as he has awaited the monthly hospital trips. However, he is not a complainer and has been obedient to you as his doctor and to us as his parents. The hearing loss was a devastating discovery, but we found out now for a reason.

This is not a time when we are traipsing around looking at any other methods of treatment. We are simply going to let go of doing anything for now.

Our question is, "How do we stop the train now that we are on it?" We would like to have his port-a-cath removed. He doesn't like it and finds it extremely uncomfortable. This is currently our primary concern.

We understand that, medically speaking, our future remains precarious. I also know that I carried a child for nine months who I thought could die like the other three, after a few months here on earth. Even though she had marvelous muscle tone and excellent health, it took about four months before accepting she was indeed healthy. (She will be five years old in a few days.) Our future remains in the hands of our Creator, and we must answer to Him for our actions. For now, we must stay obedient to other orders.

The next morning, after writing and mailing the letter, a nurse in the neurology clinic called to set up Benj's next chemotherapy treatment. I explained, with trepidation, that we had elected to withdraw from the program. Her response, "Oh, that's cool," left me feeling taken aback after such a heart-rending week.

First encounter, post withdrawal

The neurosurgeon's main nurse called the following week and asked to set up an appointment with the doctor. Our pastor and wife accompanied me to meet him again for a consultation. It was an arduous task. For the first half of the meeting, he sat with his face in his hands, not looking up or establishing eye contact. His nurse did the interacting. Dr. Wells had two questions for me. The first query, "Why did you withdraw now, after you had been informed about all the potential side effects of the treatment?" My answer was that we agreed to try this if it offered a valid alternative for our son's healing. I explained the 4-H prayer, at the risk of sounding like a complete fool. Pastor Bruce and Betty explained histories of people whom they knew had been healed through God's intervention. The doctor explained he only knew of people with liver cancer who might have a regeneration and a "spontaneous" healing. Other than that, medical science was the only solution. His second questions, "What about all the other kids on the program? What is going to happen to them?" took me by surprise. I did not know their circumstances and stated so. The thought ran through my head, Who's telling these other kids? Not I. I don't even know who they are. Given the question today, I would respond, "God has given me the responsibility to hear from Him for my child. The other parents need to seek treatment for their own children in as responsible a way as they know." He reiterated that the success rate for this procedure was 50% and that Ben had a good 50% chance (there is also a good 50% chance of flipping heads in a coin toss) of making it a few more years on this program. The doctor told us he wanted to continue to observe Ben's progress, which was a relief.

Another letter to Dr. Wells

Benj underwent an MRI a week after my first head-on collision with his neurosurgeon. The physician showed me the film of his tumor and how it appeared to have collapsed. His impression was that this was probably a result of the chemotherapy. (It could also have resulted from a reduction of the post-surgical swelling.) The three of us, Dr. Wells, Ben and I, met in the examining room. Unexpectedly, the surgeon commented, "I talked to my Sunday School teacher about you and asked, 'Don't medicine and faith mix?' He (the teacher) told me they could be compatible." His comments led me to write the following letter:

Dear Dr. Wells,

Thank you for your kindness following the MRI for Benj. You answered questions that were in my mind. My mother had sent articles regarding various forms of treatment. I am thankful the gamma knife was not an option when I referred to what I had read. You made that clear immediately. I believed you would have presented this to us beforehand. But it was still good to hear.

Please understand, we are not saying medicine and faith cannot work together. If we believed that, how could we have consented to brain surgery? When I told you on the morning of Ben's surgery that I had prayed for you all night long, that was no lie. The picture in my mind was of Abraham taking the knife to Isaac the moment the angel called from heaven, "Stop, do the boy no harm!" [7] The first comment you made to us after the surgery was, "I didn't do any damage."

There appears no correlation with our other children and Ben, but let me explain that we planned our first three biological babies. Never did I ever expect they would be less than perfect. Our fourth birth child was a complete surprise. Waiting for her birth was hardly a simple time. There was no euphoria during those nine months. After all, I had not called the shots on this one. Thankfully, months previously, I had asked God's forgiveness for not trusting Him with some areas of my life since Alyssa's death. If I had not believed that abortion was a crime against God's creation of life, it would have loomed as an actual option during those first four months. Instead, I had to trust that God knew what He was doing and that whatever the outcome, He was and is sovereign.

How does this relate to Ben? Withdrawing from the program is truly not the path we would naturally choose. We do not have any "statement" to make by doing this. It is simply a matter of feeling that we must obey. Why would God ask us to do something which contradicts human reason and common sense? Hasn't He given us minds to use? You spoke of the variables of surgical procedure. There are variables in life that reach beyond the tangible.

In reading Scripture, there are instances of God doing things which made little sense. Why would He wish to send the children of Israel into the Red Sea after they had just escaped slavery? [8] What would marching around the walls of a city do to help an army win a battle? [9] How could Gideon's army of 300 possibly withstand thousands of Midianites? [10] Who ever heard of an army which didn't fight and won simply by singing and praising God? [11] How could a man be healed of leprosy by dunking himself in "dirty" water seven times? [12]

When I heard the words, "This is the way, now walk in it," there was the sense that this was God's directive. Others heard words relating to healing. All I sensed was an order to take an alternative path—one which feels more like a trek up the mountain. But for now, there is that deep conviction that to do anything would be disobedience.

How does one know when God has spoken? That's tough to explain. To be very simplistic (there are volumes written on this topic), here are two ways I use. First, it will not contradict what the Bible says. Second, there is a thought which is impressed gently.

Remember Elijah's experience when he escaped to the cave, running from Jezebel? God was not in the mighty wind, nor in the earthquake, nor in the fire but in the still, small voice.[13] A strident harangue, when seeking guidance, is rarely from a godly source.

How do I know God will speak to me? The Bible says He will. "Your ears shall hear a word behind you saying, 'This is the way.'" [14] How do I know the Bible is true? That is one key to my personal faith. I simply must believe that it is. If it is not, then I am deceived and deluded. Either I am living a lie, or I am not.

Dr. Wells, we have nothing but profound respect for you. Discontinuing the chemotherapy intervention does not reflect on our high opinion of you and your work, nor does it negate the intense gratitude we feel towards you for using your surgical skills to aid in Ben's healing. God bless you.

Withdrawal and research

I read more information about cancer treatment. The medical community offers three basic choices in its approach to this dread disease: cut, burn and poison. After composing and sending the above letter to the neurosurgeon, we attempted some alternative methods of treating Benj's brain tumor. We no longer felt constrained to stay under total medical restrictions. A friend from church introduced us to shark cartilage therapy. We also consulted with Ben's naturopath, who encouraged the shark cartilage treatment along with some natural medications.

After speaking to Dr. Wells, my heart carried a heavy load. None of the vitamins had been effective. Another friend, who had called us from time to time since Ben's surgery, encouraged us to investigate an herbal preparation from a company he was representing. I called and spoke with him, explaining our predicament. He urged me to contact a lady familiar with the herbal tea formula. I visited with the herbalist who provided me with the tea, printouts regarding this compound, plus other natural products to enhance Ben's immune system.

Jim and I visited with the doctor together in July, after another of Ben's MRIs. Dr. Wells made a special evening appointment for us to accommodate Jim's work schedule. The meeting was congenial, and we again expressed our views on treatment we should take. We told him we were looking into more benign treatments, which Ben agreed to as far as helping him with his overall immune system and state of health. The doctor remarked that he assumed we would pursue nothing any further. We explained that after withdrawal from the program, we felt released from his protocol. We wanted to give Ben the optimum nutritional advantages. The supplements would not harm him and might indeed help in his healing.

Glimmers of sunshine and rainbows through the mist

Confronting the doctor who saved Benjy's life left me in the throes of discomfort. To remove Ben from the program, as explained in the letter, was not something I had ever predicted. During all the medical interventions, Ben's welfare remained a primary issue. Not only his physical welfare, but his emotional and spiritual well-being. When I prayed and sensed, "Do the boy no harm" before his brain surgery, this also had to do with anything that would touch our son. It might be medicine, medical personnel, supplements, friends, family. Anything or anyone could harm him. As his mother, I provided a covering through prayer and intervention. For me, with my temperament, the confrontations were far from comfortable. They left me drained and exhausted. However, my mission was to intervene, and I did what I could and what I understood.

Gathering grace gems from the bubbling waters

- When God speaks to your heart, how do you hear Him?
- Are there any specific Bible verses which have become life verses for you? When have you needed them?
- What responsibilities do you have for others? How do you act on those responsibilities?

Symptoms Return

When he withholds water, rivers dry up; when he lets them loose, they'll flood the land

(Job 12:15 ISV).

Ben had another MRI at the end of August. Dr. Wells called and spoke to me at the beginning of September. He informed us he needed to see us immediately as the tumor had resumed growing again. What a blow!

Earlier that week, during personal Bible study, several verses impressed me.

God who gives life to the dead and calls into being that which does not exist (Romans 4:17 AMP).

Such hope [in God's promises] never disappoints us because God's love has been abundantly poured out within our hearts through the Holy Spirit who was given to us (Romans 5:5 AMP).

Their fruit will be for food, and their leaves for medicine (Ezekiel 47:12c NKJV).

Hope for the needy

A devotional written by Richard Wurmbrand rang in my heart with hopefulness and eloquently expressed Whom we hope in and what we hope for. That meditation gave me reason to cling to the One who is our hope.

We... rejoice in hope Romans 5:2.

The most unfounded hope is much more founded than the most founded despair. I know it from my own experience.

I was sentenced to 25 years of hard labor. I had been deathly sick in prison, and doctors had abandoned any hope that I would recover. Under those circumstances I had a completely unfounded hope of ever leading a world-wide mission, having as its purpose the helping of persecuted Christians in Communist countries. Despair and suicide would have been logically justified. There seemed no hope that I would ever see my son again. Now, I have my grandchild on my lap.

Never give up hope. The Talmud says that if a man is sentenced to death, has his head on the block, the executioner has already lifted his axe, and he thinks, "Now I am lost," he is unfaithful. The axe can fall from the executioner's hand. It happened like this with the Romanian King Michael the Brave.

Euthanasia is false. Men doomed by all the doctors of the world can live. Hope for your business, for your children. Hope for your character even though, in spite of thousands of endeavors, it has not improved yet. We have as our hope a God who hung *the earth upon nothing* (Job 26:7). A hope which He gives holds good even without any foundation.[15]

The tumor grows back

Before our meeting took place with Benj's neurosurgeon, Jim's sister, Evelyn and her husband Humberto, had flown up from Argentina. They spent time with us to lend encouragement and advice. Humberto came into the consultation with Dr. Wells. Jim or I translated into either English or Spanish while one of us talked with the doctor. Dr. Wells clarified that Ben had only two days to two weeks to live with this tumor before it metastasized. Once it resumed growing, there would be no stopping it. He asserted, "At the very most, he has two months." He presented a few other options. One was a shunt to help with the pressure from the fluid buildup of the tumor. He warned that if the fluid had cancerous cells, the cancer could spread throughout his entire body. The doctor then asked if we had decided to implement the radiation therapy. No, that was not our intention. Third, he reiterated we could choose his program. He further explained our options to us. Although a possibility, he would not recommend any more surgery. That had been tried. This type of tumor will return, with or without continued surgical intervention. Though somewhat meekly, we explained our original position, and we had to follow the right course for Ben. We promised to come back for one more MRI.

No covering

Ben and I returned a week later for the scan. The doctor looked at it with me and pointed out the area of concern regarding this tumor. He also expressed that, because we did not care to follow his direction, he could no longer be Ben's physician. Dr. Wells would not agree to letting us use herbs as an adjunct to his regimen because it would cloud his research statistics. This put us in a hard and somewhat impossible position. We had no medical doctor with whom to consult regarding Ben's treatment. We were frightened. On the other hand, we did not detect any better guidance regarding a proper course to pursue. We would have welcomed names of other doctors who would work with us. He did not present that option. Many months later, we learned we could have pushed for a different physician. The medical world can intimidate, and we simply did not have the experience to walk through this territory. We had entered a labyrinth with no clear path.

Aunt Carolyn came for a visit after Eve and Humberto left. She encouraged us with her warmth and kindness. She had resolved to express positivity and truly kept us going with her marvelous attitude. Her support gave us the courage to continue the therapies we trusted would benefit and not harm Ben.

After starting the herbal tea, along with other vitamins and natural preparations, Ben experienced another severe bout of vomiting. Interestingly, his body purged itself of material he had not ingested. Perhaps his body was releasing some poisons which had been attacking it. He also mentioned that his neck was hurting. That discomfort disappeared within five days of starting the tea regimen.

At the end of October, Ben had a bout with apparent stomach flu. We had a harvest party at our church. Each young person or child in attendance received a bag of candy. After not eating any sweets for a few months, Ben indulged and got sick from the overload of sugar and artificial ingredients.

That same week, Jim's sister Martha and her daughter Susy came from their home in Guatemala for a visit. The kids played games, one of which was a major round of Monopoly. We drove up to the base of Mt. Hood to sled in the snow. Ben was at the point where he was vomiting regularly once again, although he did not feel as sick as he had been months earlier.

After Martha and Susy left in early November, Ben had many days when he did not feel good. During that time, I juggled his treatments. Some days he would get the herbal tea and not some of the other herbs. Other days he would not drink the tea. On those, he would take other herbs and vitamins. We worked at transforming his diet through information garnered from several books I had been reading about natural foods and cancer diets.

Preparing for a trip South

To further complicate the issue, we had made plans to visit Jim's family in Argentina for Christmas. This was a trip we, as a family, had planned for several years. However, Ben's condition was not optimum. What to do? After family discussions, we concluded the best course was to stay with our plans of traveling to Argentina. We also asked for prayer from our church, as we desperately wanted to move in the realm of God's will and not our wishes.

One request Ben had was to get rid of his port-a-cath. After wrangling with his nurse and the surgeon who had put in the device, Jim secured an agreement for the removal. The hospital scheduled Ben's surgery for December 15th, a mere few days prior to starting our journey to Argentina.

Although it was an outpatient surgery, the port removal occurred under general anesthesia. We had to wait for several hours in a ward. Ben was not feeling good, but he kept up his spirits by looking forward to extricating this extra piece of equipment from inside his body. One of his former nurses remembered him. We told her about the herbs and his new treatments. She encouraged us to pursue the course we were taking, attesting to the severity and harshness of the medical intervention. She also revealed that she herself would not go through the treatments if other options were open.

While Ben was in surgery, I settled into the designated surgical waiting room. A lady started questioning me about why I was there. She had emigrated from Lebanon and had worked as a medical secretary at the American Hospital in Beirut. The major thrust of her conversation reminded me that *"God is the healer."* She explained case histories of family members who were severely damaged by medical science. She also cited incidents in which only God could have brought patients through when medical science raised its hands in surrender. I needed the encouragement from this woman. God put her in my way.

Ben awakened and recovered from his procedure by 4:00 p.m., clearing our return home. We had two days left to pack and prepare for our next journey.

Glimmers of sunshine and rainbows through the mist

During the time of the last MRI with Dr. Wells, I could not imagine what else would come at us. It was extremely difficult to have no medical covering, as the doctor had informed us that he would no longer serve as Ben's physician. So, we had no neurologist or even a regular doctor willing to monitor his progress.

When family came from hundreds to thousands of miles away, we received the benefit, spiritually and emotionally. Loved ones prayed and advised. Although we had to arrive at our own decisions, we knew the covering of family love did not leave us abandoned and alone. Family members cared about us enough to sacrifice for us.

People who spoke encouragement with me did not appear by accident. They had divine appointments to help me stay grounded, focused. The lady from Lebanon was someone whom I could not have foreseen. Her faith and encouragement washed over my anxious heart and helped me enter peacefully into deeper trust.

Gathering grace gems from the bubbling waters

- Have you had family members surround you in times of distress? How did they help?
- We had church family also keep us enveloped in love. Have you had others, not from your family, per se, who showed you sacrificial love and care? What does that look like?

- Have you ever gone against accepted values? How did you deal with your own issues while keeping yourself calm?

Footnotes

1. Exodus 14:13 (ESV)
2. *"Don't hurt the boy or harm him in any way!' the angel said. Now I know that you truly obey God, because you were willing to offer him your only son'"* (Genesis 22:12 CEV).
3. *"I searched for a man among them to repair the wall and stand in the gap before Me"* (Exodus 33:20a BSB).
4. Isaiah 1:18 KJV
5. *Again, I say to you, if two of you agree on earth about anything they ask, it will be done for them by my Father in heaven* (Matthew 8:19 ESV).
6. Psalm 20:7 BSB
7. Exodus 22:12
8. The history of the Red Sea crossing is recorded in Exodus 13:17 to 14:29.
9. Marching around the walls of Jericho can be found in Joshua 6.
10. The battle of Gideon and the 300 soldiers is recorded in Judges 7.
11. The story of Jehoshaphat and the choir that led the army to victory shows God's mysterious ways in how He directs His people in 2 Chronicles 20.
12. 2 Kings 5 reveals the story of Naaman's healing as directed through God by Elisha.
13. 1 Kings 19:1-14
14. Isaiah 30:21
15. Wurmbrand May 10.

Section 6. Charting Unknown Waters:

Up and Away

Doth the hawk fly by thy wisdom, and stretch her wings toward the south?
(Job 39:26 KJV)

Argentine Reunion

Nevertheless, he left not himself without witness, in that he did good, and gave us rain from heaven, and fruitful seasons, filling our hearts with food and gladness
(Acts 14:17 KJV).

... And remember! I will be with you always, yes, even until the end of the age.
(Matthew 28:20 CJB).

We departed by car on the first leg of our trip to Argentina. We planned to drive from the Portland area, get as far as Doug and Gloria's (my brother and his wife) in Pasadena, and then fly out of the Los Angeles airport.

Sick in California

The farther south we traveled, the worse Ben became. By the second day, he was extremely sick and in pain. His vomiting increased to where nothing, not even

7-Up, would stay in his stomach. We called our church back home. The people prayed and asked God to show us how we were to proceed. Those who committed themselves to praying assured us that God would remain with us on our journey. We asked Ben. He adamantly insisted he wanted to continue.

By the time we arrived at my brother's home on Sunday evening, Benj's condition had deteriorated further. When Doug saw him, he expressed serious concern. Next, at their request, we drove to their church where pastors prayed for him, asking for God's intervention. Remarkably, by the next day Ben experienced a reprieve from his ailments and opted to accompany us on a trip to Disneyland. Gloria, proficient in herbal remedies, gave him her herbal drinks to keep him going; they helped considerably. Although his physical condition prevented his hopping onto active rides, like Splash Mountain, he joined us on the milder ones.

After we returned to their home, we learned Doug had spoken with a neurologist from the clinic where he worked. That doctor prescribed Decadron[1] for Ben to help with the tumor swelling and general discomfort. Doug told us, much later, that after observing his condition, he did not expect to see Benj alive again.

Flight to Cordoba

Tuesday morning, December 20th, we left from the airport in Los Angeles. We arrived in São Paulo, Brazil, early Wednesday morning and spent hours in a locked-in waiting facility at the airport. Without Brazilian visas, we could not walk around the airport. We experienced an entire day of waiting inside three large glassed-in rooms, like animals at the zoo.

Finally, the plane for Buenos Aires arrived at the gate and readied for departure. Complications occurred, including the airline officials insisting we did not have a reserved place. Jim held firm, "We are all flying on the plane, even if we have to stand the whole way." The five of us boarded the plane and found empty seats. Without specific seat assignments, we ended up in four different sections of the cabin. The three kids were all feeling sick. One of them came to sit with me. After moving closer, she leaned over and upchucked the remains of her morning meal onto my lap. Being sick, flying in a plane and enduring separation from each other made this journey arduous; but somehow, we arrived in Argentina, all in one disheveled piece.

Our next quandary was how to transfer from one airport to another. As I had experienced 20 years earlier, Buenos Aires still had one airport for international flights and another, clear across town, for in-country destinations. We piled into a compact taxi. The driver insisted that all our luggage would fit. Fitting into the cab forced Jim to sit with the heaviest piece on his lap for close to an hour. The remaining four of us wedged ourselves into the back seat.

People trying to get on flights crammed into the Ezeiza airport. Delays and flight cancellations ruled the day. Once again, we had to wait, sitting on the floor for six or seven hours. The stifling warm air in the airport left us wilted and drained. The other stranded passengers, however, were cheerful and friendly. We enjoyed the camaraderie. Since we were all stuck together, the term "Misery loves company" proved true.

With relief, we climbed onto the third and final airplane for that portion of the trip. Upon departing from the plane once we landed in Córdoba, both Jim and Benj kneeled and kissed the ground. What a joy to see so many family members waiting for us—Jim's mom, Joe and Susy, their five children, Evelyn and her three youngsters. All of us hugged, kissed and cried.

Christmas Eve in the hospital

We spent two days visiting family members. However, by Saturday morning, Christmas Eve, Ben was desperately ill. He had become weak and had started more vomiting. He also complained of a severe headache. I came in to help him. Emotionally and physically distraught, Ben pleaded with me to pray that it would not hurt when he died.

That evening, Jim's sister convinced us to take Ben to the hospital. Eve suggested we admit him to the public children's hospital, explaining that the doctors who worked there were the same ones who worked at the private hospitals. This hospital would not charge fees, and we'd have a greater opportunity for more than one medical opinion. We loaded a mattress into the rear of a covered pickup truck. Ben lay down in the back, and we left in our impromptu ambulance.

A kind, young resident physician admitted Ben and took his medical history from me. My Spanish needed polishing, but fortunately, most medical terms are similar in both English and Spanish because of their shared Latin base.

Ambulance drivers transported Benj to another place about a mile away for an MRI. We did not realize it was up to us to bring the results back to the hospital. This required my walking over to the facility two days later to request the films and hand deliver them to the hospital staff after more postponements and misunderstanding.

The four-bed room in which Ben stayed perplexed us. Fresh from modern amenities, we braced ourselves for this unfamiliar environment. The building appeared to have been constructed in the 1930s. The ceilings rose at least 12 feet high; Casablanca fans hung down to provide some air circulation. The single sink in the room constantly trickled with a dribble of water. Even though there was a drought in the city, not one plumber came to fix the damaged faucet. Torn window screens welcomed insects of diverse types, sizes and quantities into the room. The four beds held foam rubber mattresses with only a sheet covering them. If any bacteria lurked in the foam cells from past patients, those germs could not have disappeared with the draping of a clean sheet. The pillows exhibited the same treatment—bare foam rubber with only a single-layer, cotton pillowcase.

Because Ben needed someone with him 24 hours a day, I usually accompanied him, especially at night. When cousins or other relatives came for a few hours, I went to Mom Saint's to wash and change clothes before returning to the hospital. Once or twice, I could recline in a vacant bed next to Ben; most of the time, I slept on a foam mattress from home, stuffed under his bed on the floor. Another mother, with a critically ill two-year-old in the bed next to Ben's, was not as fortunate. Her bed and seating arrangement consisted of a plastic, upright lawn chair.

Outside in the courtyard, alley cats of all varieties lurked, hoping for a handout from the kitchen. Perhaps they benefited the hospital by keeping the rodent population at bay. Those feral cats never entered the building but lounged outside, ready to pounce, fight or eat.

The next evening, another physician, Dr. Sarmiento, examined Ben. Recognizing us as foreigners and realizing that North Americans rarely end up in Argentine public hospitals, he mistakenly assumed Ben spoke French and tried to communicate in French, which neither Ben nor I comprehended. The physician expressed a deep concern, along with revealing a manner of genuine warmth and kindness. Dr. Sarmiento, a highly trained neurosurgeon, never regarded us with an air of disdain or superiority. He treated us courteously, more as an adviser and a confidant than as a medical authority.

Two days later, Dr. Sarmiento insisted we consider having a shunt put in as soon as possible. The head of neurosurgery, Dr. Perez, wanted to perform brain surgery, but we resisted. We explained that his doctor in the U. S., who specialized in brain stem tumors, had emphatically refused to consider performing another surgery. Dr. Sarmiento conferred with Dr. Perez, and they both concluded a shunt insertion would offer the preferred solution.

We learned later that due to lack of funds and instruments, these Argentine neurosurgeons had to fashion their own microscopic equipment. One of their colleagues had studied the microscopic technique in Chicago. With his help, they endeavored to duplicate this method of brain surgery through "homemade" apparatuses. I commend these dedicated and committed doctors. They have my lasting admiration.

In speaking with Dr. Sarmiento, I mentioned it was our understanding this type of tumor was one of the worst. His succinct and direct response unglued me. *It is the worst.*

During that week, Jim had a few assignments of his own. On Sunday morning, he shared his testimony at Humberto and Evelyn's church, Manantial de Vida (Stream of Life). Evelyn and Humberto conducted a radio program interview with him. Jim shared about our visit and how things were turning out. He told the audience about Ben and his stay in the medical facility. The radio hosts invited the listening audience to phone the station and express their gleanings from the interview. One lady called to say that three months earlier, God impressed her to intercede for someone named Benjamin. She did not know who the person was but sensed the need for God's intervention in this person's life. She commented, "Today I know for whom God has been asking me to pray."

Emergency surgery

After several days in the hospital, and seeing no improvement, we agreed to a shunt surgery to save Ben's life. We had thought Dr. Sarmiento would perform the operation. However, the neurosurgeon on call, Dr. Moreno (not his real name), was the one responsible after we made up our minds. This gentleman was not as kind as Dr. Sarmiento; in fact, he showed outright disgust toward us.

With no other doctor available and Ben's condition worsening, we had no choice but to submit. The day of the scheduled surgery, I took a taxi to a medical supply place to purchase the shunt. We prayed this referred facility stocked the needed device. Thankfully, it was available for purchase. I charged our credit card the amount of $1800 for a French model and returned to the hospital in another taxi.

Jim endeavored to prevent the staff from shaving Ben's head, explaining that medical personnel before his brain tumor surgery had removed a small section of hair. However, this was not their standard procedure and caused a rift in the relationship between us and Dr. Moreno. (Dr. Sarmiento had earlier explained why this was unavoidable, "You can see for yourself that the hygiene is abysmal here. We must do everything we can to assure cleanliness.")

Our next problem occurred when Dr. Moreno decided not to do the surgery before the weekend's festivities. Seeing Ben's weakening and declining condition, Dr. Romain, an older pediatrician who appeared to live at the hospital, convinced the neurosurgeon of our son's desperate need. The surgeon relented and scheduled surgery for that evening, December 30th. We waited. When the doctor arrived with his wife, I handed him the box with the shunt, and he walked into the operating room. Nausea and dread welled inside me as I gave the surgeon the very device that would provide a drainage pathway for the brain fluid buildup. We said goodbye to Benjy as we lingered outside the door and prayed.

Finally, the waiting ended. The surgeon emerged from the operating room and assured us that all had gone well. After the hour-long surgery was deemed successful, Jim returned to his mom's house to take care of our daughters, and I turned to walk downstairs to await admittance into the intensive care unit. While still in the hallway, an American lady approached me and asked, "Are you Lynn?" *Who is she?* After introducing herself, Margaret explained why she had come. She and her Argentine husband pastored a church in Carlos Paz, a small town close to Córdoba.

The lady I had befriended whose son was also hospitalized was a friend and neighbor to Margaret. She had told Margaret about an American Christian whose son was in the bed next to her son. After hearing her friend's story, Margaret felt a yearning to meet and talk with me. Margaret rode for an hour, standing on a crowded bus, driven through rutted roads, to reach the children's hospital. Upon arriving, she began a search for the American lady. I am assuming it wasn't too difficult as we must have been the only Americans in the entire hospital.

God knew I needed someone to encourage me and to pray for us. We filled a lightning-brief hour with talking and praying. Then she hurriedly left to catch the last bus for that night, back to Carlos Paz. We have not seen one another again, but her kindness left its mark on my heart. Strangers can be our angels unaware.

Later that evening, a young pastor, his wife and their two children came to encourage me during my isolation from Benjy. I remembered José from when he was about 10 years old. Their efforts to visit and uplift me endued me with a stronger sense of God choosing His own to bring heavenly messages. What support we need from one another!

The doctor prescribed a two-day stay for Ben in ICU. I rested in Ben's bed. At about 2:00 a.m., someone from ICU entered the room to tell me that Ben was asking for me. Generally, family members are not allowed in Intensive Care unless they comply with the strict schedule. However, they showed us compassion by letting me help Ben with his needs. (Because they did not speak English, they were more willing to open the unit.)

Critically ill children filled the intensive care unit. Babies with serious birth defects and injuries comprised the majority. Their plaintive crying broke my heart. The department was scrupulously clean. The attending nurses and physicians treated Ben and me with great kindness. Nevertheless, I learned that after I left, a new nurse came on duty and refused to allow anyone to get me to help care for him. He had spent several hours asking for me. Ben told me this when the staff finally allowed me re-admittance, after I had stood in the queue with the other parents.

Medical staff sometimes requested items from patient families to help stock the supply shelves, which were at a minimum. They asked me to purchase bandages for the unit along with pain pills. I was happy to have something to do with my time and energy besides waiting in the room or in the ICU hallway. It took walking a mile or two to find a drugstore with the two required items, but I found a pharmacy with both bandages and aspirin.

In the daylight hours, I stood in line, waiting my turn with the other family members of those children who were in ICU. Young mothers came from great distances to see their babies for an hour in the morning and another hour in the later afternoon. Being allowed to stay with one's critically ill child is a privilege not all enjoy.

By New Year's Eve, the doctor relented from requiring that Ben remain in ICU. Benj showed strong vital signs; plus, he needed to stay in a location where someone could understand his requests and meet them. He was already eating with no ill effects. The outlook was highly favorable.

Glimmers of sunshine and rainbows through the mist

Rife with obstacles, our trip to Argentina started off and continued with more potholes in the road, both in the skies and on the land. We could not have anticipated Benjy's condition would head onto a downward path after arriving in Córdoba. Taking our son to a public hospital in another country, after having him treated at a more modern facility in our area, was more challenging than I could have imagined.

Meeting and knowing the stories of people at the children's hospital stretched my heart for the better. So many others had to endure greater challenges and hardships. Even the doctors sacrificed themselves to do their work. Their income at the children's hospital reflected what a laborer here might earn. They held memberships in private clinics where they earned higher salaries. On the other hand, they also chose their work locations and elected to donate their skills, with light compensation, to those families who had little to no income and no insurance. We felt stranded with stateside insurance and no international coverage to absorb our costs. By God's grace, we received mercy through the hands of the medical team, through family members, through caring friends, through divine interventions.

Gathering grace gems from the bubbling waters

- Have you ever come up against a wall with circumstances beyond your control?
- Can you identify people who opened your heart when you wanted to escape from a situation?
- If there are others who touched you, can you recall how they increased your understanding? Your compassion? Your appreciation?

Continued Hospital Stay

He opened the rock, and water gushed out; it flowed through the desert like a river (Psalm 105:41 ESV).

Benj gratefully returned to the ward, even if it meant the ambient comfort level was not as pleasant (the ICU was air conditioned). On the main floors, summer weather made the rooms uncomfortably warm. During the day, the indoor temperature soared close to 90 degrees. Ben slept well that night. In the morning, on awakening, his head wrap fell to the floor. I told him not to worry, as putting the same wrap back on after it had fallen on the floor would be too unsanitary. If only I had realized what would happen later, I would have stuck the contaminated wrap onto his head.

One night away

On the evening of December 31st, New Year's Eve, 1994, Jim's family wanted me to join in the fireworks celebration with them. Ben's cousin, Mikaela, offered to stay with him while I attended a family outing. I was thankful to leave the hospital for a night, but apprehensive about not being available to care for his needs.

While the family celebrated at Eve and Humberto's house, back at the hospital, Dr. Moreno made his rounds and discovered Ben without his head wrap. He responded with a major tantrum, yelling at and degrading the resident on duty. He caused Ben further pain through his rough and brutal treatment. Ben was running a slight fever. This, more than likely, was the expected result of his recent surgery, coupled with the extreme heat in his room. Because of the fever, the doctor insisted on giving Ben IVs again. The IV medication he prescribed for him contained Dilantin, an anti-seizure medication best given by mouth. Ben could have swallowed pills, as he was having no trouble keeping foods or liquids down following the surgery. When given by IV, the drug clogs the veins and causes damage, resulting in their collapse. Ben experienced severe pain and discomfort.

Hospital drama

Evidently, the doctor had also screamed harsh threats against "these Americans who think they can come in here and..." He alleged, "If this boy's parents think he is going to get out soon, they have another think coming. The boy will stay until at least Thursday." This meant that most of our vacation would comprise spending time with Ben in the hospital.

We had provided our own large thermos of cold water for Ben to drink. On seeing the thermos, the doctor ordered Mika to use the cold drinking water for sponging him to bring his temperature back to normal. When Jim arrived for the night shift, there was no clean, cool water available.

After spending a restful night at Mom Saint's home, I returned to the hospital on Sunday morning to learn what had transpired the night before. I stayed with Ben for the remaining hours on Sunday. He felt miserable, especially because of the anti-seizure medication via drip IV.

When Dr. Moreno walked into the room on Sunday afternoon and read on the chart that Ben's temperature had dropped to normal, he turned and challenged, "Do you see that? I healed him myself."

Not wanting to further antagonize him, I meekly said, "That's good to hear."

Feeling braver after his self-congratulation, I addressed him with the smoldering question. "When can we expect Ben's discharge?"

"It won't happen until the end of the week," he quickly answered with a nonchalance that mocked my raging emotions.

The conversation ended as he abruptly turned and left the room. I felt trapped. Benjy felt trapped. This contradicted what the other doctors had originally advised. There was little chance for further dialogue. Dr. Moreno held the lock and keys to release, and he wasn't about to hand them over.

The incident regarding Dr. Moreno's tantrum had been noised throughout the ward, and with the way word spread, probably most of the hospital. The mothers of other patients came and talked to me about the situation. Each new story unearthed more dirt.

Then the medical staff started confiding in me, including the young resident doctor who had received a severe raking over the coals. One nurse reported that Dr. Moreno's easily triggered temper was notorious. She had worked with him in surgery; it was not uncommon for him to throw instruments across the room when an assistant mistakenly handed him the wrong implement. The feeling of helplessness became more intense as the hours passed.

The IVs were causing Ben excruciating pain. Each time a nurse came to exchange the emptied glass container with a full one, she would locate another vein to inject the IV needle into Ben's tender arms. No pain killers made the application more bearable. The discomfort continued to increase. It took Ben hours to fall asleep. He could not relax from the IV pain coupled with the apprehension of having another IV insertion. He agonized and moaned throughout the night. I asked the resident if Dr. Moreno's orders could be rescinded. She responded that since he was the operating surgeon and Ben was his patient, his word was law. I lay on my mat under Ben's bed, crying and praying through the night. *God, we need a way of escape. I do not see any solution, but You know of one. We are desperate, Lord. Please answer quickly.*

A way out

The next morning, Dr. Sarmiento arrived early, with a smile on his face. He asked optimistically, "Well, how are things going today?" I reported the entire scenario. After listening, he responded, "He's out of here." I was incredulous. Did he hear what I said? Does he know what he's doing? Dr. Sarmiento quickly removed the IV and explained that as soon as we could arrange for transportation, Ben was free to go. Seriously? A burden lifted! God had heard our cries.

I ran to the public phone to call Jim.

"*Hola*," he answered.

"Hi, Jim. Dr. Sarmiento is dismissing Ben."

"What?! Who are you?"

"It's me. Your wife. Dr. Sarmiento just examined Benjy. He removed the IVs and told me Ben was released."

Within the hour, Jim arrived to retrieve us. We left the hospital in such a hurry that we neglected to extend the expected farewells to the medical staff. This caused hurt feelings, as our quick departure was perceived as ungrateful. A day or two later, we tried to make amends by returning to the floor to offer our formal thanks to the nurses and medical community who had cared for Benjy and for us.

At our last hospital appointment, we took Ben to have his stitches removed. We talked with Dr. Perez, the head of pediatric neurosurgery, and with Dr. Sarmiento. It was a bittersweet goodbye. We hugged and kissed farewell. (As a note of reference, *Sarmiento* means grape vine. This gentleman truly was a source of life and encouragement for us.) Both doctors cautioned us to take Ben to a medical facility on our return to the States, warning that his medical condition was still fragile. A parting word from Dr. Perez gave me a different way to focus on the illness. He advised, "You must remember, the boy has cancer. Cancer does not have the boy."

Right after that appointment, a dozen of us Saints departed for Valle del Lago. We enjoyed five days of meaningful visits with new friends, old friends and family. The doctors had warned that Benj could not enter the swimming pool for fear of wound contamination. Although he had to forego pool privileges, Ben joined all the other excursions and activities we planned for the family.

We rode back to Córdoba and spent a few more valuable days before returning to the States. True to form, the airlines surprised us with a minor glitch regarding our tickets. After calling to confirm our reservations, the local office informed us we had none. Fortunately, we had our pastor's telephone number. His wife Betty called the stateside travel agent, who responded wholeheartedly, vigorously pursuing our cause. Prayers continued. A few calls later, our reservations were swiftly reinstated. As an extra motivation, the agent had told the airlines she might have to discontinue her business with them if they did not straighten up their act. They straightened up and flew right, at least this time.

Glimmers of sunshine and rainbows through the mist

Dealing with an irate and vengeful doctor left me perplexed and mystified. Perhaps he despised us because of our nationality and put it on himself to set the record straight as far as who was in control. Clearly he intended to hurt the one we loved just to watch us writhe in pain. I protected Ben in any way I could. Facing the surgeon with the predicament was not the way out. I had tried to respond in as non-combative a way as possible, swallowing words I might have preferred to speak. At the least, I would have preferred a friendly dialogue without causing a major conflagration. We were trapped and at the mercy of this man's unrestrained temper and clear disdain. From Dr. Moreno's reported actions, others were trapped by him, too.

We didn't stay trapped. God gave us a way out. Dr. Sarmiento took up our cause and immediately responded when he heard our plight. One can only imagine the volcanic eruptions that took place when the surgeon realized his patient had made a hasty withdrawal, securely away from his dictates. Dr. Sarmiento showed us God's mercy and kindness by his willingness to receive the hateful invectives Dr. Moreno would have preferred to pour on us.

Gathering grace gems from the bubbling waters

- Have you ever encountered attacks on someone you care about, even yourself, because you differ from most around you? What did you do? How did you manage this and still maintain your integrity?
- Have you faced an apparently impossible life event and then had it turn around? What happened?
- How has God intervened on your behalf as you have encountered impassable mountains?

North and South to Mexico

As they pass through the Valley of Baka, they make it a place of springs; the autumn rains also cover it with pools
(Psalm 84:6 NIV).

Daniel made up his mind to eat and drink only what God had approved for his people to eat. And he asked the king's chief official for permission not to eat the food and wine served in the royal palace
(Daniel 1:8 CEV).

Then your light shall break forth like the morning, your healing shall spring forth speedily (Isaiah 58:8 NKJV).

We enjoyed an uneventful flight back to the States and arrived in Los Angeles 20 hours after leaving Buenos Aires. Doug and Gloria welcomed us into their home once again. They had done a lot of homework regarding choices for Ben's next course of treatment. Packets of information with video tapes from various medical facilities awaited our perusal. We spent a whirlwind day trying to nail down a decision as to our next destination. Prayers provided us clearer direction.

Finally, we decided to try the Contreras clinic, Oasis of Hope, in Tijuana, Mexico. One of Doug and Gloria's family members had battled Hodgkin's[2] while in his teens. To determine the value of both the treatment and the doctors, this young man contacted his wholistic doctor in Indiana, who affirmed the clinic would offer excellent opportunities for us.

The decision was not an easy one. Our family would separate for an unknown length of time, hoping to offer Benjy a chance at recovery. Jim faced a long drive back home with Chelann, 11, and Katelyn, 5. Meanwhile, I concentrated on a shorter journey with Ben, headed in the opposite direction. At least my Spanish had improved after practicing extensively at the hospital in Argentina.

Two directions

Sunday, January 15, 1995, we bid a tearful goodbye to one another. Katelyn did not understand that she and I were also being separated until Jim loaded both girls into the car, while Ben and I stood on the curb to wave as they drove away. Recalling Katelyn's face and hands pressed against the back window as she cried, "Mama! Mama!" still makes my heart weep.

Once back home, Jim had a daunting task on his hands. He found himself needed: by the girls, his job, the bill collectors, the house, the vehicles. Loving and generous church friends brought in meals several times a week. The girls took care of themselves during the day, with neighbors and church friends checking in. Chelann did her homeschool work, directed Katelyn in hers and performed prearranged household chores. Some of their major altercations stayed under the radar for decades. Thankfully, they endured and survived each other.

After Jim and the girls returned to Oregon, Gloria, her daughter and her baby grandson drove Ben and me to the Oasis of Hope medical clinic in Tijuana. We could not have made it to the clinic without their concerted effort. We needed, and they gave, their encouragement to stay on task as the weight of the battle rested on our shoulders.

Once we entered the clinic, Ben and I encountered additional problems. Blood is taken routinely from all cancer patients. His oncologist notified us that Ben had close to the highest counts he had ever seen. The cancer marker test examines the body's immune system—the higher the score, the lower the immune system, and therefore, the more active the cancer within the body. A high score on that test was not a good sign.

Within a week of starting on the Alivizatos Greek vitamin IV treatment, Ben became gravely ill. The doctor on duty admitted him to the Oasis Hospital.

Benjy spent days eating no food. He started vomiting again and lost any desire to eat. His right eye migrated to the side of his face, causing his vision to blur. As he lay in the bed, separated by a curtain from the other patient, I sang songs and read Scripture verses to him, especially the ones that encouraged us to believe God for his healing.

Losing a new friend

Steve, the man on the other side of the curtain, had liver cancer, externally evidenced by extreme jaundice. Benjy confided, "Mom, I think Steve should transfer into an intensive care unit. He's really sick." Unbeknownst to Ben, we were in intensive care even though it didn't look like the units we had seen in the States.

One afternoon, after I sang out of the Bible for three hours, we heard Steve climb out of bed. When his feet touched the floor, he collapsed to his knees. Within minutes, he died. A couple of days afterward, Steve's dad, came and told me both he and Steve had appreciated listening to the music I sang. Those songs had ushered Steve into the ballads of heaven.

With Steve's death, Benjy seemed to go into a state of shock and depression. It was as though his *fight* had drained from him. An American liaison worker secured a transfer for Benj into a private room. All the while, he grew weaker. I asked him if he wanted something. He sighed, "I just want to go home." Watching him continue to spiral downward, I knelt by his bedside and surrendered. Jesus, here is Ben. You love him far more than I do. I trust You to do the most loving act for him, even if that means taking him to heaven. Do what You wish.

One of the most restful nights I had in days allowed me to experience uninterrupted sleep. I figured the Lord would take Ben while he slept. However, Benjy wasn't finished here, and God didn't call him home. When I awoke the following morning, he sat up in bed, with more color in his face and a stronger presence. He even asked for breakfast. He had wanted little to eat since our arrival ten days earlier. Dr. Jr. came into the room for the morning exam; with one look at Benjy, he chuckled. The previous day, he had muttered, *"Ay Yi Yi Yi,"* in exasperation as he left the room.

The physicians on staff showed exemplary care and concern for their patients. An on-loan neurologist had earned highly admired status with the nurses and anyone else who knew him. Few individuals have crossed my path who exhibit the courtesy, grace and gentleness of Dr. Navarette. Not only was he a gentleman, but the clinicians held him in high regard because of his reputation as a neurologist. They consulted him about brain issues, from reading the MRIs to advising on medication.

One serious dilemma, during Ben's days in the hospital, was his vomiting, which invariably occurred once his four drugs were administered through the IV. A few times of asking what medications were being given alerted me to the fact that he could not tolerate his pain medication, morphine. The nurses changed the order of the medications, thus helping me pinpoint which drug was creating havoc. Without fail, Ben immediately started heaving after the morphine injection. I expressed my concerns with a handful of staff members who insisted that morphine was the gold standard for pain maintenance. However, I continued to see Ben vomiting on each shift after receiving morphine.

The morphine issue quickly resolved after telling Dr. Navarette my observations. Without hesitation, he wrote out a different drug prescription based on my concerns. This same doctor exhibited such gallantry that whenever he left a room, he would bow and then back out, facing the patient until he reached the door. He showed profound respect for each of us. I wasn't looking for a bow, but I appreciated his bowing his ears to listen to me and then heeding the matter.

One of Ben's nurses observed that his veins showed signs of abuse from having received Dilantin in the other hospital. She insisted, "His collapsed veins have been seriously compromised." According to her, a better solution would involve having another *"port"* installed. A Hickman catheter could be inserted on the right side of his chest. This would prevent further collapse of his veins while Ben continued with IV therapy. At the time, this appeared an effective alternative for continued treatment. He came out of the surgery fine but was sore for days following. The port proved a bother, as it required constant irrigation to keep the line clear. It fell out the day we returned home weeks later. Hindsight has better vision, but we didn't have that then.

We secured Ben's MRIs from stateside to allow the medical team in Mexico to review them. In comparing the medical report from Argentina to the American notes, it appeared his tumor was larger on leaving Argentina than it was when Ben originally had brain surgery. The size in question relates to a matter of three to five millimeters. However, at this location on the brain stem, any growth signals a warning alarm.

Because the first vitamin IV treatment did not work as quickly as predicted, the medical staff suggested a regimen of specific radiation. Dr. Jr. addressed Ben and presented this option to him to decide. Ben would receive radiation therapy focused on the site of the tumor itself. Had we opted for the same remedy here in the States, the treatment would blast radiation throughout his entire head, causing an expected drop in IQ points, lowering his cognitive abilities.

Benjy decided in the affirmative, which meant we would visit another clinic where radiation was administered. Trips to radiation each day took the entire morning. Other individuals from the Oasis Clinic, who also needed the treatment, traveled with us. Appointments were handled on a first come, first served basis. Patients could spend upwards of an hour or two before receiving therapy, followed by a wait for everyone in the group to complete their round.

Our new friends who joined us on the radiation clinic trips kept us entertained. Two older gentlemen enjoyed making the experience almost cheerful. A thorn in our side was the taxi driver, Juanco, a self-appointed expert who failed to endear himself to the patients because of his rudeness. During one of our trips, while driving maniacally down the street himself, Juanco honked and yelled at a police officer to "get off the road or learn how to drive." Then he stuck out his arm and banged on the side of the police car with his hand. *Oh, dear Lord, please help us get to the clinic without getting arrested.*

Don devised ways to irritate Juanco by thwarting his plans of returning to the clinic "on time." Juanco incessantly complained that he had a schedule to keep, not, we observed, because he had anything else required of him. Usually, we saw him hanging around chatting with patients and medical staff for hours. The prevailing scuttlebutt hinted the clinic had finally agreed to let him transport people to other locales simply to get him off the premises for a while. True or not, the reports appeared plausible.

Jim's two weekend visits with us bolstered our spirits. Ben ached for his dad our entire stay in Mexico. Jim's energy and spirit spurred Benjy to keep on with the treatments. Spending time with his dad gave Ben the sense this was a temporary stay and not a permanent one.

Girls on their own

Back in the States, the girls had a special friend, Bonnie-jo, who volunteered her love and her time to care for our daughters during Jim's two weekends in Mexico. The first time Jim landed in the San Diego airport, the Portland area experienced a snowstorm which caused the sliding doors in the house to freeze shut. To open the glass door on the patio, the girls poured hot water into the glide. The door immediately opened. Once it was shut again, a greater problem resulted when trying to unjam the bulk of ice that had formed in the crevices. It never shattered. Getting into and out of the house presented a conundrum in the ice and snow. Somehow they managed.

On another weekend, while under Bonnie-jo's care, Chelann almost spent the night at a neighbor's house. Once Katelyn observed her caregiver had fallen asleep on the couch downstairs, the five-year-old put on her dad's boots, stealthily exited the house and sneaked through the darkness to where Chelann was staying, three lots away. Chelann's friend's mom called Bonnie-jo to ask if she were missing someone. On searching, she realized Katelyn's bed was empty. She ran to the neighbors' home to retrieve the escapee.

"Katelyn, why did you leave home?"

"I missed my sister."

Katelyn returned with a proviso. Chelann and her friend had to spend the night at our home just to avoid any extra escapades on Katelyn's part. When asking her decades later about the escape, Katelyn vividly recalled the incident, "I was so scared!" Her fright fueled her desire to reach her sister even faster. Mission accomplished.

Renewing hope in God's plans

On Jim's second trip to Tijuana, he made special arrangements to have Ben's neighborhood friend, Jason, come along. We filled that weekend with as many events as possible. In one of our photos, both boys pretended to break through the chain link border fence to get to the U. S. The fence had a human-size hole in it, so there must have been others who had exited. That visit with Jason and

Jim gave Ben an extra boost and further increased his determination to stay the course.

During our months in Mexico, we met incredible people—the staff at the clinic, the cancer patients and their family members. The atmosphere at the clinic exuded hope. God permitted us to create special bonds as we prayed, shared and wept with one another. The forged relationships resembled those that develop in a foxhole with life and death encounters.

A favorite event for me was chapel time in the clinic's basement. Often, Dr. Contreras, Sr., played choruses on his guitar. Another young man also led us in worship, explaining that even though he was a Mexican national, he had been born in America. Further clarification let us know America is where he found Jesus and was born again. A Russian gentleman gave challenging Bible studies, presenting observations as a seasoned follower of his Savior with a slightly different slant. Among the congregants were a few Amish families. The men sat together in their dark suits. The women, in plain, long dresses, gathered in their group with the children, from babies to young teens. I studied their interactions. The small children sat as quietly and obediently as their older siblings.

Doctors and medical staff presented treatment with politeness and respect. Despite Ben's youth, the physicians honored Ben's ideas, discussing the next steps with him. Although many of the brochures they gave us are gone, I saved a quotation from a booklet we received at the clinic. The statement reflects their philosophy regarding the individual who is beset with a severe illness:

> Being a patient at the Contreras Hospital is an entirely different experience than in traditional hospitals and clinics. Historically, when a patient is under the care of an allopathic doctor, complete power is given over to the physician for the direction of the "healing" process. The patient is a "victim" of some such disease and whatever the doctor and medicine can do for the person is entirely out of the patient's hands. Most often, drugs are given, the patient is told to eat anything he/she wants because it doesn't make any difference anyway, and then told to go home if he is able and do the best he can. The patient resigns himself to his fate.
>
> At the Contreras Hospital, your role is different. The doctor is your

partner and is counting on you for your part, which, by the way, is the most important of all. The doctor deeply cares about you and wants nothing more than your complete healing or remission. Your doctor can help you select which treatment is going to be the most effective for your particular situation and can help administer it. He can advise you, share a compassionate ear when needed, and even pray with you.

… A part of you yearns to live, to have more meaning, more purpose to your life, to be free! You want to feel the sweet peace and gentle love of God. Your heart and soul's desire is to come to the end of your life and hear the words, "You are my beloved in whom I am well pleased."[3]

Besides the expertise of the doctors, joyful anticipation added to their protocol. They did not base their hope on *"feel good"* psychology, but on a deeply grounded faith in Almighty God. The founding physician, who trained at Boston Memorial Children's Hospital, Dr. Ernesto Contreras, Sr., in his 80s, radiated a captivating smile, reflecting a deep and abiding relationship with Jesus Christ. One small comment in their informational brochure states: "We do the difficult—treatments, diet, discipline, prescriptions, etc. God does the impossible— the miracles of life, health and healing." Also scattered throughout their booklet were Scripture verses. The following selection from Romans 8:24-28 (NKJV) encouraged my heart:

For we were saved in this hope, but hope that is seen is not hope; for why does one still hope for what he sees? But if we hope for what we do not see, we eagerly wait for it with perseverance. Likewise, the Spirit also helps in our weaknesses. For we do not know what we should pray for as we ought, but the Spirit Himself makes intercession for us with groanings which cannot be uttered. Now He who searches the hearts knows what the mind of the Spirit is, because He makes intercession for the saints according to the will of God. And we know that all things work together for good to those who love God, to those who are the called according to His purpose.

The weeks continued to pass. Finally, days before spring, we readied ourselves to return home. Dr. Jr. forewarned us that Ben would most likely need further radiation therapy, probably at a clinic in Seattle. The doctor ordered a CAT scan to see how things were progressing, not necessarily for any diagnostic purposes. In amazement, he saw the tumor had shrunk significantly. According to his calculations, the residual effects of the radiation Benj had received should more than take care of what remained of the tumor. He called in his brother, his father and several other doctors to rejoice with us at the astonishing progress Ben had made in the almost two-month stay. Benjy's recovery had been remarkable. Dr. Jr. extolled, "Ben, you are a miracle! This is far more than I ever expected. Thank God!"

We prepared for our leave-taking. This included buying essential vitamins and herbs, a continuation of the treatment. Also, I received further instruction on the care of Ben's Hickman catheter, which ended up unnecessary. It fell out when we arrived home.

At last the day came to exit our hotel room. In my haste, I neglected to drop the room keys off and found them much later in a purse pocket. We were both heading back home, much to our relief. A gracious gentleman, Roberto, took us back over the border. Because we were early, he good-naturedly took us on a tour of Catalina Island. Benj was getting antsy, but we reached the airport on time. As a parting farewell, Roberto encouraged Ben to trust in God and to continue to seek Him in all that he did in his life.

Too much time sightseeing meant we showed up at the airport later than originally projected. Time was now of the essence. I hurriedly handed our tickets to the agent, only to discover the ones I gave her were the older ones from our Argentine excursion. Poor Ben wanted to find an efficient model of a mom right away. Fortunately, the ticket agent allowed us to purchase tickets at the lowest price available that day; she assured me I could receive a reimbursement for the lost tickets once they were found. Indeed, the tickets were located when we arrived home; they had been tucked in between our clothes. Returning those tickets to the airlines granted us our full refund.

Glimmers of sunshine and rainbows through the mist

The time in Mexico, despite hard places with Ben's erratic physical condition, brought refreshment. The doctors could certainly have insisted on worst-case scenarios, as they often saw extremely ill patients. However, they gave us hope. It wasn't a hope that ignored the hard and crushing times. Rather, it was a realistic hope, throwing all our cares on the only One who could carry us in this or in any season. I learned to continue to embrace hope, to look at the possibilities of

God's interventions instead of facing what could be the result without His divine presence. For some, things worsened. Because the atmosphere exuded hopefulness, the patients and their companions also learned to cling to an eternal perspective and not one limited to the earthly realm.

Gathering grace gems from the bubbling waters

- In the story about Steve, where was God? Has God ever used you to give someone hope, courage or a drink of cold water?
- How do you think hope was given and restored to patients at the clinic?
- How can we spread hope to others who have lost theirs?
- What words encourage you to persevere?
- Can you think of people who have stepped in for you? Strangers?
- How would you want someone to encourage you in a hard place? A place which feels like life and death?
- Are there Scriptures you recall that give your heart encouragement?

Footnotes

1. Dexamethasone, the chemical name for Decadron, is an adrenal cortical steroid. This drug is specific for inflammation. In Ben's case, it helped to reduce the swelling in his brain. Uncomfortable side effects commonly accompany this medication. Cortisone meds provide quick results but take a long time for withdrawal as severe symptoms often accompany a failure to continue with at least some of the dosage, admittedly a small percentage.
2. Hodgkin's' disease is a cancer that attacks the lymphatic system. One of my cousins died of the illness as a young adult. Her death was one I couldn't face. Although I lived an hour or two away at college and could possibly have obtained a ride, I had not matured enough to embrace her family and allow my sadness to blend with theirs.
3. This section is from an Oasis of Hope pamphlet. Because over a quarter of a century has passed, the material cannot be secured again. The words come directly from the information we received upon arriving at the clinic. The Scripture referenced is a paraphrase from Mark 1:11.

Section 7. Weighing Anchor: *One Year*

He shall be free at home for one year
(Deuteronomy 24:5 KJ21).

Free at Home

You attend to the earth and water it; with abundance You enrich it. The streams of God are full of water, for You prepare our grain by providing for the earth
(Psalm 65:9 BSB).

What a relief to get back home again! Jim and the girls had kept the house clean and in order. A man of details, Jim had meticulously stacked all the mail (every piece that had arrived in the past two and a half months) in neat piles on the dining room table. I plowed through, but the task swallowed up hours and days.

Diet dos and don'ts

The requirement for me, at this stage, was to re-educate all of us in the nutritious and wholesome food department. Ben's restrictive diet demanded a considerable amount of time to prepare. This resulted in the whole family eating food based on his dietary boundaries, which they did not particularly care for. But it was the only alternative. Of course, they had the options of not eating or else preparing their own meals, but no one hopped onto those band wagons. Beforehand, Ben and I had agreed that I would stick strictly to his diet; I demanded harsher food limitations for myself than for him. I also gave up consuming chocolate for two years as my Daniel[1] fast.

I prepared most of the food from scratch. Food additives, excess salt, refined sugars and flours occupied the forbidden list. Ben needed as many fresh fruits and vegetables as possible, plus foods with low acid and low dairy. Most meat was excluded as well. Further, he took mega doses of prescribed vitamins, along with a few herbal formulas. He swallowed approximately 10-15 pills three times a day. Many of the pills I made by hand with empty gelatin capsules and the powdered ingredients.

The next few months we spent renewing acquaintances, making up goals for the next year and visiting a newfound medical doctor. Our visit with Ben's physician encouraged us when he asked, "What is **my** role in this?" Dr. T. did not pass out a dictum telling us what we could not do or what we had to do. He frankly informed us he had limited knowledge about cancer, and more specifically, about brain tumors. To our immense relief, he agreed to engage as Ben's primary physician. Dr. T. ordered MRIs, scheduled every six months. He oversaw the bi-monthly blood tests to determine Ben's immune system levels. He sent cold-packed blood samples, by air freight, to San Diego. The Contreras laboratory, in a nearby border town, tested the blood and returned the results to Dr. T.

Driver's permit and travels

In June, days following his 15th birthday, Ben passed the exam for his long-awaited driver's permit. Somehow this rite of passage holds great significance in a young person's life, and Ben was no exception. He enjoyed talking about the make and the model of the car he would be getting. When we pointed out that he could have our old yellow van, he formed endless plans about how to jazz it up and make it a streamlined vision of beauty.

Ben traveled that summer. He spent two weeks in Michigan's Upper Peninsula with Aunt Carolyn and my mom. Uncle Jon and Aunt Jane also invited him to visit their cottage in Cedar River, Michigan, where Uncle Jon took him sailing on his catamaran in Lake Michigan's Green Bay (not the town in Wisconsin). Ben loved it and remembered that excursion for months. Uncle Jon later confided that Ben had calmly remarked about a time restriction and the need to return to shore. Perhaps he wasn't as ecstatic as we assumed, but it was memorable.

Not wanting to miss out on any social opportunity and to make up for lost time, Ben accompanied another friend and his family to a beach house they'd rented on the Oregon Coast. While there, the boys rode horses, climbed rocks, jogged the beach and played billiards.

Because Chelann wanted more social involvement, she begged to start public school that fall. I assented and signed her up for sixth grade. She also took piano lessons, showing a natural affinity for the keyboard. Katelyn didn't pine for the public life; perhaps she welcomed more one-on-one time with her mom as I had spent months missing in action, both in Argentina and in Mexico.

Socializing

In September Ben started back to school. He eagerly returned as a sophomore to the thick of activities. After school, he and his friends competed in "bike olympics," which amounted to riding up ramps and performing aerial tricks with their bicycles. He never divulged to me how much he took part, but I'm positive he didn't demur when the opportunity presented itself.

Ben and his friends spent afternoons at Shawn's place. He even spent the night there once. Later he confided that Shawn's mother did not learn that both Ben and another friend were there until later in the evening. Evidently Shawn received a corrective lecture in front of his friends about letting his mom in on his plans. Chagrined, Ben promised not to camp out at anyone's house unless he had prior knowledge that at least one parent was informed. I made a mental note to make sure I also knew the parents were on the same planning page.

In September Ben had a routine blood draw at the doctor's office. One of the staff airmailed the sample in a freezer pack to Mexico for analysis. The results disclosed that his immune system had arrived at a super mark. A "normal" reading was around 2.5. Ben's came in even lower at 2.3. How thankful we were for that outcome!

He welcomed school and worked painstakingly on the assignments in all his classes. One of Ben's burning desires was to return to soccer. He talked about meeting with his soccer coach, Mike, to see when he could get back onto the team. To train, Ben walked home from school every day, about two and a half miles from where we live. Because our house rests at the top of a steep butte, the last mile was all uphill.

Pain in the neck

At the beginning of October, Ben complained of neck pain. Initially, we assumed that his overloaded backpack stressed his body and increased his discomfort. He hauled the backpack around in school and on the walk home. In mid-October, he started going to a chiropractor twice a week. His doctor showed great interest in his medical history and assured me he would manipulate him gently, as he was unsure about this neck problem. The chiropractor approached Ben's treatment with the premise that it could be stress related, but always reminded me that this could be a problem with the tumor recurring.

Meanwhile, we had welcomed two foster sons, two brothers ages 8 and 10, who were to stay with us for the duration of the school year. Because Ben had extra bunk beds in his room, we took those out for the boys. Ben supposed he'd feel better sleeping on the floor than on a soft bed, since a hard surface should be better for a neck and back problem. Eventually, we settled him onto a wooden-framed futon with a sturdy mattress.

As time passed, his neck ache continued. We called his physician, Dr. T., for a consultation. He advised that Ben have an MRI, as his condition did not appear to be improving following the onset of the neck problem. He had also started complaining of numbness in his feet and mentioned that he had little feeling in his ankles.

The MRI revealed the tumor had metastasized into his spine and had grown larger at his neck. It had progressed, seeding itself into other areas along the entire length of the spinal column. In addition, the tumor had extended into other regions of his brain.

Dr. T. set up appointments on a Thursday with two of the hospital oncologists, a radiation therapist and a chemotherapist. The radiation therapist, a portly man in his early 60s, asked questions about Ben's treatment and medical history. I visited him alone, not taking Ben with me, as this was a setback enough; Benjy didn't need to listen to more devastating news from another physician. After grilling me for an hour, the physician insisted I return in two hours for more discussion. At the afternoon appointment, he launched more scathing criticisms regarding the actions we had taken. He seemed livid about our medical interventions and stated that we "really cared little about the boy." Once I could escape from the diatribe, I ran to the car and cried the entire drive home. His acerbic tongue lashing had blistered my soul.

The appointment with the chemotherapist was scheduled for late afternoon. Betty, our pastor's wife, willingly consented to accompany me, for fear there would be similar opposition. Our fears were ungrounded. This doctor demonstrated grace, kindness and understanding. He, himself, had been a missionary kid and recognized the Saint name. He reassured me that he promoted health and healing. I asked him about an approach developed by a doctor in Texas. Although he was unaware of the treatment, he promised to work with the suggested protocol, if possible. Additionally, he divulged that the radiation therapist, with whom I had met earlier, was simply on loan for less than a week and rarely consulted with patients or their families. It was good to receive assurance that he wasn't necessarily their man of choice and presumably would not advise other unsuspecting families. Maybe I prevented someone else from enduring a heartbreaking consultation.

Calling friends and other organizations, I collected information about the less invasive procedure, which had some outstanding results. After hours of research, we learned the National Institute of Health had phased out their experimental work with the antiangiogenesis therapy. Therefore, regardless of his willingness, the chemotherapist could not assist us in administering the medication since this was no longer a viable medical alternative at his hospital.

The only other option available was to meet with another radiation oncologist, who seemed sympathetic to our situation. She took pains to attend a seminar at the hospital where Ben initially had surgery and his first treatment. This doctor asked what kind of help they could give, but she returned disappointed, with no more answers than when she started. She suggested a course of massive radiation. After this treatment, Ben would stay in his present condition regarding his movements and muscle strength. This would supposedly prevent, or at least mitigate, the severe pain from the tumor. However, the side effects included loss of all his hair, continual sore throat, constant nausea and terrible stomachaches. When asked if this would affect his cognition, her guarded answer revealed this would not be an issue. In short, he would die before we would even notice any change in his mental state.

She then turned to Ben and asked, "What would you like to do?"

He had sat silently, listening to the ominous predictions. His eyes filled with tears as he choked out a reply. "I just want to play soccer."

Her response eliminated the soccer possibility when she inquired, "Don't you like to read?"

I am not sure why she offered him a choice. Perhaps she had been trained to ask open-ended questions. Unfortunately, she couldn't offer much hope. She was kind but couldn't address or fulfill his dreams. From a human standpoint, no one could.

The doctor then informed us she would order more tests. She wanted us to return for bone scans soon. The following day, the hospital called while Ben was in class. They had scheduled a bone scan, and I arranged to take him after school.

On picking him up, I announced, "The bone scans have been scheduled. We'll go this afternoon."

Ben answered, "No, I am not going."

"Why?"

"Because every time they do a test, the results are worse than they were before. I'm not going through this anymore. They cannot help me, anyway. Only God can."

I would like to say that Ben's impassioned statement persuaded me to leave him alone. My mind raced. Perhaps another diet. Of course, there was always the radiation. At least something would be done. Isn't it better than nothing? I begged him while we were in the car to consider the radiation option.

"Ben, I don't want to see you suffer." (Radiation promised more suffering. Who was I kidding?)

He answered, firmly and quietly, "I will not go through with it."

No more discussion. His responses showed he had studied this carefully. We had left some decisions in his hands, knowing and respecting his wisdom and maturity. Critical to supporting him was learning to hand him the reins, and essentially, to hand God the reins and trust Him.

Glimmers of sunshine and rainbows through the mist

With the return of the tumor and Ben's increased discomfort, I was beside myself. How could I help him? I wasn't always consulting God on this matter. What could I do to improve the situation? There were few options open; I planned to continue investigating possibilities. I read more books, searching for a better way out.

Dr. Contreras, Sr., offered me a treasured conversation soon after we learned of Benjy's condition, when he called and spoke with me, offering his kind understanding. It amazed me he took the time to call, long distance, to express, not only his concern, but his faith in an all-sustaining God, the One who knows the number of our days and who is ready to take us home with Him to a celestial land, not a temporal abode here on earth. He understood Benj's condition. He didn't sugarcoat it with platitudes but made the simple statement, "We know where he is going."

Gathering grace gems from the bubbling waters

- When facing tough decisions, what is your usual way to handle the situation? Do you look for other ways around the inevitable? Do you accept there may not be more answers?
- When is faith a matter of accepting what we don't want to endure? How is it characterized in your own life?
- Has anyone ever contacted you to breathe the breath of God into your weary soul? How was it done?

Fret Not

Be patient, then, brothers, until the Lord's coming. See how the farmer awaits the precious fruit of the soil—how patient he is for the fall and spring rains

(James 5:7 BSB).

A pointed devotional from *My Utmost for His Highest* by Oswald Chambers on November 15th pierced my heart as I recognized my complicity in not releasing God's activity into Ben's life. I tried using my best arguments to exercise my influence. The problem is, God didn't want my influence. He was moving in another direction. He was holding sway over Ben's life, but not on my terms.

> John 21:21,22: "*Lord, what shall this man do? What is that to thee? Follow thou Me.*" One of our severest lessons comes from the stubborn refusal to see that we must not interfere in other people's lives. It takes a long time to realize the danger of being an amateur providence who is interfering with God's orders for others. You see a certain person suffering, and you say—He shall not suffer, and I will see that he does not. You put your hand straight in front of God's permissive will to prevent it, and God says, "*What is that to thee?*"
>
> Most of us live on the borders of consciousness—consciously serving, consciously devoted to God. All this is immature; it is not the real life yet. The mature stage is the life of a child which is never conscious; we become so abandoned to God that the consciousness of being used never enters in. When we are consciously being used as broken bread and poured-out wine, there is another stage to be reached, where all consciousness of ourselves and of what God is doing through us is eliminated. A saint is never consciously a saint; a saint is consciously dependent on God.[2]

His terms

The words struck home. Ben was willing to suffer on his own terms. I was trying to protect him because of what I dreaded; I was unwilling to release him to what I feared. Simply put, I attempted to protect myself from his pain.

Agonizing over the distressing news, I felt the same hopeless abandonment I had experienced years earlier when the doctor diagnosed Alyssa with her illness.

For five days, I fasted and cried impassioned prayers for some word from God. I longed for something that would tell me He was part of all of this. From my personal diary, I composed the following prayer:

> Dear God, I desperately need to hear from You. I need Your peace, Your joy. You have promised to answer from heaven when I cry out to You. I am crying out, Lord. What is it You want to say to me—to us? Your ways are beyond finding out, but in Your word, it says, "'Come now, let us reason together,' saith the Lord." (Isaiah 1:18)
>
> "Precious child, let go of the future. Let go of today. I will work out a plan for you. I LOVE you. My love is immeasurable. I have not abandoned you. Listen to Me. Let your heart and mind be quiet. I have words for you to hear. Be still. Your worries are My concern. Release them to Me. I can and I will take care of things.
>
> "Don't you trust Me? I am a gracious, good and loving Father—no good thing will I withhold from you. Look up. Keep your eyes stayed on Me. I will not disappoint you. My work is not only in you. Remember that. My concern is that all come into My glory, not just you. Let not your heart be troubled, neither let it be afraid. In the world you will have tribulation, but be of good cheer, for I have overcome the world. There is nothing I ask you to do that I can't handle. Nothing. Be a vessel, a channel. You are not My machine. You only hold that which I have entrusted to you.
>
> "There is now therefore no condemnation to those who are in ME, Christ Jesus. I have redeemed you. I have called you by My name. You are Mine."

Trust God

Finally, on November 18th, the sixth morning of my fast, the familiar words found in 2 Corinthians 12:9 came again: *"My grace is sufficient for you."* Those same words had encouraged me exactly ten years earlier, prior to our move to Oregon. All right, Lord, it doesn't look like I have much choice. I will stop worrying and trust you to do the very best for us. You know what I can handle. And you know how to keep Ben and our whole family in Your loving arms.

Sunday morning Jim and I spoke briefly to the congregation at church about Benjy's latest medical prognosis. Jim made the statement, "No matter what, I trust God." I shared what God had revealed to me about grace and the Oswald Chambers passage that had addressed our situation.

Fret not

The guest speaker, Rev. Paul Hawkins, had changed his entire sermon emphasis right before the start of the service without realizing why, but sensing he was obeying God. His emphasis was: *Trust God.* As he knit his sermon with the few words we had shared, he also mentioned that in other cultures, there is a sense of *we*. In English-speaking cultures, the message is *I*. He challenged our church body to think in terms of *we* when various ones of us encounter severe trials. He intertwined Psalm 37 (AMP) with his message, starting with the beginning verse, "*Fret* not yourself..." "Trust (lean on, rely on and be confident) in the Lord," continuing on in verse 3 and then to: "Delight yourself also in the Lord... Commit your way to the Lord... Be still and rest in the Lord; wait for Him and patiently stay yourself upon Him; fret not yourself." The word *"fret"* encompasses uncomfortable definitions when considering God's command not to fret. He enumerated the meanings of the word: crossness, tantrum, tizzy, fume, pet, fit of temper, burst of anger, stew, ferment, agitation, gnaw, fray, make ragged, caterwaul, squall, boohoo, whine, whimper, wail, mewl, pule, weep, yammer, moan, sigh, sob,[3] to cause to be uneasy, to disturb the surface, brood, become corroded.[4]

Rev. Hawkins did not leave us any room or excuse for *fretting* after explaining this word's various definitions. Primarily, the Lord did not leave any room for such behavior. The speaker also referred to selections from Oswald Chambers' writings.

> Never trample in with religious common sense and say, "Oh, yes, with a little more Bible reading and devotion and prayer, I see how it can be done."
>
> It is much easier to do something than to trust in God; we mistake panic for inspiration. That is why there are so few workers with God and so many workers for Him. We would far rather work for God than believe in Him. The degree of panic is the degree of the lack of personal experience.[5]

What are you dreading? You are not a coward about it; you are going to face it, but there is a feeling of dread. When there is nothing and no one to help you, say, "But the Lord is my Helper, this second, in my present outlook." Are you learning to say things after listening to God, or are you saying things and trying to make God's Word fit it? Get hold of the Father's say-so, and then say with good courage, "I will not fear." It does not matter what evil or wrong may be in the way; He has said, "I will never leave thee." [6]

Baptism

During the season of Thanksgiving, the next issue we encountered was not physical, but spiritual. Although each of our children had made decisions to follow Jesus, none of them had been baptized. I spoke to Ben frequently about this during the week after November 18th. There were several verses of Scripture that I shared with him. The one which moved me and convinced Ben of his need to be obedient in this matter was Matthew 3:15 (ESV): *But Jesus answered him, "Let it be so now, for thus it is fitting for us to fulfill all righteousness."* Then he consented. On a Saturday afternoon, in a small, private ceremony, Pastor Bruce baptized Ben, Chelann and Katelyn, with only a few present: our pastor and his wife, our two church elders, two members of the diaconate, our two foster sons, my mother (visiting from Arizona), Jim and me. There was nothing more to do but wait and see what God would do. Humanly speaking, we had done all we knew to make a way for Ben's healing.

Ben continued to attend school until after Thanksgiving. He could barely walk, and we feared that if he fell, he would not have the strength to get up; but he insisted he must attend his classes. The last few weeks of November, he tired easily and returned home to sleep for several hours after half days at school.

Several staff members from the high school—his counselor, the school psychologist and the school nurse—scheduled an intervention for his benefit. We discussed ways in which he could better attend school and still be protected. They suggested letting him use the staff elevator, assigning students to carry his books, etc. Someone also asked about securing a wheelchair. I noted he would probably lose the use of his hands before he lost the ability to walk. In the end, he would allow no one to treat him any differently than the other students. His goal was to stay as normal as possible for as long as he could.

Benj worked hard and pursued his subjects with fervor. He needed to write and compose reports. I recall one he had to rewrite for a combined English and humanities class. He labored relentlessly for hours on the word processor. His strength was quickly waning. Painfully, he struck the keys with feeble hands. He did not make, nor did he allow anyone else to make, excuses for him. Often he made me think of a poem I had memorized in sixth grade, "If" by Rudyard Kipling.[7] In reviewing the poem, I would change the last section to read, "If you can trust the Lord and keep on trusting, despite all that life slings at you, you will receive your crown in glory and be God's own man, my son."

Finally, the day came in early December when Ben acknowledged he could not continue attending classes. His grades, up to that point, were excellent, all As. Although we notified the school of his condition, some teachers continued to grade him, factoring in the missing assignments as zeros. By the time the term ended in February, his grades had plummeted, although there were merciful instructors who granted him As. He still cared about his marks and wanted to know what he had received. He worried about making up the courses he was missing. Lacking physical strength, Ben could not even attempt home studies. He often asked me, "How am I ever going to make up for all the time I have lost?" I gave him some platitudes, but he wasn't convinced as he continued to express concern.

Dad shadow

Taking Ben to work thrilled Jim (and Benjy). In early December, the two rode in Jim's 18-wheeler together, with Ben gently letting his dad know that he (Ben), if given the opportunity, could have handled the difficult maneuvers with ease. He met many of the men at Jim's work and several of the customers with whom Jim had shared about his condition. Ben could not get out of the truck because he lacked the strength, but he endured and returned home, beaming from the experience.

A week later, on a sunny December Sunday afternoon, Jim and Ben decided to make a day of it, driving along the scenic Columbia River Gorge. They talked of the countless familiar places our family had enjoyed since moving to the Northwest 10 years earlier. Their trip, however, only lasted about 12 minutes as they became involved in a minor car accident before leaving Gresham. The other driver admitted his fault; the damages were eventually covered monetarily, eliminating that concern; but we still had a damaged vehicle. Although it was the last time the two of them traveled alone together, the accident was impressive. Right after the crash, Ben's first words were, "Wow, Dad, that was awesome!" He also joked about having whiplash. His neck was unbearably stiff and sore, not from the accident, we all knew, but from the metastasized tumor at its base.

Glimmers of sunshine and rainbows through the mist

Releasing Benjy to the latest unknown physical onslaught cost me. I looked for another way out. As Rev. Hawkins quoted Oswald Chambers, for me, I was learning to do nothing. That week had wrung out my energy and inventiveness. I had foolishly believed that if I were involved in actively promoting his health through some interaction or intervention, I would contribute to his welfare. I could not. The more I investigated, the more the focus was on me and my agenda. Truthfully, I was not moving in a positive direction and finally had to let go and trust. God had His plans, and I had to get out of the way to let God have His way.

Gathering grace gems from the bubbling waters

- Have you ever faced a dilemma in which you had to wait and do nothing else?
- What did it feel like? How did you respond? What took away the discomfort?
- Are there ways that you cope in the times of hard challenges? Do you pray, read Scripture, read other books, sing?
- How do you find peace?

Five Months—Sufficient Grace

My soul thirsts for God, the living God. When shall I come and appear in God's presence?

(Psalm 42:2 BSB).

But He said to me, "My grace is sufficient for you"

(2 Corinthians 12:9 NIV).

An early Christmas gift in December of that year was a new puppy for Ben. For months after school, Benj had studied the classified ads in the newspaper, searching for the dog of his dreams. Men at work heard that he wanted a Shar-Pei. He had wanted a pug, but somehow this was translated into a Shar-Pei, maybe because it was a gift. I read about Shar-Peis and learned they were high need. With extra kids in the house, we had more than enough love and attention to meet those needs. My interpretation and the facts were located poles apart. They are high need because of their health care issues and their powerful personalities.

Dogged determination

Steve, a sales representative at Jim's work, had explained to me about the dog. I was hesitant, knowing Ben wanted a different breed, but Steve extolled the virtues of the dog and insisted the puppy would fit inside a shoe box. We did not realize the box he referred to would have fit Paul Bunyan's shoes. He even told me he felt this was a divine plan because this dog was offered to them. That convinced me. Who was I to argue with a divine plan? Many of Jim's coworkers had collected funds to give Ben a special gift. They strategized to buy a dog with the money, but a breeder offered to give Ben the puppy. The woman and her husband delivered Sterling to our home. He was a three-month-old black pile of wrinkles who gave Benjy hours of enjoyment, just because Sterling was Ben's own designated pet.

Due to his progressive weakness, Ben could not attend Jim's company Christmas party. He allowed us to take his puppy inside the office to show Sterling to the people gathered. The puppy had suffered from an infection that week. After one dose of antibiotic from the vet earlier in the day, he suddenly developed a hyperactive personality. He became more of a handful as he grew out of puppyhood. Ben doted on Sterling, calling him "one rad dog." The dog gave him an incentive to plan on training techniques when he would recover. Therefore, we endured this blessing for months.

As a family, we celebrate each Christmas with an annual tree-cutting expedition. Jim carried Ben to the front seat of our van; we five piled into the back. At the tree farm, Chelann, Katelyn, Brandon, Randall (our two foster sons) and Jim actively engaged in choosing the best tree. Ben and I sat in the van and visited while the troops searched for the elusive evergreen. Finally, they made their choice. We returned home to put it up and decorate it. "Merry Christmas!"

Christmas visitors

A week after the kids started Christmas vacation, Ben and I both succumbed to a flu virus. A severe ice storm left us without electrical power. One morning, I found Ben collapsed on the floor of his bathroom. Severely weak, he could not move. Both of us ran a fever, but Ben's state was obviously far more severe than mine. Somehow Jim kept the other four children busy upstairs for part of the day while Ben and I languished, sick and feverish, on the couches in the den. The wood stove burned bright and warm. There was no heat upstairs.

The next day, two greathearted men, Harley (his clown name) and Jerry, from the Make a Wish Foundation, arrived to ask Ben about a wish he would like to make. In reaching our house, they lived out the postman's motto of "neither rain, nor sleet, nor dark of night shall keep these men from their appointed tasks." They had slipped and slid up our street, having to walk on a slick roadway about half a block up to our driveway from where they had left their cars. We were stunned to see them on our front doorstep that Sunday afternoon, knowing full well we would not have attempted the trip ourselves.

Given the chance to make a special wish ignited Ben's imagination. We had spent several days joking about the wish being something we could all use. He would make up an imaginary conversation. "No, sir, my parents had nothing to do with my wanting the house painted as my special wish." He ended up telling them he would like a PlayStation or a remote-control car. Within a week, they brought him a PlayStation with 11 games and a TV set. Not being a TV fan, this did not look like such an ideal arrangement to me. However, I was wrong. It was a blessing for Ben, in the weeks of being confined to his bed, to have a television to watch, especially when I was unavailable to read to him or talk with him. His hands had weakened so rapidly within the week that he could not use the controls from the PlayStation. However, because he understood the idiosyncrasies of the games, he directed others when they ran into obstacles as they played.

More hard places

By Christmas, my mom from Arizona and Aunt Carolyn from Michigan had joined us. Ben could no longer walk and needed to rely on his dad to carry him where he needed to go. He spent more and more time in his bedroom. We celebrated Christmas, not by the Christmas tree upstairs, but down in the den, next to his bedroom. Even though we had some gifts to exchange, all nine of us mostly appreciated the gift of spending time together.

Following Christmas, Ben's condition declined rapidly. He regressed from being unable to walk to being unable to sit up unaided within two to three weeks. Besides the severe pain Ben experienced in his neck, similar, I believe to having a stiff neck for months without end, he also suffered from painful leg spasms when lying down. After a month, those subsided, giving way to other discomforts.

The Portland Adventist Hospice program agreed to enroll Ben, something for which we were most grateful. He has been the only young person they accepted. To this day, they haven't had another youth. A hospice volunteer came to stay with Ben so that I could attend Bible study for a couple of hours once a week. Sherri, Ben's nurse, gave me invaluable support. I shared Ben's and my needs with her while she encouraged and advised where needed. When he endured bad days (more severe pain and greater nausea), she ordered medication changes immediately. Benjy was not comfortable with others looking in on him. So, his nurse became my major support as she looked in on me.

Day in and day out, we kept up the battle against the emotional ravages caused by this illness. I read books, Scriptures and letters. We also prayed together. John Michael and Terry Talbot, brothers whose lyrical songs speak of God's love and care, encouraged us during those days. Ben's favorite Talbot song narrated a story about Jesus as He was walking through a town, healing all the sick. He and I also sang together. One Scripture I clung to over the many months of Ben's illness affirmed (Isaiah 58:8 KJV):

Then shall thy light break forth in the morning,
And thine health shall spring forth speedily.
Thy righteousness shall go before thee.
The glory of the Lord shall be thy reward.

The Heart of Praise by Jack Hayford emphasizes the importance of maintaining songs in one's heart. Tenets in the chapter entitled "Aggressiveness in Worship" became a driving force in my life and in Ben's:

Let the saints be joyful in glory; let them sing aloud on their beds. Let the high praises of God be in their mouth, and a two-edged sword in their hand

(Psalm 145:5,6 NKJV).

In 2 Chronicles 20:2, King Jehoshaphat, undermanned and relatively powerless, has been brought word that *"a great multitude is coming against you."* You know, or know someone who knows, the empty feeling: word comes of a dread disease leaving only weeks or months to live… business going under… broken relationship… abandonment. This text gives direction on what can be done in such moments, something besides resigning to a passive prayer for strength.

Uncommonly threatening situations call for [an] uncommonly strong response: for taking up a "two-edged sword" in a spiritual sense—aggressively trusting God, forcefully throwing ourselves in worship at His feet, and boldly brandishing the spiritual weapons Jehoshaphat used. They still work to put doubt and fear and anxiety to flight.[8]

Some days we delved into discussions about his life plans. Ben shared about his thoughts and dreams for the future. College, marriage and a family of four children were among his goals. He also fretted over the lost credits in school and asked if he would have enough credits to graduate from high school with his classmates. He hoped to buy a car so that he could drive to school. My mother, back home in Arizona by this time to oversee my dad's care, helped to spur this on by offering him her Toyota. He enjoyed contemplating the offer for about a week. Then he confided, "Mom, I can't take her car. I don't want to hurt her feelings, but it just wouldn't be right."

One day while Ben was watching TV, the narrator referred to people suffering from paralysis. Ben commented sympathetically, "Being paralyzed would be really hard." Although he could not move his legs and had only slight hand movement, he never perceived his bedridden condition as paralysis.

Benjy showed extreme reluctance to invite friends to visit, especially those who had known him on the soccer field. Finally, in exasperation, I confronted him one day and asked, "Ben, why aren't you letting any of your friends come to see you? They want to visit you and do something for you." Wearily, he replied, "Mom, I just want them to remember me the way I was when I was healthy."

We did not talk about his dying in those weeks and months of pain and debilitation. We talked of hope and healing, of the Lord's coming. Ben had heard enough medical prognoses to know where he was headed if God didn't choose to heal him here. For hours a day, he was quiet and still. He did not whine or complain, but with firm determination, he met what was ahead, whatever it might be.

In March, Ben had a severe episode of pain. It appeared he was dying. Jim rushed home early from work. Aunt Carolyn, who had stayed months to help with the household, was in the room. His nurse came. Pastors Bruce and Betty arrived to offer support. Dan, a young man from church, joined us to pray. An emergency run for medications was made to a location on the other side of town (most times, his medications arrived at the house). With the administration of new drugs, his crisis subsided. However, he was not as cognizant as before and seemed to experience more of a haze, which remained for five days. Then he improved somewhat. His mind returned to an increased awareness. He had little memory of the previous week and regretted that he had lost time.

Benjy did, however, remember people praying for him in his room. He asked me who had come and how many were at his bedside. I listed the names of each person who had joined us and explained there were seven of us. Undeterred, he insisted, "No, there were eight people in my bedroom. There was someone else. Who was it?" I didn't see anyone else. Did Jesus come to minister to him? Was there an angel?

Amazingly, God preserved Ben's ability to reason. His mind stayed sharp in several important areas, especially during conversation. He didn't always remember events from weeks prior and felt devastated that he had no recollection of his summer vacation.

His sense of humor stayed with him during those trying days. With his droll wit, he often countered my pronouncements with a one-liner that caught me off guard. One day, while talking about his need to tutor his younger sister, Katelyn, I suggested he do a task with her, which she didn't like. He rejoined, "Mom, she hates to do that." I urged, "That's okay. Have her do it anyway." Showing strained patience, he wryly observed, "Mom, that's the difference between you and me. I ***want*** her to like me."

Ben met the humiliation of bed care with the dignity and presence of a nobleman. He continually showed gratitude. That is one change Benjy exhibited; he became more effusive in his language. In the past, he rarely used flattering or flowery language. During those months of isolation and confinement, he constantly expressed appreciation. Instead of becoming surly and bitter, he evidenced even greater tenderness and love.

Glimmers of sunshine and rainbows through the mist

Of great value to me were those who talked to me on the phone or sent cards, either to me or Benjy. One young woman called me late at night from back East. She had been a patient in Mexico at the same time Ben was there. She shared how God had touched her heart in the days after she left and the changes He had made in her life. Another lady, whose daughter had died in the winter from the same kind of tumor as Ben had, contacted me with life-encouraging words as she shared about her daughter's writings and experiences. My brother, whose mind is like Ben's in both humor and manner, would call to encourage me. He didn't talk about Ben's condition. Instead, he discussed creation and the stars of the heavens, the amazing varieties of colors. Hearing about God's care for the stars gave me an incredible peace and reassurance in realizing He also cared about me and the ones I loved.

Considering the challenges presented, I thank God for preserving Ben's mind, except for brief periods. I know there are many with brain tumors who have become non-verbal for months. God graciously kept the communication window open.

Through our hours together, Benjy and I entered sacred ground in our conversation. I looked into the windows of his soul, into rooms we had never previously entered. There wasn't much we didn't talk about. He was living a lifetime with me as the beneficiary of his words of wisdom and understanding. As his primary caregiver, I accepted Ben's dependence on me for his emotional, spiritual and physical support. God endowed me with a rare opportunity, a gift of immeasurable value and cost.

Gathering grace gems from the bubbling waters

- Has someone much younger than you taught you any life lessons? What did you learn that has kept you more aware and more grounded in life?
- What have you learned from someone who is ill? What can that person impart that healthy individuals cannot share?
- How would you support or encourage someone who is afflicted with an incurable disease?
- Can you think of a way to inspire caregivers who are weary of well doing?

Favored Smiles

I thirst

(John 19:28 NKJV).

But those who drink the water I give will never be thirsty again. It becomes a fresh, bubbling spring within them, giving them eternal life

(John 4:14 NLT).

Although Ben only had a couple of severely traumatic periods of unresponsiveness and pain, each time he returned from one of them, he, himself, noted a more severe weakness. Each siege left him with a little less that he could accomplish.

I continued to log into my diary to preserve a record of the daily events. Those written words helped me stay focused. The act of writing gave me more purpose and more hope for what I was walking through. It defined the experiences. In early April, I wrote about God's work and Benjy's condition:

Ben is sleeping more now than before. He is weak, eating little. Physically, there have been no improvements that I can detect—he's not noting any either. This is discouraging for me to believe and confess and expect and hope.

Faith is the substance of things hoped for

But God…

But God…

But God…

Since his hardest episode over a month ago, he has not experienced difficulty speaking or communicating except for a midnight event last week. I prayed against confusion, and the difficulty lasted only a few minutes.

Ben is not complaining. He keeps on each day, facing it courageously. He is not whining about how long this is taking. Occasionally, he expresses frustration. That is the exception. He suffers so much—beyond any level of endurance I could reach. Through this, I must believe that God is doing a deep work in his heart. I know that God's love for Ben is limitless.

God is allowing him to pass through this trial, not only for a ministry here on earth but also for an eternal weight, one that surely cannot be fathomed or measured by me.

This walk of blind faith has been the most challenging yet. It is simply **hard**. *I have asked, often, for a sign. Nothing. No visible evidence of any improvement. So, should I take it that is the sign? Is the observation that Ben's not improving a sign, a sign of God's intention to take him to heaven? Or is it simply that He is waiting to heal Benj at the most opportune moment? Also, Ben is still alive when others do not survive this beyond days and weeks. He has been here months with no extra medical intervention. That could be a sign, too. Right now, God is not telling. I feel that I have passed the place of handling this—more than I can bear. Yet, we endure because we must. During the night, the song kept ringing in my ears: "Nothing is too difficult with Thee."*[9]

April 10, 1996

On Easter Sunday morning, April 7, 1996, I awoke with the thought, "I am the resurrection and the life…"

Ben's days since Easter have been far improved over his days last week. I am so thankful for these good days when he does not feel dreadfully sick and nauseated. Also, the pain is less than that from last week.

Thursday afternoon, April 18th, Sherri, Ben's nurse, came for her twice-weekly visit to check on his condition. She rarely physically observed Ben, understanding and respecting his desire and need to have few caregivers. She realized his pain level had increased considerably after talking with me; so she dialogued with him about how this could be regulated. She carefully tried to convince him that an IV would offer much better pain management than the medication he was taking. He was adamant. He refused an IV. After she left, he asked, "Doesn't she know how much I hate needles?" My hatred for needles might have dissolved to experience some relief from pain. That was not Ben's inclination; his wishes were respected.

A friend of ours came to visit Ben on Friday evening. His brother had recently died of cancer. Perhaps because of this, his heart displayed a distinct tenderness towards Benjy. Even though we received meals from our church, he had organized other friends to bring in meals, too. He brought Ben a signed Trailblazers basketball. This was the last time Ben could sit up and the last time he felt like eating anything.

The next morning, Saturday, Ben's physical condition worsened. His quantity of pain medication remained the same. He wanted nothing to eat or drink. By Sunday, he was in a semi-delirious state, talking about events from the past. While Jim cared for Benjy on Sunday morning, I attended church and shared about his condition with friends. That evening, he was still in the same place physically. We were standing outside his door, talking about putting a call in to the Yoshiwaras. Ben called out their phone number from his bed. We had doubted he knew what was happening around him. Yet he responded to our conversation.

That night, instead of sleeping in Ben's bedroom, I slept in the adjoining den with the monitor on. He was talking constantly, and I needed some rest. Toward early morning, I awakened to hear him calling out to various family members and our pastor. First he called, "Mom!" When I did not respond right away, he called on others: "Dad! Chelann! Katelyn! Grandma! Aunt Carolyn! Uncle Joe! Pastor Bruce!" Curious, I continued to listen. "Would someone please take this weight out of my hands? It is so heavy! I can't carry it anymore." Then I realized the pain level had increased in his neck. I ran in and gave him medication. In a deeper sense, the weight of the illness would allow none of us to take that out of his hands.

Talking through memories

On Monday Ben talked through his life. Subject to the person he was talking to or about and the surroundings he was relating to, I could usually determine which life event or stage he was envisioning. For some inexplicable reason, I could interrupt his reverie by asking him what was going on or what he had been doing. He would then answer me coherently. For example, once he asked if we had one or two catamarans. We do not have any, but Uncle Jon owned one, the one on which Ben had sailed the previous summer.

Pastor Bruce and Betty also came over for an hour to see Ben in the early afternoon. Pastor detected Ben was not responding to his comments. As they prepared to leave, Betty reassured him, "Ben, I love you." He called out to her, "I love you, too."

In the evening, I came in and found Ben softly laughing. This was not a typical reaction of his, especially during any of his more troublesome episodes. Curious, I asked, "Ben, what on earth are you finding to laugh about?"

"It's a new building. It's being built. You wouldn't understand."

"Have you been talking to Jesus?"

"Yes."

"You saw Him? Oh, what did He say?"

After I posed those questions, he looked at me, rolled his eyes and responded in exasperation, "Oh, Mom." He didn't say it, but he probably wanted to say, "When will you ever grow up?"

That evening, Ben called out to his little sister, Katelyn, who had been standing quietly near his doorway. With a bounce, she happily entered the room to see her big brother. Katelyn walked to the head of his bed to look at him, face to face. Ben told her he needed a kiss and a hug from her. She leaned over and kissed his head.

Last day not a lost day

He slept more restfully that night. Toward early morning, Jim came into the bedroom and stood for a few minutes, seeing him for what he suspected could be the last time. He quietly withdrew and reluctantly left for work.

I woke up soon after that and made a quick assessment of Ben's condition.

His skin felt clammy, and his breath came irregularly. As we lay there in the stillness, we talked together. He was lucid and aware of what was happening. I asked, "Ben, are you ready to go to heaven to see Jesus now?"

He replied, "I know it's not fair, Mom, but I've been ready for a long time."

"Oh, Benjy, what's not fair? You've endured so much in these past months. We don't want to hold you back."

Our hospice volunteer came over that morning to watch both Ben and Katelyn so I could attend Bible study. However, I was so weary that instead of leaving, I climbed the stairs to take a nap. Rest did not come, but I lay down for an hour to replenish my sagging strength. Afterwards, I called the church to ask Bruce and Betty to come to our house. Within 15 minutes, they arrived.

From pain to joy

Ben's pain had exploded. He moaned that his head hurt. Whenever one of us massaged his temples, he responded, "Thank you, thank you." I strained to hear his comments as he spoke in a barely audible whisper.

"Could I have some water?"

After a small spoonful, he said, "Thank you. That's all I needed."

Besides saying "Thank you," I heard him whisper, "one six."

I asked, "Did you want to live until you were 16?"

He gently nodded his head.

As he labored with each breath, I quietly announced that I should leave the room to call his dad. Benjy heard me.

Weakly, he cried out, "No, no!"

I then assured him, "I'll stay."

Within minutes, his breathing became more strained. Because his pain level was still high, I gave him one more dose of painkiller. He relaxed. Shortly, he started to smile. He smiled three of the most radiant smiles he had given in months. And then he left. He left us for his eternal home, maybe for that building he had seen the night before. He left to enter Jesus' presence.

After Benjy passed, I ran to the phone to call Jim's work, knowing he would want to have first-hand information. I spoke to his dispatcher, who promised me he would let Jim know he needed to come home.

Via the company-issued radio, the dispatcher contacted Jim on what became a party line for the other drivers in their trucks as they listened in.

"Hi, Jim. This is John in dispatch. You need to come back to the terminal. There are things going on at your home."

"Why do I have to come back? Does this have something to do with my boy?"

"Yes, it does."

"Could you please tell me what's happening with my son?"

"Do you want me to share over the radio?"

"Go on ahead and tell me."

"Are you sure you want me to tell you?"

"Yes, I'm sure."

"Ben is no longer with us."

At that point, Jim had already pulled over.

"Thank you. I'll go on ahead and finish my last stop."

Then, as he sat and tried to absorb the news through his tears, he heard coworkers coming onto the radio to express their condolences. This lasted for several minutes.

Jim recalls, "John came back on to ask me how long I would need to finish unloading at the construction site. When I finished that assignment, I headed back to the terminal and talked to my supervisors. They even offered to have someone get me and drive me back, but I assured them I could handle the return drive, which I did. When I got to the terminal, I was supported and encouraged by the other co-workers, dock workers, truck drivers, office personnel and mechanics."

Glimmers of sunshine and rainbows through the mist

Early in the morning on the day Ben died, Chelann had a dream in which she was picked up at school by the hospice volunteer who was helping to care for Benjy and Katelyn at home. She recalled the color of the car and the clothes the volunteer was wearing. When Chelann walked through the front door, she saw our pastor and his wife at the top of the stairs. She recognized the styles and colors of the clothes they had on. She saw people crying. All that she experienced in her dream came to pass that afternoon.

So many prayers were given and so many words were received. We were waiting for God to heal Benjy. God did. Several times, He did. Then Ben's time here was complete. Even though it was not the number of days we would have chosen, God had a greater plan for him. At last He called Ben to eternity, and Ben radiated with joy as he left.

Since the time of an autumn Bible study in 1993, I had announced Proverbs 4:23 as one of my life verses. In the NIV it reads: *Above all else, guard your heart, for out of it flow the wellsprings of life.* Within days of Ben's passing, I realized that key Bible verse, the one that had meant so much to me over the past two and a half years, held the date of his home going, April 23 or 4/23.

Two years after Benjy's death, Chelann composed a poem for herself about her heartache. It had been difficult for her to resolve his death, as we had focused so many of our prayers for his healing. She wasn't prepared. In some ways, none of us were.

Gone,
Yet Not Forgotten
You left my heart so empty,
Yet you left my heart so full.
You left my heart aching with pain,
Yet you left my heart aching with joy.
My heart is so empty of your presence,
Yet you left my heart so full, with memories of you.
My heart aches with pain from your absence,
Yet my heart aches with joy from the absence of your pain.
You are gone from my life,
Yet you are not forgotten from my heart.
Chelann Saint (Holmes)

Gathering grace gems from the bubbling waters

- What do you do to help others deal with or face difficult circumstances?
- Even though years have passed, we still miss our son, brother and friend. How do you honor or remember loved ones who have died?
- Did you note anything about Benjy's life that might enhance your own?

- Is there something you would like to remember from this episode in our lives? Is there a takeaway?

Footnotes

1. Personally, I looked at the chocolate fast as relinquishing something I enjoyed as a prayerful sacrifice to God while listening to His voice. The story of Daniel's fast can be found in Daniel 1:8-14, 10:3.
2. Chambers 320
3. The Original Roget's Thesaurus of English Words and Phrases
4. The American Heritage® Dictionary of the English Language
5. Chambers 153
6. Chambers 157
7.

If

Rudyard Kipling

If you can keep your head when all about you
Are losing theirs and blaming it on you;
If you can trust yourself when all men doubt you,
But make allowance for their doubting too;
If you can wait and not be tired by waiting,
Or, being lied about, don't deal in lies,
Or being hated, don't give way to hating,
And yet don't look too good, nor talk too wise.

If you can dream - and not make dreams your master;
If you can think - and not make thoughts your aim,
If you can meet with Triumph and Disaster
And treat those two impostors just the same:
If you can bear to hear the truth you've spoken
Twisted by knaves to make a trap for fools,
Or watch the things you gave your life to, broken,
And stoop and build 'em up with worn-out tools;

If you can make one heap of all your winnings
And risk it on one turn of pitch-and-toss,
And lose, and start again at your beginnings,
And never breathe a word about your loss:
If you can force your heart and nerve and sinew

To serve your turn long after they are gone,
And so hold on when there is nothing in you,
Except the Will which says to them: *"Hold on!"*

If you can talk with crowds and keep your virtue,
Or walk with Kings - nor lose the common touch,
If neither foes nor loving friends can hurt you,
If all men count with you, but none too much;
If you can fill the unforgiving minute
With sixty seconds' worth of distance run,
Yours is the Earth and everything that's in it,
And - which is more - you'll be a Man, my son!

8. Hayford, pp. 153-155
9. Chance.

Section 8. Filling Our Cups at the Waterfall: Such Sweet Sorrow

It was also called Mizpah, because Laban said, "May the LORD keep watch between you and me when we are absent from each other"
(Genesis 31:49 NIV).

The Artful Dodger and Oliver

"I have placed my rainbow in the clouds. It is the sign of my covenant with you and with all the earth"
(Genesis 9:13 NLT).

Baptism, which corresponds to this, now saves you, not as a removal of dirt from the body but as an appeal to God for a good conscience, through the resurrection of Jesus Christ
(1 Peter 3:21 ESV).

Two young brothers joined our home in the fall of 1995. They had come to my Sunday school class from a home across the street from the church. As soon as I met them, they charmed me with their sweet dispositions and engaging manners.

After the service, I walked them back to the house where they were staying. Because it was a temporary, emergency placement, the foster mom explained that the state was looking for a home where they could be placed as their biological parents could not care for them, each having extenuating circumstances. Oh, how I wanted them to come to ours!

Foster parents

Benjy's health appeared stable, so that worry was put aside as a probable reason for not taking on new boarders and new people to love. Jim and I attended the state-mandated classes to receive our foster parents' certification. Within weeks, we welcomed Brandon and Randall into our home. An alcove in our living room accommodated their bunk beds. They stored their clothes in bed boxes beneath the bottom bunk.

The boys could have stepped right out of the musical, *Oliver*, based on the Charles Dickens' novel, *Oliver Twist*. The older brother Brandon, the Artful Dodger, had a charm that could melt an iceberg. He modeled the proverbial saying of being able to sell ice boxes to Alaskans in deep midwinter. With his ability to peddle merchandise, he won an award at school for selling the most chocolate candy bars. Suspicious, I later realized he had eaten over half the merchandise himself. So much for giving kids an allowance when they aren't ready for it. We didn't have control over that as it was mandated by the State. All kids need instruction in handling funds. I tried but am not sure the lessons took hold.

Randall, the younger brother, possessed a gentle disposition. As Oliver, in the musical, reflected a rare innocence, so did Randall. He was not prone to shenanigans and tried hard to obey the rules. He often despaired of Brandon's tendencies and worked hard to prove he was cut from different cloth even though he deeply loved his brother.

Occasionally, in the fall, Brandon's teacher called me to discuss some of his homework assignments. After seeing his papers, I agreed they were unacceptable, but he had not asked for advice. So, we worked on re-dos a few times to make sure the material was appropriate. For one assignment to use magazine or newspaper pictures showing nouns, as an example, he had cut out pictures of lingerie ads. We had a talk about what is suitable and to ask before jumping in with what might seem a great idea. Ofttimes great ideas need finessing.

Speaking of great ideas, once Brandon left a spoon in a cup, which he put into the microwave. The brilliant fireworks impressed him, as evidenced by his dancing and clapping to the rhythm of the sparks. My failure to join in the festivities resulted, in part, because the appliance broke irreparably. On the plus side, no one forgot any metal objects after that.

The boys loved learning. The older one, especially, longed to play an instrument. Unfortunately, we had to put that on hold, as we could not fit music practice into the schedule. Their enthusiasm for schoolwork and assignments amazed me. In looking back, I know they felt protected and accepted at school. It was a safe place for them.

Understanding God's direction

The brothers attended church with us and continued to absorb Bible lessons. A lesson they took to heart was the one in which Peter and the other apostles had been warned about not preaching the gospel. When the authorities challenged them, their reply, as observed in Acts 5:29, resounded within both the boys, *"We must obey God, not man."* Brandon had wanted to be baptized, but after talking with his father, he was upset because his dad refused to allow him to express his faith in this way. However, after learning the Bible verse, Brandon and his brother felt convinced they must obey God's orders. Without speaking with us, they asked the pastor to baptize them. So he did.

During their time with us, they had supervised parental visits at the Children's Services office. Every week I took them for time with either their mom or their dad. Eventually, employees from the county retrieved them from school as my time became more limited while caring for Benjy.

Before Ben died, we knew we could not keep the boys in our home permanently. According to state counselors/case workers, they needed to join a family that could give them a forever home. This knowledge filled me with a deep ache. I set out to find people who would qualify as parents. The older brother had a teacher who had told me about her desire to adopt a child while the boys were living with us. She and her husband expected to adopt a baby. However, the Lord had another plan for both the children and the adults.

New parents

I still remember calling Paula while I knelt on the floor in our bedroom, trying to keep my voice soft so that no one could hear me. It was difficult to look for someone else to parent the boys. I loved them deeply and did not want to let them go. However, our home dynamics would not permit them to stay beyond the end of the school year. I prayed, and I sobbed. My heart broke, but I knew I had to release them into God's hands and allow Him to direct their paths. *"Father, if You are willing, take this cup from me; yet not my will, but Yours be done."*[1]

The boys spent one weekend with Mark and Paula, their prospective parents. We didn't tell them why they would visit with them at their home, as each side needed to stay somewhat neutral. An out-of-town family wedding opened another opportunity for the boys to stay a second weekend with them.

The couple fell in love with the two brothers and started the process of adoption. One afternoon, at the close of a school day, their future mom, Paula, and I met in a classroom with Brandon and Randall to let them know about the new home they would be joining. I told them I had prayed to God, asking Him for clear direction where they were to live. I loved them dearly but knew they would be taken care of and loved in their new forever home. My heart felt heavy as I sobbed out the words that needed to be said. It was also hard for the boys to hear. They had experienced enough tearing, trauma, and turmoil in their first decade of life... more than I could fathom.

We started our transition, allowing the boys to become accustomed to the idea that they would no longer be living with us. My heart felt torn as we continued to spend our days together. I endeavored to improve the transition as we talked through the changes we would all be experiencing. When they left, our older foster son wrote us a letter revealing his tender heart:

> Dear Jim and Family,
>
> Thank you for sharing your home with me and Randall. If you didn't become our foster parents, we would have been separated. I can't think of anything more sad to lose someone you love and grew up with. I know you are very sad of the loss of your son and brother. Ben was very

close to all of you. He was a great boy and accomplished many things while he was alive. Now you are losing two more boys. It's hard to say goodbye to a family that you have been with through a death. You are very lucky to have each other and to be a whole family!

Love you lots.
Sincerely,
Brandon

We saw the brothers occasionally that first summer. Knowing they left our home for a permanent home answered my prayers. "Goodbye" created additional sadness, but my mind and heart knew they would receive extra special care. Their new parents spared nothing to ensure a rich life. They enhanced their lives with school participation, sports activities, music lessons. What else? Mark and Paula introduced greater discipline, love and affection, along with the comforting and firm embrace of a family.

Then life started happening, and we didn't see them as frequently. After they became adults, we saw them a few times. On one visit to our home, Brandon surprised me with a question. "Lynn, do you know my favorite memory from living here?" I thought of multiple lessons learned: their morning send-offs with the full armor of God, concerts we attended, a Christmas party at Jim's company, nighttime prayers and Bible stories. I didn't answer him, clueless about where he was going. "What do you remember?" Finally, he said, "I remember coming home from school. When I walked in the door, I saw you making apple sauce. I had never seen anyone do that, but that made me think, 'This is what home should look like.'"

Glimmers of sunshine and rainbows through the mist

During a difficult time, we welcomed two young boys into our home. They won my heart. Their presence instilled more hope within me. They let me know that life will continue. I knew God had more in store. Caring for Benjy was hard, sad and significant, but I also had four other children who needed me. Somehow, having extra youngsters in the house kept me from feeling weighted down. Even when Benjy left this earth, there were still others who encouraged me to continue walking forward.

Gathering grace gems from the bubbling waters

- Have you cared for someone who gives your life more purpose?
- How have you handled separation from someone you love? What has given you hope when you understand you cannot keep that person with you?
- What represents home to you?

Aunt Carolyn, Family Recorder

Therefore, you will joyously draw water from the springs of salvation (Isaiah 12:3 NASB).

Aunt Carolyn filled the role of a bonus mom my entire life. As the oldest of the nieces and nephews, I laid the first claim on her heart and she on mine. When she developed cancer in 2003, I flew to Michigan for two weeks in August to care for her following a hysterectomy, intended to stop the spread of the illness. Not only was she a cooperative patient, but her nursing skills also equipped her with general procedures, which helped me tremendously in giving her care. After she came home from the hospital, we tried several specific comfort measures. However, as soon as one was tried, or so it seemed, she moved to a better level of pain management and didn't require the previous method. Her healing progress and her strength showed her remarkable propensity to persevere.

Another butterfly visit

Because God often reminds us of past events with new experiences while harking back to old ones, He gave me one that touched my heart. Attached to Aunt Carolyn's garage was a sun porch surrounded by summer flowers, zinnias, cosmos, lilies of the valley, tiger lilies and forget-me-nots. As I opened the porch door, a butterfly started circling around me. It had been sipping nectar from the flowers and then came near. Fascinated, I studied this bejeweled creation. Looking at it closely, I realized it was an exact duplicate of the velvety black swallowtail butterfly Benjy and I had released in Arizona 20 years earlier. That former butterfly had been hard to surrender and so was this one, as it visited me for 20 minutes and then fluttered away into the sky. I wanted it to return, but it was destined for other flowers in other fields. Another opportunity to learn to let go.

A week of encounters

Almost a half-dozen years later, in midwinter, I returned to Michigan's Upper Peninsula for Aunt Carolyn's last week of life. Uncle Jon had arranged to meet me at the airport in Green Bay, Wisconsin. While waiting for him, Aunt Jane, who was in Arizona, called my cell phone to report that Aunt Carolyn had just been taken to the hospital. Instead of driving me straight to Aunt Carolyn's home, Uncle Jon took me to the Bay City Hospital in Marinette, next to her hometown of Menominee.

God scripted each day. Instead of sadness, there was expectation and joy, even though we all knew we were waiting for her to leave her earth house. One gem after another made the week shine.

Aunt Carolyn's nurse on the oncology floor gave me profound encouragement. The first time Theresa entered the room and tended to Aunt Carolyn, checking her vital signs, she delicately commented, "She'll be going soon. She'll be running and dancing just like children do." Her remark infused me with hope, which kept me singing in the following days.

Theresa shared a few stories with me about cancer patients she had known over the years. One that stands out is the story of a 16-year-old boy who had been in and out of the hospital during his cancer battle. He died at home. However, his mother shared his last seconds with Theresa. As he lay dying, he exclaimed, "Do you see the light? All the light? It's beautiful! It's Jesus! He's so beautiful!" And then, he finished his earth life.

After recounting the incidents to my friend, Sharon remarked, "Theresa is a hidden one—God's secret agent." Previously, I had not thought of these sublime encounters with special people as finding a secret agent. Since that time, I have searched for the ones He has concealed for me to identify. The Bible reveals *that they may be encouraged in heart, knit together in love, and filled with the full riches of complete understanding, so that they may know the mystery of God, namely Christ, in whom are hidden all the treasures of wisdom and knowledge.*[2] The second portion of another verse reminds us, *and now your true life is hidden away in God in Christ.*[3] Each of us possesses a special hiddenness of which we are caretakers.

On our second night in the hospital, I heard Aunt Carolyn stirring. I suspected she needed to get up for something, so I left my chair and stood at her bedside, ready to assist her. As I stood there, she calmly stated, "I'm ready to go." That was it. No more movement and no more comments. She was getting ready.

Many people visited with Aunt Carolyn. She had friends from her high school days, from church, from her work. Even her doctor recalled exchanging information with her while she was working as a plant nurse for American Can, a local paper-producing company.

Most who came brought light and encouragement. One young man, with a voice like the tenor Josh Groban, came and serenaded her with praise music. Others arrived and shared their own miracle stories of God's intervention. More friends showed her their respects because they loved her. Naomi, one of her more dour visitors (perhaps the only one), upon seeing her resting in bed, cried out, "It's the end! It's the end!" I wish I'd had the clarity to counter, "Oh, it is just the beginning. It is truly the beginning. She will be so happy soon." However, I doubt Naomi would have heard me. She was too engrossed in her own hysteria.

A concern for Uncle Jon and for me was if the hospital would not allow her to stay. Because of insurance regulations, certain protocols had to be met. Taking care of her at home would have been difficult with the required 24-hour care. We had to consider extra equipment, such as a hospital bed, plus instructions and supplies for administering pain medication. Taking her home remained a real and worrisome threat as the doctor had addressed the possibility with me on Sunday morning.

"You know we cannot keep her here to die, right?

"Well, no. But, yes, I guess I understand."

"Her insurance coverage does not permit her to stay in the hospital without some medical intervention. Are you prepared to provide for her needs at home?"

"It doesn't look as if we have much choice. If we must, we'll find a way."

When he left, I prayed. *Dear Lord, how will I keep Aunt Carolyn comfortable? She needs pain meds. She needs repositioning. She needs personal care. She needs so much that I don't know how to give. But, Lord, You know her needs. Will You please take care of her? Thank You for Your help. Amen.*

The following day, Dr. M. came into the room and addressed me as he cleared his throat. "I don't want to upset the family's wishes, but I want her to stay here in the hospital until her life passes. I will take responsibility for her care and ensure she has insurance coverage." Upset? Hardly. Uncle Jon and I were relieved and thankful, as we had started counting the cost.

With each new day, Aunt Carolyn spent more hours sleeping. Although nurses and doctors tended to her needs, she did not rally as much as she had earlier. The night before she passed, she opened her eyes and winked at me. Was it her secret? Was it our secret?

Time to go home

Months before returning to Michigan, a friend had spoken to me about bells. He advised, "Look for the bell. When you find it, you'll know you are home." On January 15th, in mid-afternoon, Aunt Carolyn lay resting in bed. She started coughing, a cough for which there was no remedy. I predicted a long night and settled into a rocking chair for a quick nap. At 6:15, I started hearing bells from the IV stand, signaling the feeding solution had drained. I checked on her and realized she was gone. The bells rang. She was home.

Uncle Jon joined me within 45 minutes of her passing. All the arrangements had been made with the funeral home ahead of time. They came and took her earthly remains while we gathered her personal items. As the two of us worked, someone quietly entered the room. We turned to see Zane, the young man who had serenaded her earlier in the week. His face clouded as he realized she was no longer here. This time he came with his guitar. I asked him to sing for us anyway. He played as he sang, "Thy Word", based on the Scripture which declares, *Thy word is a lamp unto my feet and a light unto my path.*[4] Zane's voice and playing closed our day at the hospital, trusting that He was near us and with us at the end.

By the next day, family members arrived: her other brother, Jerry, his wife, Carolyn, Aunt Jane, a few nieces and nephews. We planned a special meal treat at Mickey Lou's, a local hamburger joint, which was interrupted by a tiny incident.

Uncle Jerry had turned on the ignition of his rental car to keep the engine warm before leaving for the restaurant. He warned Uncle Jon, "Don't touch that door. The keys are in..." Too late. There was no way to get back into the vehicle. Fortunately, a locksmith in this small town willingly left his own family events to open the car door. One more wink from God.

On Sunday, I attended the morning worship service, appreciating the people and absorbing the atmosphere of a church I had known since I was a little girl. The closing song interrupted my reverie. The congregation was singing "Thy Word," the same song Zane had played for us on Thursday night in the hospital room. In His synchronicity of divine coincidences, God gifted me with another assurance of His careful attention and His watchful care over each event as He guides us to the end.

In the afternoon, a memorial service was held for Aunt Carolyn. All the songs and readings she had requested were included. Except for the date of her death, the bulletin had been composed days before, as she had her say on the order. Aunt Jane had typed it up. A year prior, Aunt Carolyn elected to include a poem about Sister Caroline in her memorial bulletin.

Go Down, Death

James Weldon Johnson—1871-1938

(A Funeral Sermon)

… While we were watching round her bed,
She turned her eyes and looked away,
She saw what we couldn't see;
She saw Old Death. She saw Old Death
Coming like a falling star.
But Death didn't frighten Sister Caroline;
He looked to her like a welcome friend.
And she whispered to us: I'm going home,
And she smiled and closed her eyes.
And Death took her up like a baby,
And she lay in his icy arms,
But she didn't feel no chill.
And death began to ride again—Up beyond the evening star,
Into the glittering light of glory,
On to the Great White Throne.
And there he laid Sister Caroline
On the loving breast of Jesus.

And Jesus took his own hand and wiped away her tears,
And he smoothed the furrows from her face,
And the angels sang a little song,
And Jesus rocked her in his arms,
And kept a-saying: Take your rest,
Take your rest.
Weep not—weep not,
She is not dead;
She's resting in the bosom of Jesus.

Glimmers of sunshine and rainbows through the mist

Staying with Aunt Carolyn as she made her last trek home to heaven allowed me a distinct life privilege. It's not something everyone can plan. Somehow our kind God allowed me to spend her last few days and moments with her. As mentioned, she had written out her earthly memorial service months earlier. She understood how each person would play a part and designed the service with methodical anticipation.

Her planning included her possessions. The only perfume bottle I found, upon returning to her home, was Eternity. She counted her last days and provided for others. Mary Lou, her caregiver, shared that Aunt Carolyn told her she would teach Mary Lou how to die. She held deep feelings and embraced deep purposes for her life. She challenged others to grasp their own purposes. It encourages me that she accomplished what she had set out to do. God granted her last wishes to her as she submitted to His grand plans.

God's ways are beyond our finding out. We don't see the future of His divine plan or even in the present while we are walking through life's labyrinth of twists and turns. Scripture reminds of God's intentionality for our lives. Acts 13:36 has become a new promise and affirmation: *When David had completed the purposes God intended for him, he died.* When we know him, we are not too early or too late. We must complete our purpose. When it is complete, eternity awaits.

Gathering grace gems from the bubbling waters

- Are there steps you are taking to prepare others for your trip to eternity?

- How might you plan for your heavenly journey?
- What can you do to prepare your own heart to meet Jesus?

Never Heal a Broken Heart

You have taken account of my wanderings;
Put my tears in Your bottle.
Are they not in Your book?
(Psalm 56:8 BSB)

"Never heal a broken heart," tenderly advised the speaker, Rev. Richard Wurmbrand, as he opened his sermon. That statement captured my attention. What did he say? During the entire sermon, my thoughts kept crying out and shouting, *But God, You promised to bind up the wounds and heal the brokenhearted.*[5] *Don't You want to heal broken hearts? What good is a broken heart, Lord? I want a healed heart. Can't life get better, and can't things return to normal?* Rev. Wurmbrand elaborated, "Everyone has suffered from a broken heart. It is impossible to find someone who has not suffered loss." He elaborated the losses one might experience:

- ruined or strained relationships with a spouse, a child, a suitor, a sibling, a loved one, a friend, a co-worker, a neighbor
- death of a beloved
- shattered hopes and dreams

He continued, "No one is immune from disappointment and broken heartedness. The one who suffered the greatest broken heart was Jesus. However, His broken heart is still revitalizing and drawing men to Himself today. The energy of Jesus' broken heart at Calvary is the greatest force we can know."

Rev. Wurmbrand shared in 1980, six months following Jeremy's death. Those cool January days provoked me to despair. All that week, I agonized over his sermon. The speaker's background was not unfamiliar to me. While in high school, I had read *Tortured for Christ*, one of the first books he wrote after his emigration out of Romania and then, eventually coming to the United States. The Nazis imprisoned him during World War II for being a Jew. Later, because he was a Christian, the Communists jailed and tortured him for 14 years in Romania, including three years in solitary confinement.

He recounted, at another time, that he had been kept in the dark for so long he had forgotten there were colors. Why would this man want to keep his broken heart? He endured such despair. My areas of need paled in comparison. However, those places still caused me pain. How could I move forward?

Who heals the broken heart?

After a week of meditating on and railing about Pastor Wurmbrand's message, I cautiously arrived at the following conclusion: *Healing my broken heart is not my responsibility. Of course, God wants to heal my heart. That is a promise in His word. However, if I heal my heart, I will damage the work God wants to do. As in a physical wound, scar tissue forms. Scar tissue has no nerves, no feeling. Stick pins into a scar and there is no pain. If I attempt to heal my own broken heart, I will protect it with knotted scar tissue.* God's Word holds the promise: *"I will give you a new heart and put a new spirit within you; I will take the heart of stone out of your flesh and give you a heart of flesh."*[6]

All right, Lord, help me receive a heart of flesh. Give me a heart that will still feel pain, that will not forget how to cry or to laugh. Grant that I may possess a heart that will reach out in love and compassion. Give me a heart that weeps with those who weep, that rejoices with those who rejoice.[7] *Give me a heart like Yours.*

Five months prior, I had recorded thoughts about a broken heart in my diary. It's as if God had prepared me for the sermon, but I didn't connect that writing for many years. Five days after Jeremy died, I wrote, *A broken heart can be filled. A twisted heart, bitter and festering, cannot know healing because it remains unsurrendered.*

No breaks, no breakthroughs

Don't Waste Your Sorrows, by Dr. Paul Billheimer, outlines the attitudes of a broken heart. He reveals the necessity of retaining a broken heart to minister and truly touch the heart and life of anyone else.

An unbroken heart:

- has resentment and rebellion against God and man
- takes offense
- retaliates against criticism and opposition
- lacks appreciation

- indulges in self-justification and self-defense
- reveals discontent and irritation with providential circumstances and situations

A broken heart reveals:

- usually years of crushing heartache and sorrow
- emptiness—empty of plans, ambitions and self-promotion
- surrendered, yielded and submitted
- agape love—the love that took Jesus to the cross as seen in 1 Corinthians 13[8]

Hope reborn in the brokenness

Each heart is a seed. *"Unless a grain of wheat falls into the ground and dies, it remains alone: but if it dies, it produces much grain."* [9] A whole seed lying comfortably in the ground produces nothing. However, a broken seed, as a broken heart, can produce much harvest. Brokenness is not fruitful. It still requires the divine ingredients, the divine touch, to produce the growth and fruitfulness of His intentions.

Out of tremendous gloom, hope can be reborn. The prophet Jeremiah eloquently describes his journey from total despair to expectancy in Lamentations 3. Each of the first 19 verses shouts discouragement and depression. Verses 6, 7, 15 and 17 portray a bleak outlook.

He has caused me to dwell in dark places, as those long dead. He walled me about, so that I cannot get out; He has weighted down my chain. He has filled me with bitterness, He has made me drink to excess and until drunken with wormwood—bitterness. And You have bereft my soul and cast it off far from peace; I have forgotten what good and happiness are.[10]

Suddenly, the writer reverses his course and changes his outlook. Starting in verse 21, he declares a God of faithfulness in Whom we can hope.

But this I recall, therefore have I hope and expectation: It is of the Lord's mercies and loving-kindnesses that we are not consumed, because His (tender) compassions fail not. They are new every morning; great and abundant is Your stability and faithfulness. The Lord is my portion or share says my living being;

therefore will I hope in Him and expectantly wait for Him. The Lord is good to those who hopefully and expectantly wait for Him, to those who seek Him.[11]

Songs in the night

Mrs. Charles Cowman's *Streams in the Desert* became a fountain of life for me during the days of physical, mental and spiritual struggle. The words she recorded encouraged me to embrace the "songs in the night." [12] Dated one day before Ben's earthly birthday, the meditation invites me to sing.

> There are songs which can only be learned in the valley. No art can teach them; no rules of voice can make them perfectly sung. Their music is in the heart. They are songs of memory, of personal experience. They bring out their burden from the shadow of the past; they mount on the wings of yesterday.
>
> St. John says that even in heaven there will be a song that can only be fully sung by the sons of earth—the strain of redemption...
>
> No angel can sing it so sweetly as I can. To sing it as I sing it, they must pass through my exile, and this they cannot do. None can learn it but the children of the Cross.
>
> And so, my soul, you are receiving a music lesson from your Father. You are being educated for the choir invisible. There are parts of the symphony that none can take but you...
>
> Your Father is training you for the part the angels cannot sing; and the school is sorrow. I have heard many say that He sends sorrow to prove you; no, He sends sorrow to educate you, to train you for the choir invisible.
>
> In the night He is preparing your song. In the valley He is tuning your voice. In the cloud, He is deepening your chords. In the rain He is sweetening your melody. In the cold He is molding your expression. In the transition from fear to hope, He is perfecting your lights.
>
> Despise not your school of sorrow, O my soul; it will give you a unique part in the universal song. George Matheson[13]

Glimmers of sunshine and rainbows through the mist

Some may recoil at the concept of a broken heart. Perhaps the words are too strong or unhopeful. If it hurts too much, I don't take offense. It is hard.

Because I felt broken and bleeding in grieving over my children, and later felt the same with others, brokenness presents the only way I can describe the experience. None of us can ever compare our sorrows with another's griefs and pain. Each of us, individually crafted, has hurts and wounds that cannot be measured on someone else's scales. Only the Creator can reach us in tender compassion to embrace and comfort us in our sorrows. Still, He has also given us hearts that can bleed with others. As Native Americans joined slashed wrists to blend their blood to become blood brothers, so we can symbolically bleed with and bleed into one another when the pain of feeling alone in sadness causes us to cry out. He settles the solitary in families.[14] Many, if not most, of these families are forged, not through biology, but through a divine mystery, one only our loving Father could devise and plan. Those families are birthed in shared sorrows which can grow into shared joys.

In *Nobody Left Out*, Michael Murray, a man who lives with cerebral palsy, quotes theologian Matthew Henry. In his explanation of Luke, Henry speaks of the broken heart. "None can truly appreciate how precious Christ is, and the glory of the Gospel except the broken-hearted."[15]

A decade ago, I attended a funeral for a toddler who had died in an accident. During the memorial service, my heart was smitten. As I sat and listened to the family and friends share their thoughts, I started to cry. Soon I could not keep myself from sobbing. Although our last child had died at least 15 years previously, somehow I had never grieved all my children at once. I desperately needed this cathartic passage. My heart bled and my eyes flowed. In the heaving sadness, healing entered. I wasn't looking for it, but the healing came unexpectedly. A waterfall of sorrow and a waterfall of comfort entered my soul at the same time. My broken heart experienced new comfort and new tender mercies. We don't know when we will find a crack in the structure… as water flowed from the rock in the wilderness. The water ripped open the rock and quenched the thirst for thousands. So, our hearts break and living waters can flow, mingled with the tears.

Gathering grace gems from the bubbling waters

- Has your heart been wounded and broken?
- What are some gems you have collected in the whirlpool of sadness?
- Have you joined with others to become a family? With others who share the loneliness? With others to share in the unforeseen delights?
- What is a promise you can embrace in the brokenness?
- What jewels of mercy and grace have you encountered?

Footnotes

1. Luke 22:42 (NIV)
2. Colossians 2:2,3 (BSB)
3. Colossians 3:3 (TPT)
4. Psalm 119:105 (KJV)
5. Paraphrase from Psalm 147:3
6. Ezekiel 36:26 (NKJV)
7. Paraphrase from Romans 12:15
8. Billheimer 75
9. John 12:24 (NKJV)
10. Lamentations 3: 6, 7, 15 and 17 (AMP)
11. Lamentations 3:21-25 (AMP)
12. Psalm 77:6a (NIV)
13. Cowman pp. 162-163
14. Psalm 68:7a (NKJV)
15. Murray 38

Section 9:

Flowing with the River of Time: Parting Words

So may the words of my mouth, my meditation-thoughts,
and every movement of my heart be always pure and pleasing,
acceptable before your eyes, Yahweh,
my only Redeemer, my Protector
(Psalm 19:14 TPT).

Water from the Author of Life

Jesus replied, "Anyone who drinks this water will soon become thirsty again. But those who drink the water I give will never be thirsty again. It becomes a fresh, bubbling spring within them, giving them eternal life"
(John 4:13,14 NLT).

Continuing to face our losses and those of others

Over two and a half decades have passed since we said "Goodbye" to Benjy. Losses reflect life. The challenge is to receive those losses as the way God works out His eternal purposes in our hearts. Death is the last enemy… but it was not God's original design in creation. So we learn to accept losses while knowing heaven awaits with gain. Many lessons are arduous, but they need to be learned and applied in order to grow, to survive and to thrive.

One of my highest goals is to reach out to others with kindness and compassion, knowing they, too, are experiencing their own woes and sorrows. Keeping my heart tender towards those who hurt and ache is the purpose of maintaining my broken heart. Too often, we want to dismiss someone else's heartache because our own feels raw. However, we are called to walk in pain with them as Jesus so readily reached out when His own heart felt crushed by the burdens He was carrying.

So, so different

Jim and I possess disparate personalities. Having been raised in Argentina, he reflects a temperament with effortlessly surfaced emotions, allowing him the ease of expressing words and feelings. He is not half-hearted about many issues and prefers to address concerns in the open. Verve, energy and tenacity radiate from within. He does not quickly back down. Not easily intimidated, he prefers confrontations when difficulties arise.

Gregarious by nature, Jim seeks out conversations with friends and strangers alike. He learns about people's past histories because he is curious about and interested in them. For instance, while shopping together at a local grocery store, Jim frequently finds someone he wants to talk to. Shortly, both are sharing their life stories with each other while I run back and forth, filling the grocery cart. By the time the cart is filled, he ends the conversation, having made a new friend he will never see again this side of heaven.

More cautious than my husband, I enjoy talking with people but am careful about sharing my political views, for example. My modus works through placating. *"Let's keep the peace and no one will get hurt"* has been my motto. I understate my reactions, harking back to Scandinavian roots. It's just my personal temperament. Because I try to avoid strong and immediate confrontations, I take more time to evaluate each situation and the individuals involved. Hopefully, I contribute godly wisdom to the process.

What have I learned through the years? One major area is to face sadness and not run from it. As reflected in my original butterfly story, I know I fluttered past the difficult and uncomfortable. I longed to help, but I lacked both the experience and the understanding of how to lend a hand. Not understanding the gift of weeping with those who weep prevented me from walking with those in pain. I needed more depth and that could only come by diving past the surface. Living through pain wasn't my choice, and it hurt. Enduring the pain opened me to areas I could only skim over previously.

Our marriage endured many blows with the deaths of our children. Our deeply embedded cultural and temperamental differences created an innovative combination that didn't always produce sweet music or a thing of beauty. Jim takes a hands-on approach. As a truck driver, he is accustomed to dealing with emergency situations. He has a crisis mentality. When the tough issues came, he instantly faced them. He would run in where angels feared to tread. If Jim were upset, he'd express himself. He has not changed. I now rely on his willingness to address issues, and I trust his openness.

In the past, I escaped trying circumstances, desperately attempting to return to comfort. I had to mature and face the hard places, the rocky roads, the pits and valleys. On this journey of growth and renewal, I was forced to listen to His still, small voice. Because of that, I pray my life now reflects a greater, more sensitive response to nudges from heavenly realms. Even though I cannot run in and save anyone, I can offer personal sadness and wounds as my tears mingle with the tears of the one who is hurting.

Our olive trees

As they grew up in our home, both our daughters lived through their own griefs and pains. Katelyn cried more easily, expressing her feelings openly. Katelyn was almost seven when Ben passed; she displayed her emotions and didn't hide them. Our older daughter, Chelann, exercised more caution as she shielded her feelings. I found it hard to minister to her needs; I was probably more guarded, too. When she was upset, instead of crying, she would sometimes confront and direct her words at me, which led me to withdraw, leaving both of us at an impasse.

When Chelann took ownership of Ben's bedroom the week after his passing, I was in a stupor. It was painful for me to accept another person in Benj's bedroom, at first, as I was trying to work through my personal grief of losing him. By the same token, so was my daughter. Finally, I realized it was her way of reclaiming a bit of her brother. At least she had his room and could somehow embrace some of his life.

Chelann is now married to Ben (that is his name), a man who had three children when they married. They also have a precious daughter together, Jolynn, named for my mother (Joyce) and me. Jolynn is the image of Chelann when she was young. She has the same physical energy, emotional attributes and organizational gifts.

Although her walk has been fraught with challenges, Chelann reflects firm determination. She tirelessly devotes herself to raising her own family and establishing order and consistency for her two sweet daughters, Elle and Jolynn, at home, and regularly shows hospitality to family and friends. Highly organized, she also enjoys working at a home business, which she coordinates with Ben. Her heart is tender towards the needs of others. As a gift giver, she looks for ways to bless through the things she either makes or finds, and that includes delivery drivers who benefit from her gifts and snacks.

Katelyn and her husband, Ehsan, gave birth to their little girl, three years from the time of this writing. Three days before Avery's birth, they learned the baby was afflicted with hydrocephalus, fluid on the brain. Jim and I accompanied them two days later to the prenatal doctor's visit which felt as heavy and as discouraging as the ones we had experienced with our own children when they were seriously ill. The medical staff wanted to discuss the ramifications of the tests and statistics.

Dr. Richardson conducted our family interview in a darkened room. The only physical light came from the ultrasound screen illuminating the unborn infant's features. Each pronouncement from the doctor predicted more dire circumstances. What little hope we held was steadily shredded.

After the consultation, a member of the medical staff ushered us into a bright, sun-filled room to confer with a high-risk pregnancy nurse. When Sonja walked through the door, she poured in light as she dismissed many of the doctor's dark words. Where minutes before our hearts ached and grieved in sorrow, Sonja's words offered us rays of sunshine filled with promise.

Our granddaughter arrived the next morning. Within two days, Avery had brain surgery to implant a shunt to remove the excess fluid from her brain. She stayed in the NICU (neonatal intensive care unit) for two weeks and then was released home. Later, doctors diagnosed her with cerebral palsy, which carries its own challenges. However, she has received early intervention from a plethora of therapists. Each week, Avery meets with one or two professionals at the hospital therapy center or at home. She has five different therapists assigned to her care. Avery's memory for music, lyrics and stories is astounding. God turned our sadness into dancing with her life.

Both Katelyn and Ehsan have tasks they did not envision when first learning about their expected baby. Katelyn confronts Avery's health issues with a natural energy to intervene and help. As the mother of a child with different abilities, Katelyn faces the challenges with the expectation of a future full of hope.

God grants us ways to reach out and touch

We have received miracles in our life. Our marriage alone is a testimony to God's faithfulness and wonderful work. At times, it appeared easier to jettison the entire package. However, owing to nothing less than divine intervention, we have endured. Despite all we faced, we are now, decades later, looking at each other and enjoying each other's company. No small feat. No less a miracle.

Our journey has become a trust walk, a trust fall. We have learned to take steps without seeing the way ahead. We have simply had to depend on God's ability to work out the plans that did not meet our expectations. And He has.

Trusting each other's instincts is what we are working on. This didn't always happen. We sometimes hit a few glitches, but we have become better at agreeing on some major issues that would have caused serious breakdowns in the past. Despite our differences, we can share more and risk more, depending on the other one to help.

We have arrived at a place in which we are freer to trust each other. We aren't in competition. Our personalities have remained the same. He's bold and I am more laid back, but we persevere in trusting our faithful and loving God. We can look each other in the eye and laugh. We like each other! God's miracle.

Our broken hearts are still beating. We know what we have walked through and can still sit and cry together when the memories are stirred. The tears keep us tender and help us focus on Him to touch others who need more of what He has and what we have found—joy in the mourning. We are refreshed and offer refreshment to others from the flowing waters that pour into and through our hearts.

Works Cited

Alcorn, Randy. *"Heaven as Substance, Earth as Shadow." Eternal Perspectives*, Patheos, 21 June 2021, www.patheos.com/blogs/randyalcorn/2021/06/heaven-substance-earth-shadow/?utm_medium=email&utm_source=BRSS&utm_campaign=Evangelical&utm_content=254. Accessed 27 June 2021.

Bevere, Lisa. *"God Doesn't Love His Children Equally." ChurchLeaders*, 3 Aug. 2017, churchleaders.com/children/childrens-ministry-articles/307307-god-doesnt-love-children-equally-lisa-bevere.html. Accessed 2 Apr. 2022.

Billheimer, Dr. Paul. *Don't Waste Your Sorrows.* Fort Washington, Pennsylvania, Christian Literature Crusade, 1977, pp. 1–131.

Brother Lawrence. *"The Practice of the Presence of God." Gutenberg.org*, 2012, www.gutenberg.org/cache/epub/5657/pg5657.html. Accessed 26 Mar. 2021.

Chambers, Oswald. *My Utmost for His Highest.* New York, Dodd, Mead and Company, 1963, pp. 153, 157, 320.

Cowman, Mrs. Chas. E. *Streams in the Desert.* 1925. Ninth ed., Los Angeles, The Oriental Missionary Society.

Gallagher, K. *"Tikvah (Hope)." GRACE in TORAH*, 27 Oct. 2013, graceintorah.net/2013/10/26/tikvah-hope/. Accessed 10 July 2020.

Gaston, John. *"'I Will Never Leave You nor Forsake You!'" Sermon Central*, Sermon Central, 11 Apr. 2019, www.sermoncentral.com/sermons/i-will-never-leave-you-nor-forsake-you-john-gaston-sermon-on-god-s-presence-239006. Accessed 11 Dec. 2020.

Goldberg, Stephanie. *"What Is Werdnig-Hoffmann Disease?" www.nursingcenter.com*, Journal of Christian Nursing, July-September 2007, www.nursingcenter.com/pdfjournal?AID=728372&an=00005217-200707000-00009&Journal_ID=642167&Issue_ID=728360. Accessed 11 July 2020.

Harris, Kirby. *"NEVER, NEVER, NEVER, NEVER, NEVER (Leave You or Forsake You)." A Slave's View*, The Master Design. A Rivendell Web Services Company, 8 Feb. 2011, christslave.kirbyharris.com/2011/02/never-never-never-

never-never-leave-you.html (Accessed 11/5/2020).

Hayford, Jack. *Fill Your Heart with the Riches of Praise.* 1992. Ventura, California, Regal Books, 1992, pp. 153–155.

Hopkins, Rebecca. *"The Missionary Kids Are Not Alright." ChristianityToday.com*, 25 Mar. 2022, www.christianitytoday.com/ct/2022/march-web-only/third-culture-missionary-kids-trauma-deconstruction-church.html. Accessed 2 Apr. 2022.

Layton, Marta. *"The New Testament Parable That Is Les Miserables." Think Christian*, 16 Jan. 2013, thinkchristian.net/the-new-testament-parable-that-is-les-miserables. Accessed 22 Mar. 2021.

Michael Jr. *Funny How Life Works.* Southlake, TX, Breakfast for Seven, 2020, pp. 45-53, Chapter 5. "Funny Thing About Having a Gun to Your Head."

Murray, Michael. *Nobody Left Out: Jesus Meets the Messes: A 40-Day Devotional for Messy, Broken People (like Me!)*. Archangel Ink, 2020.

Napier, Chad. *"What Does Ebenezer Mean in the Bible? What's an Ebenezer Stone Used For?" Christianity.com*, 30 May 2019. Accessed 24 June 2020.

Piranha Guide. *"Piranha Eating - Can They Strip Humans and Cows to Bones within Minutes?" Piranha Guide*, 7 May 2019, piranhaguide.com/piranha-eating-can-they-strip-humans-and-cows-to-bones-within-minutes/. Accessed 6 Nov. 2020.

Smith, Hannah Whitall. *The God of All Comfort.* 1956 edition ed., Chicago, Moody Press, 1997, pp. 84, 120.

Soroski, Jason. *"What Does Shalom Mean & Why Is It Important?" Crosswalk.com*, 3 Mar. 2021, www.crosswalk.com/faith/spiritual-life/what-does-shalom-mean.html. Accessed 11 June 2021.

Spurgeon, Charles Haddon. *"Never! Never! Never! Never! Never!" Bible Hub*, 26 Oct. 1862, biblehub.com/sermons/auth/spurgeon/never_never_never_never_never.htm. Accessed 25 Mar. 2021.

Talmon, Noelle. "An Experiment Took Monkeys Away from Their Mothers to Prove, Scientifically, That Love Exists." Ranker, 14 Nov. 2018, www.ranker.com/list/what-were-the-harry-f-harlow-monkey-love-experiments/nicky-benson. Accessed 22 Mar. 2021.

Acknowledgements

Years ago, my mother asked me to write about some of my life experiences and life lessons. She must have felt I had something to share. Then again, many mothers are convinced their children have insightful thoughts.

Some friends have also suggested I write my story. I am indebted to them because many times their words echoed my mom's encouragement. Perhaps my friends would not exercise the same biases in encouraging me. Would they?

In the not-too-distant past, I took a course at the behest of my friend, Sharon, who suggested that now might be the time to embrace some of the God-given lessons. Not only that, she also mentioned that this would be, if nothing else, a way to honor my mother's years of waiting for me to present her my memoirs. Mom entered heaven's portals half a dozen years ago, so she'll have to observe from lofty heights. Perhaps the Lord has told her to check out the progress, or perhaps not.

In these past two years, I have learned so much from Nika Maples, the instructor of the Keep Going course I joined, not by accident nor by my design. I spotted an advertisement on social media, and God drew me into the lessons. The class participants have buoyed my intentions. Several have conducted online Zoom meetings, called pomodoros, in which we write for a prescribed length of time, break to breathe and talk, then return to the task at hand. Kay Nell Miller, Isabel Baker and Linda Powell have plugged in their computers and committed to online Zoom writing, day after day, week after week, month after month. Fellow writers who have joined work and prayer include Laura G. Anderson, Mish Graham, Lyla Peterson and Janine Preuss.

Besides writers who have worked alongside are friends and family who have encouraged in their reading, proof-reading and editing suggestions. Janet Albers jumped to willingly share her expertise. Years ago, a family member asked Dad to wash her car. He expected a scrub brush but was handed a toothbrush. I expected Janet to use a scrub brush, but instead she used a toothbrush to find all the corrupt commas, missing margins and wayward words in the manuscript. My undying gratitude goes to her for lending me her thoughts and ideas with her extremely gracious and kind attitude.

My sister-in-law, Evelyn Saint Jimenez, kindly agreed to look over the text for inconsistencies, which has helped me see more clearly with another set of eyes. Another writer friend and neighbor, Becky Hanchett, has helped push the project along as we have prayed each other into authorship.

Hidden behind the scenes is our nephew, Ariel Jimenez, who skillfully and carefully operated on editing the page designs. Not only that, he applied his expertise on the outside cover. We have talked back and forth on this project and I am so thankful for his gentle ministrations. Another word of gratitude goes to Leon Burkholder who provided the beautiful waterfall scene. What he presented was exactly what I had asked.

Friends from HUGS, a long-standing Bible study group, wove in their prayers – Maura Buker, Liz Hammett, Sharon Hazlett, Lisa Jennings, Susy Saint, Liz Sheeley, Bea Soff and Patti Whitney. My daughters, Chelann and Katelyn, have been curious about when I would get to the finish line, giving me extra impetus to swim against the current of my own resistance. Jim, my husband, has offered me time and atta boys when my enthusiasm has flagged.

Ultimately, this is an act of obedience to Him. He permitted my experiences, and He gave the insights. So, dear Lord, this is what You and I have worked on. Thank You for helping me as the waters didn't always look crystal clear. They looked downright murky. But You were there. Your faithfulness carried me through. You are here.

Bible References by Sections

Section 1

1. Leviticus 25:23 (HCSB)
2. Proverbs 21:1 (ESV)
3. Deuteronomy 8:7-9 (NASB)
4. I Corinthians 13:6
5. Acts 22:16 (ESV)
6. Isaiah 30:21 (NKJV)
7. Genesis 24:13-14 (ESV)
8. Mark 3:17 (NKJV)
9. Isaiah 35:6 (NIV)

Section 2

1. Job 1:21 (CSB)
2. Isaiah 25:8 (AMP)
3. Isaiah 8:1 (LB)
4. Psalm 90:12 (KJV)
5. Psalm 84:6 (TPT)
6. Psalm 116:15 (KJV)
7. Revelation 7:17 (NASB)
8. Psalm 139:23 (NASB)
9. Isaiah 30:21 (ESV)
10. Psalm 84:11 (TPT)
11. Isaiah 40:11 (paraphrase)
12. Jeremiah 1:5-6 (NIV)
13. Psalm 63:1 (NLT)
14. Jeremiah 8:11 (KJV)
15. 1 Kings 17:10 (NASB)
16. Job 3:11 (WEB)
17. Exodus 15:22-25 (BSB)
18. John 7:37 (NKJV)
19. Romans 12:15 (paraphrase)

20. Jude 1:23 (AMP)
21. 1 Corinthians 13:4b (TPT)
22. 1 Timothy 6:6 (paraphrase)

Section 3

1. Romans 11:19 (ESV)
2. Job 14:7-9 (NIV)
3. Romans 12:1 (NIV)
4. 1 John 4:7,8 (KJV)
5. Ephesians 1:5,6 (NLT)
6. Isaiah 49:20-22, 23a, c (NASB)
7. Psalm 133:1-3 (BSB)
8. Psalm 36:8-9 (NASB)
9. Jeremiah 14:21-22 (BSB)
10. 2 Timothy 4:2 (NIV)
11. Proverbs 18:4 (NASB)
12. Genesis 13:5-10 (ISV)
13. 1 Corinthians 13:5 (ESV)

Section 4

1. Ecclesiastes 3:2 (NET)
2. Psalm 139:9,10 (NLT)
3. Psalm 87:7 (NASB)
4. Exodus 17:12 (NLT)
5. Joshua 1:9 (paraphrase)
6. 2 Corinthians 10:5 (KJV)
7. Isaiah 57:1 (KJV)
8. Joel 3:18 (NASB)
9. Mark 15:34 (NKJV)
10. Hebrews 13:5 (referenced)
11. 2 Peter 3:8 (BLB)
12. Ephesians 1:4 (CSB)
13. Psalm 23:2 (ESV)
14. Deuteronomy 6:6 (AMP)

15. 2 Samuel 23:12 (ESV)
16. Isaiah 61:7
17. Isaiah 55:10,11 (BSB)
18. Psalm 113 and 115 (selected verses for song)
19. Hebrews 6:7 (NIV)
20. 1 Corinthians 9:25 (WEB)
21. 1 Corinthians 9:27 (NKJV)

Section 5

1. Psalm 140:7 (BSB)
2. Psalm 63:1 (NLT)
3. Exodus 14:13 (ESV)
4. Isaiah 58:11 (NIV)
5. Malachi 4:2 (KJV)
6. Isaiah 58:8 (KJV)
7. Isaiah 58:11 (KJV)
8. Jeremiah 17:14 (KJV)
9. Exodus 14:13 (ESV)
10. John 5:7 (NASB)
11. Genesis 22:12 (CEV)
12. Exodus 30:20 (BSB)
13. Job 13:15 (paraphrase)
14. Psalm 147:8 (NKJV)
15. Romans 5:2 (NKJV)
16. Isaiah 1:18 (KJV)
17. Psalm 42:7 (KJV)
18. Matthew 8:19 (ESV) (reference in endnote)
19. Psalm 20:7 (BSB) (reference in endnote)
20. Exodus 22:12 (paraphrase)
21. Exodus 13:17-14:29 (referred to)
22. Joshua 6 (referred to)
23. Judges 7 (referred to)
24. 2 Chronicles 20 (referred to)

25. 2 Kings 5 (referred to)
26. 1 Kings 19:1-14 (referred to)
27. Isaiah 30:21 (paraphrased)
28. Job 12:15 (ISV)
29. Romans 4:17 (AMP)
30. Romans 5:5 (AMP)
31. Ezekiel 47:12c (NKJV)
32. Romans 5:2 (quoted in meditation)
33. Job 26:7 (quoted in meditation)

Section 6

1. Job 39:26 (KJV)
2. Acts 14:17 (KJV)
3. Matthew 28:20 (CJB)
4. Psalm 105:41 (ESV)
5. Psalm 84:6 (NIV)
6. Daniel 1:8 (CEV)
7. Isaiah 58:8 (NKJV)
8. Mark 1:11 (paraphrase)
9. Romans 8:24-28 (NKJV)

Section 7

1. Deuteronomy 24:5 (KJ21)
2. Psalm 65:9 (BSB)
3. Daniel 1:8-14, 10:3 (referenced, not quoted)
4. James 5:7 (BSB)
5. John 21:21,22 (quoted in meditation)
6. Isaiah 1:18 (referenced, quoted)
7. 2 Corinthians 12:9 (NIV)
8. Psalm 37 (AMP, some sections quoted)
9. Matthew 3:15 (ESV)
10. Psalm 42:2 (BSB)
11. 2 Corinthians 12:9 (NIV)
12. Psalm 145:5,6 (quoted in meditation)

13. John 19:28 (NKJV)
14. John 4:14 (NLT)
15. Proverbs 4:23 (NIV)

Section 8

1. Genesis 31:49 (NIV)
2. Genesis 9:13 (NLT)
3. 1 Peter 3:21 (ESV)
4. Acts 5:29 (referenced)
5. Luke 22:42 (NIV)
6. Isaiah 12:3 (NASB)
7. Colossians 2:2,3 (BSB)
8. Colossians 3:3 (TPT)
9. Psalm 119:105 (KJV)
10. Acts 13:36 (NASB)
11. Psalm 56:8 (BSB)
12. Psalm 147:3 (paraphrase)
13. Ezekiel 36:26 (NKJV)
14. Romans 12:15 (paraphrase)
15. 1 Corinthians 13 (referenced)
16. John 12:24 (NKJV)
17. Lamentations 3:6,7,15,17 (AMP)
18. Lamentations 3:21-25 (AMP)
19. Acts 13:36 (NASB)
20. Psalm 77:6a (NIV)
21. Psalm 68:7a (NKJV)

Section 9

1. Psalm 19:14 (TPT)
2. John 4:13,14 (NLT)

Bible Translations Used with Permissions and Copyright

Amplified

"Scripture quotations taken from the Amplified® Bible (AMPC), Copyright © 1954, 1958, 1962, 1964, 1965, 1987 by The Lockman Foundation Used by permission. www.lockman.org Berean Literal Bible

The Holy Bible, Berean Literal Bible, BLB
Copyright ©2016 by Bible Hub
Used by Permission. All Rights Reserved Worldwide.Berean Study Bible

The Holy Bible, Berean Study Bible, BSB Copyright ©2016, 2020 by Bible Hub
Used by Permission. All Rights Reserved Worldwide.The Christian Standard Bible. Copyright © 2017 by Holman Bible Publishers. Used by permission. Christian Standard Bible®, and CSB® are federally registered trademarks of Holman Bible Publishers, all rights reserved. Contemporary English Version

Scripture quotations marked (CEV) are from the Contemporary English Version Copyright © 1991, 1992, 1995 by American Bible Society. Used by Permission. English Standard Version

The ESV® Bible (The Holy Bible, English Standard Version®). ESV® Text Edition: 2016. Copyright © 2001 by Crossway, a publishing ministry of Good News Publishers. The ESV® text has been reproduced in cooperation with and by permission of Good News Publishers. Unauthorized reproduction of this publication is prohibited. All rights reserved.Holman Christian Standard Bible

Scripture quotations marked HCSB are taken from the Holman Christian Standard Bible®, Copyright © 1999, 2000, 2002, 2003, 2009 by Holman Bible Publishers. Used by permission. Holman Christian Standard Bible®, Holman CSB®, and HCSB® are federally registered trademarks of Holman Bible Publishers. International Standard Version

Hours before Lynn leaves Argentina, the two posed for a picture in Buenos Aires

August wedding day with newlyweds, plus Lynn's parents, Vernor and Joyce Hulstedt, and her brother, Doug.

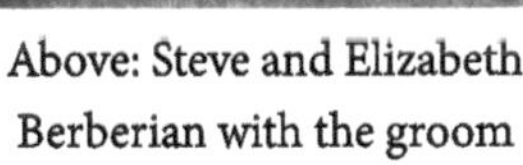

Above: Steve and Elizabeth Berberian with the groom

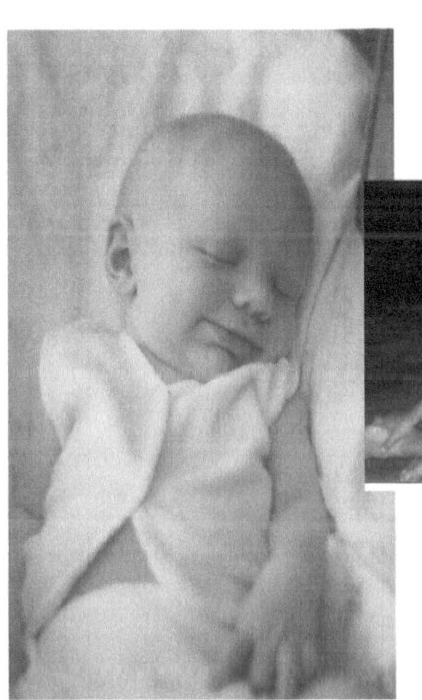

Nathaniel smiling when awake and smiling in his sleep. Now, he sleeps with the angels.

Martin and Jeremy

Jim holds Jeremy, who wears his Argentine poncho.

Martin displays Benjy and Mikaela.

Benjy, our pioneer woodsman, in the White Mountains of Arizona

Eve and Humberto with Phil and Ruth Saint on Christmas Day

Lower left: Benj and Humberto with companion dog Whitey

Lower right: Joe and Martin rescued the Jim Saint family when the car's fuel pump broke in the mountains, hours from home.

Welcome to Baby Chelann.

Benjy, four years old, proudly displays his first fish catch.

Adoption day
with Duane Olson holding Chelann.

Below: Goodbye to Joe, Susy, Martin,
Mika and Becky.

Siblings at the Pacific Ocean.
Benjy calls out, "Hold my hand!"

Benjy holds Alyssa,
2 months.

Jim, Benjy, Chelann overlooking waterfall vistas.

Left: Benjy and
Chelann in a
quiet moment.
Lower left: Benjy
and Chelann with
newborn Katelyn.

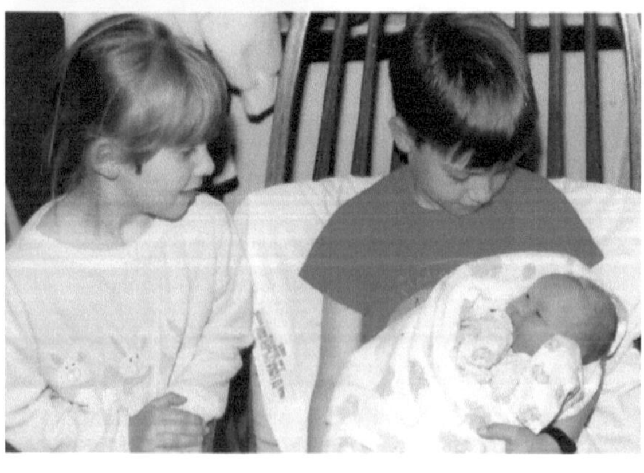

Katelyn enjoys eating sand.

Lynn's brother, Doug, and his wife, Gloria, visit from California.

Soccer buddies, Ben and Grant, take a time-out after a soccer game.

Duke and Joyce Hulstedt visit with the three grandchildren. Chelann quiets Katelyn.

Poking the fire on a camping trip.

Beloved family: Grandma, aunts, uncles and cousins abound at Valle del Lago, the camp founded by Grandpa Felipe Saint.

Below left:
Chelann and Katelyn
at Plaza San Martín
in Córdoba.

Below right:
Eating ice cream
on the *peatonal*-
sidewalk street.

Above: Benjy, Chelann
and Katelyn
at the Dique la Viña
power plant.

You are the wellspring of our lives. Our words are deep waters;
wisdom's fountain bubbles as an artesian spring.
Psalm 36:9 and Proverbs 18:4

Avery at 2 years.

Katelyn and Ehsan's wedding with Holmes, Saints, Hulstedts and Bruemmer.

Jim and Lynn at birthday and Christmas outings.

Ben and Chelann with all family members at tree cutting.

www.ingramcontent.com/pod-product-compliance
Ingram Content Group UK Ltd.
Pitfield, Milton Keynes, MK11 3LW, UK
UKHW041636190726
13854UKWH00006B/2519